STREET

TOTTENHAM

a Theatre
fe

E STREET

e Fitzroy
avern

DMILL STREET

GOWER STREET

MALET STREET

London
University

Senate House

COURT ROAD

PERCY STREET

The Eiffel Tower
(The White Tower)

The Wheatsheaf

The Bricklayer's
Arms

The Adelphi offices

Bedford
Square

BLOOMSBURY STREET

Time & Tide

GREAT RUSSELL STREET

British
Museum

Russell
Square

MONTAGUE STREET

Brunswick
Square

Horizon
offices

GUILDFORD STREET

Hospitals

SOUTHAMPTON ROW

Bloomsbury
Square

The Plough

Poetry Quaterly
Offices

UBONE PLACE

The Black Horse

FORD STREET

NEW OXFORD STREET

CHARING CROSS ROAD

Soho
Square

FRITH STREET

GREEK ST.

Fava's

The Caves de France
The Colony Room

OLD COMPTON STREET

The Patisserie
Valerie

ROMILLY STREET

ch

FTESBURY AVENUE

Fitzrovia
1900-1955

0   100   200   300 Yards

THE FITZROVIANS

THE FITZROVIANS
A PORTRAIT OF BOHEMIAN SOCIETY
· 1900-55 ·

HUGH DAVID

MICHAEL JOSEPH   LONDON

To
my mother and my father,
and to Mike

MICHAEL JOSEPH LTD

Published by the Penguin Group
27 Wrights Lane, London W8 5TZ, England
Viking Penguin Inc., 40 West 23rd Street, New York, New York 10010, USA
Penguin Books Australia Ltd, Ringwood, Victoria, Australia
Penguin Books Canada Ltd, 2801 John Street, Markham, Ontario, Canada L3R 1B4
Penguin Books (NZ) Ltd, 182–190 Wairau Road, Auckland 10, New Zealand

Penguin Books Ltd, Registered Offices: Harmondsworth, Middlesex, England

First published in Great Britain in 1988

Copyright © Hugh David, 1988

Typeset by Cambrian Typesetters, Frimley, Surrey
Printed in Great Britain by
Richard Clay, Bungay, Suffolk

ISBN 0 7181 2879 6

A CIP catalogue record for this book is available from the British Library.

Contents

List of Illustrations	vii
Foreword	ix
PROLOGUE: Cleaning the Stables	1
CHAPTER ONE: Scandals in Bohemia	6
CHAPTER TWO: La Vie de Bohème	20
CHAPTER THREE: Bohemia in London	31
CHAPTER FOUR: 'Give up Verse, My Boy'	42
CHAPTER FIVE: Augustus and the Demi-Johns	60
CHAPTER SIX: 'Welcome, Gentlemen, to Tot'nam Court'	78
CHAPTER SEVEN: Café Society	99
CHAPTER EIGHT: At the Eiffel Tower	118
CHAPTER NINE: Enter Dylan Thomas	137
CHAPTER TEN: A District of the Mind	157
CHAPTER ELEVEN: Whistling in the Blackout	181
CHAPTER TWELVE: Te Palinure Petens	202
CHAPTER THIRTEEN: Sohoitis	218
CHAPTER FOURTEEN: Deaths and Entrances	237
EPILOGUE: Gin, Whisky, Sloth, Fear, Guilt and Tobacco Revisited	249
Notes and Sources	253
Bibliography	266
Index	270

List of Illustrations

between pages 84 and 85

1. Oscar Wilde and Lord Alfred Douglas ('Bosie'), *c.* 1893. (*BBC Hulton Picture Library*)
2. Algernon Charles Swinburne, a caricature by A. Bryan. (*National Portrait Gallery, London*)
3. Oscar Wilde in his 'Aesthetic' lecturing costume, 1882. (*National Portrait Gallery, London*)
4. A cartoon by George du Maurier from *Punch*, 1881.
5. Henry Mürger. (*BBC Hulton Picture Library*)
6. The Café Boulogne, Soho.
7. The London Sketch Club 'Smoker'.
8. W. B. Yeats (*National Portrait Gallery, London*)
9. Augustus John (*National Portrait Gallery, London*)
10. Walter Sickert, *c.* 1920. (*BBC Hulton Picture Library*)
11. *19 Fitzroy Street*, 1913–14. (*Laing Art Gallery, Newcastle upon Tyne, Tyne and Wear Museums Service*)
12. George Gissing, *c.* 1905. (*BBC Hulton Picture Library*)

between pages 180 and 181

13. Michael Arlen, *c.* 1920. (*BBC Hulton Picture Library*)
14. Interior of the Cave of the Golden Calf. (*By permission of the British Library*)
15. Spencer Gore's deer-hunting mural in the Cave of the Golden Calf. (*Yale Center for British Art, Paul Mellon Fund*)
16. *The Eiffel Tower Restaurant*, 1930, a drawing by William Gaunt. (*Michael Parkin Fine Art*)
17. Nina Hamnett, 1932.
18. The French, *c.* 1938. (*BBC Hulton Picture Library*)

19. The Fitzroy Tavern, 1949. (*BBC Hulton Picture Library*)
20. Dylan Thomas, 1946. (*BBC Hulton Picture Library*)
21. *Landscape with Figures – III*, by Osbert Lancaster. (*The Lancaster Estate and John Murray Ltd*)
22. Ruthven Todd in 1934. (*Christopher Todd*)
23. John Minton in 1954 (*Collection of Roger Mayne*)
24. The Colony Room, *c.* 1950. (*Denise Hooker and Constable and Company Ltd*)
25. Robert Colquhoun and Robert MacBryde, 1951. (*BBC Hulton Picture Library*)
26. The 2i's Coffee-Bar. (*Topham Picture Library*)

Foreword

FITZROVIA takes its name from a pub – the once-famous and then notorious Fitzroy Tavern which stands on the corner of Charlotte Street and Windmill Street just north of Soho in the West End of London. But although the massive building itself dates from 1897, the term Fitzrovia, in both its geographical and vague, literary-critical applications, was seemingly not coined until after 1945. Indeed, according to the *Oxford English Dictionary* it did not appear in print until as late as 1958 (in a *Times Literary Supplement* review of the autobiography of Phillip O'Connor who 'emigrated into what he called Fitzrovia – a world of outsiders, down-and-outs, drunks, sensualists, homosexuals and eccentrics').

Clearly, then, the writers and artists who gathered in the Fitzroy and many smaller pubs in the tight huddle of roads and mews around the lower end of Charlotte Street from the early 1930s did not see themselves as 'Fitzrovians'. Nor was there any public conception of Fitzrovia at the very time when it was ostensibly at its height for, like 'the Nineties', 'the Roaring Twenties' and even 'the Swinging Sixties', Fitzrovia is a posthumous construct.

But, although this has undoubtedly proved convenient for the critics and headline-writers who have retrospectively given asylum in its saloon bars to an amazing assortment of the characters of the thirties and forties ranging from Charles Laughton to Pablo Picasso, the *real* Fitzrovia was rather different – if, indeed, it ever really existed.

As many latter-day chroniclers and archivists have separately commented, for one reason and another the day-to-day doings of writers and artists in the 1940s (commonly held to have been the heyday of Fitzrovia) are among the least well documented in the century or so in which there was a perceptible London Bohemia. While the Blitz and, for instance, the London Tube shelters were extensively photographed, even Fitzrovian figures then as eminent as Julian Maclaren-Ross, Nina Hamnett, Augustus John and Dylan Thomas seem to have been virtually ignored by the camera throughout the 1940s.

The definitive written record is equally sketchy, as well as being subjective and irremediably self-interested. Depending on one's sources that 'real' Fitzrovia can be depicted as anything from a principality of frail freelance Bohemians increasingly under the heel of a bleak, *Nineteen Eighty-Four*-ish dictatorship of bureaucracy, Arts Councils and a ruthlessly expansionist BBC, to a boozy Never-never land which rivals (and occasionally even betters) the territory of the *post hoc* legend.

In what follows I have tried to chart a course between the two extremes, tempering the hortatory, End-of-Life-as-We-Know-It sermonising of the former with the later, but more picaresque, memorialising of the latter. Throughout it all, however, my main aim has been to try to understand Fitzrovia in the context of the particular brand of Bohemianism which grew up in London in the early years of this century in the immediate aftermath of the trial of Oscar Wilde in 1895.

For an outsider – someone, indeed, not born until virtually every event described in this book had taken place – the task has not always been easy. In the course of my research I have spoken to a large number of surviving Fitzrovians (and contacted several more who, for their own reasons, preferred to have nothing to do with the project); but what follows is inevitably as much a work of synthesis as it is of dispassionate interpretation. I am happy to acknowledge the debt I owe to the many previous volumes which have dealt with or touched on Fitzrovia and the London *vie de bohème*. All those to which I have had any more than passing recourse are listed in the Bibliography.

There remain various personal debts of honour. Frank Delaney provided the initial push which got this book started, while the late Geoffrey Grigson ensured that it at least began on the right lines. For later leads, contacts, lunches and cups of coffee, and for their patience in answering many questions and their forebearance in listening to my half-formed theories, I am especially indebted to

Norman Balon, Gaston Berlemont, Cecil Collins, John Craxton, John Heath-Stubbs, Adam Johnson, Alfred Marnau, Richard Mervyn, Andrew Motion, Michael Parkin, Alan Ross, Victor Sassie, Rosemary Say, Alan Smith, Ken Thomson, Christopher Todd, Elisabeth Welch and David Wright.

Except where they are directly attributed, for better or worse all the opinions expressed are my own. For believing that I had any at all to express I am deeply grateful to my agent Bill Hamilton, and to Roland Philipps of Michael Joseph.

The staffs of the London Library, the Swiss Cottage and Holborn Local History Libraries of the London Borough of Camden, the London Borough of Bromley Central Library and the British Library Reading Room, were all unfailingly helpful and efficient in tracking down the more recherché written records.

I am indebted to the following for kindly allowing me to quote from copyright sources: the Estate of the late Michael Arlen and Messrs William Collins Ltd for extracts from *Piracy*; Mrs Eva Reichmann and the Oxford University Press for extracts from *Seven Men* by Sir Max Beerbohm; Rogers, Coleridge & White Ltd for material from *The Unquiet Grave* by Cyril Connolly; Dan Davin and the Oxford University Press for passages from *Closing Times*; Graham Greene, William Heinemann Ltd and The Bodley Head Ltd for a passage from Graham Greene's story *Men at Work*; the executors of the Estate of the late John Lehmann for extracts from *I Am My Brother* and *New Writing and Daylight*; the Estate of the late Arthur Ransome and the Oxford University Press for extracts from *Bohemia in London*; the Trustees for the Copyrights of Dylan Thomas and J. M. Dent & Sons Ltd for material from the poet's *Collected Letters*; A. P. Watt Ltd, on behalf of Michael B. Yeats and Macmillan London Ltd, for material from *Memoirs* and *Autobiographies* and some lines from 'The Pilgrim' by W. B. Yeats.

The extract from Louis MacNeice's 'Autumn Sequel' is reprinted by permission of Faber and Faber Ltd from *The Collected Poems of Louis MacNeice*. Ezra Pound's poem 'Mr Nixon' forms part of the sequence 'Hugh Selwyn Mauberley' and is reprinted, by permission of Faber and Faber Ltd, from *Collected Shorter Poems* by Ezra Pound.

Every effort has been made to trace the copyright-holders of material used, but in a few cases this has proved impossible. The publishers apologise for any omission – most particularly to the representatives of the late Julian Maclaren-Ross – and will be happy to fill any omissions in any future edition of this book.

Hugh David
London, April 1988

Cleaning the Stables

'E'LL 'ave 'is 'air cut reg'lar now!' shouted a prostitute as Oscar Fingal O'Flahertie Wills Wilde was led away from the Central Criminal Court at around six o'clock on Saturday, 25 May 1895. He did too. At Pentonville a prison barber made short work of the elaborate waves which had previously received the daily attention of a hairdresser, and within forty-eight hours all the other necessary processes had been completed. Bathed and disinfected, kitted out in ill-fitting prison garb and securely handcuffed to a warder, the playwright was taken across London in a closed horse-drawn van to begin his sentence in Wandsworth Prison.

Public executions had ceased only a little more than thirty years previously, and crowds in the streets outside the Old Bailey during the closing stages of notable trials were by no means uncommon at the end of the last century. But it was not just the naively optimistic prospect of an increase in trade as one more bugger was put behind bars which caused the nameless prostitute's outburst. Neither was it mere prejudice which, according to more than one contemporary writer, brought about the swirling of a petticoat or two in those normally calm City streets that Saturday evening. It was something altogether more basic, an atavistic belief shared, if not so uninhibitedly shown, by all levels of society that at long last 'reg'lar' service was being resumed.

The trial of Oscar Wilde was one of those events which, even as they are happening, can be seen to be irrevocably altering the climate of their time. It is hardly an exaggeration to say that as soon as it was announced, following Wilde's arrest on 5 April 1895, a shiver ran through the whole artistic, 'Bohemian' com-

1

munity in which he had previously moved. And by the time Wilde and Alfred Taylor, the proprietor of a male brothel with whom he was sentenced, were taken from the dock, the ripples had spread far wider. It had become clear that in some intangible way things would never be quite the same again. Even the judge had recognised this when he dispatched the jury with the words: 'Whatever your verdict may be, gentlemen, it cannot leave things precisely as they were before this trial.'[1]

It was not merely that the sordid details of Wilde's 'feasting with panthers' had been paraded in public. Indeed, the fact that he had been charged with offences under Section 11 of the 1885 Criminal Law Amendment Act ('The Blackmailer's Charter', which remained on the statue book until 1967) was in itself largely irrelevant. The case would not have had such prurient appeal, but its seismic consequences would have been virtually the same if the playwright had been convicted of not paying his income tax or of stealing from one of the shops he frequented in the Burlington Arcade. The crucial point about the whole business was not that Wilde was charged with homosexual offences (although there seemed to be a certain inevitability in the connection between 'The Love that Dare Not Speak its Name' and the perceived feyness of Wildean Aestheticism). The crucial point was that he had been arrested at all.

'Dans ce pays-ci il est bon de tuer de temps en temps un amiral pour encourager les autres', Voltaire had said of the English after the execution of Admiral Byng in 1757; and now they were at it again. Wilde was the *amiral* of the day, but at the same time as his personal reputation was being destroyed by the shaky testimony of a succession of 'rent-boys' and hotel bed-makers, implicitly a whole generation was being brought to book. Bohemia was being invaded; and the languidly beautiful Aesthetes, its effete young denizens, were also being encouraged to 'ave their 'air cut reg'lar. For, through its prosecution of Wilde, society seemed to see itself as effectively bringing to an end a prolonged *fin de siècle* which had existed in various guises for the previous twenty-five years – or at least that is the impression one gets from reading contemporary accounts.

By putting one man in the dock, it believed it could clean the stables. Imbued with a smug belief in self-help, Victorian society hoped to be seen as purging itself of the fevered, fleshy excesses of Pre-Raphaelite art and Swinburnean verse by the application of no more than what the *St James's Gazette* called 'a dash of wholesome dignity'.[2] The Central Criminal Court proceedings can thus be seen as the manifestation of an abrupt change in its self-image. It paid the piper, but, publicly at least, by the spring of 1895 it was announcing that it had become bored with Wilde's tune. (Privately, of course, it behaved rather differently: a super-Wildean society raffishness survived to become one of the hallmarks of the Edwardian era.)

It no longer mattered that 'Oscar' had been the licensed fool of London society during the whole of the previous decade, the trendsetter in whose name all the young men of London (or so it seemed) had grown their hair and flouted covention. The interior decoration of its own suburban villas might well have owed everything to a wholly Wildean concept of 'the house beautiful', but the public had simply tired of him and the artificiality for which he stood. The Marquess of Queensbury's famously mis-spelt accusation that he was 'posing as a somdomite' merely proved the last straw.

In a shabby compromise between public probity and private profit, a full three weeks before the trial began, the actor-manager George Alexander had the author's name erased from playbills in front of the now demolished St James's Theatre where *The Importance of Being Earnest* was doing good business. His action was immediately followed by Lewis Waller who was presenting *An Ideal Husband* at the Theatre Royal, Haymarket. That play was already nearing the end of its run, but on 6 April 1895, its last performance before transferring to the much smaller Criterion, it too appeared with Wilde's name missing from all placards and programmes. Friends demanded their letters back, and burnt any of Wilde's which they had kept. He might privately have quipped that 'the working-classes are with me – to a boy!' but every time Wilde ventured out in public he was booed by the lower orders and ostentatiously shunned by a previously adoring aristocracy.

Only a little over four months previously, on 3 January, the Prince of Wales had been among the audience at the opening of *An Ideal Husband*. The following month Aubrey Beardsley and the cream of London society had braved one of the worst blizzards of the decade to be seen at the first night of *The Importance of Being Earnest*, a glittering occasion after which 'the audience rose in their

3

seats and cheered and cheered again', according to the actor Allan Aynesworth who created the role of Algy.[3] But by 20 May the world had changed; and the moment Wilde stepped into the dock the extent to which he was to be made the whipping-boy of a generation became frighteningly clear.

There is no suggestion that he received anything other than a fair trial. It was enough that he was subjected to what the judge, the Honorable Mr Justice Wills, called 'the cold, calm, resolute administration of justice' and, for the first time in years, treated like any other citizen. It was to prove a novel experience for all concerned. It was a public humiliation for Wilde but hardly less of a disaster for his friends in the public gallery. Like him, they could only watch in silence as the lush, over-heated sophistry of the Aestheticism they had all so enthusiastically espoused, wilted and died in the cold light that illuminated the Central Criminal Court. Two of Wilde's letters to Bosie were read aloud, but their sentimental, high-flown prose was ludicrously inappropriate to the occasion and cut little ice with the severe, thin-lipped judge:

> I may be dull myself, but speaking personally I cannot see the extreme beauty of the language said to be used. However, opinions may well differ on this point. But suppose that the letters are 'prose poems', suppose that they are things, of which the intellectual and literary value can only be appreciated by persons of high culture, are they thereby any the less poisonous for a young man?[4]

Like many judges before and since, in his charge to the jury Mr Justice Wills confessed himself at something of a loss. 'I would rather try the most shocking murder case that it has ever fallen to my lot to try than be engaged in a case of this description,' he said before going on to attempt to make some sense of the lifestyles of the defendants. It proved a difficult task. Wilde's in particular had been lived in a different world, in restaurants, clubs and hotels of which Mr Justice Wills had no knowledge. He had been 'spending £40 or £50 a week' and entertaining young men overnight at the Savoy, said the judge, adding rather disingenuously that, although 'the mere fact of two men sleeping together' was not a punishable offence, 'it seems astonishing to me that he should not get at least the whole use of a bed for his money'.

It was not prurience so much as genuine bewilderment which

lay behind his remarks. (The Bow Street magistrate who presided over Wilde's committal proceedings a month before had had similar problems, demanding to know precisely what Kettner's was, although the doors of the then-fashionable Romilly Street restaurant were less than a mile from his court.) Even the cost of a light supper became the subject of puzzled judicial reflection: 'I know nothing about the Savoy, but I must say that in my view "Chicken and salad for two, sixteen shillings" is very high. I am afraid I shall never have supper there myself.'[5]

Only after the jury had returned a unanimous verdict, pronouncing the playwright guilty on seven separate charges of gross indecency, did Mr Justice Wills give any indication of his personal feelings. Passing sentence on Wilde and Alfred Taylor, he left the defendants in no doubt that, despite his wig and gown, he was a normal member of society, and like everyone else felt for them only a deep revulsion:

> It is no use for me to address you. People who can do these things must be dead to all sense of shame, and one cannot hope to produce any effect upon them. It is the worst case I have ever tried . . . That you, Wilde, have been the centre of a circle of corruption of the most hideous kind among men, it is impossible to doubt. I shall, under the circumstances, be expected to pass the severest sentence that the law allows. In my judgement it is totally inadequate for such a case as this. The sentence of the Court is that each of you be imprisoned and kept to hard labour for two years.[6]

'And I? May I say nothing, my lord?' cried Wilde as he was led from the dock. His request was turned down, doubtless out of a feeling that in recent years he and his kind had been given ample opportunity to have their say.

CHAPTER ONE

Scandals in Bohemia

IN the twenty years leading up to the arrest of Oscar Wilde the isle had indeed been full of noises. Since the early 1870s the most insistent of all had been the cry of 'Art for Art's Sake', a tribal ululation which – even before Wilde began writing – had accompanied the self-conscious attempts of a loose, amorphous group of 'Aesthetes' to appropriate the equally loose mantle of English Bohemianism.

Neither term is easy to define. Although individual Aesthetes were immediately identifiable by their style of dress, studied poses, devotion to beauty in all its forms and their effusive vocabulary in which the adjectives 'utter', 'total', 'consummate', 'blessed' and 'precious' were unduly predominant, it is misleading to speak of an Aesthetic movement. Unlike the Pre-Raphaelite Brotherhood, say, which had both a mixed membership and a revolutionary manifesto, Aestheticism which had its origins at the universities of Oxford and Cambridge in the 1870s was never formally constituted. Even after its translation to London, its adherents remained individuals – poets, painters, poetasters and mere poseurs who had in common little more than a notional allegiance to that always contentious doctrine of Art for Art's Sake.

Indeed, their very self-conscious individuality became one of their trademarks. Few of them would have known, and fewer still cared, that the Aestheticism they were so casually espousing actually had its origins in Kantian ideas about the essential disinterestedness of art, and that the term itself had first been used by the aesthetic philosopher Alexander Baumgarten as far back as 1750. For to them – at least until the arrival of Wilde, and more particularly of Walter Pater – its philosophical pedigree was largely irrelevant. The watered-down, popular Aestheticism which infected Oxbridge in the 1870s and 1880s merely seemed to offer a way out, a gaudy, adolescent egress into individuality and personal fulfilment. In 1877 the *Oxford and Cambridge Under-graduates' Journal* had noted that it gave *'implicit* sanction [. . . for] Pagan worship of bodily form and beauty',[1] and even today that remains as accurate as any other definition.

'Bohemianism' is a similarly vague term, the connotations it has acquired during the twentieth century retrospectively colouring its wider, still more imprecise meaning in the eighteenth and nineteenth centuries. Feckless womanising, a cheerful contempt for fashion and seemingly obligatory drunkenness are only part of the story, for in the late nineteenth century in particular the term conveyed something more.

At its most basic this was the intangible 'differentness' which artists (in the broadest sense) had come to perceive in themselves. Arthur Conan Doyle caught this very well in his story 'A Scandal in Bohemia', first published in *The Strand Magazine* in July 1891. In the title he refers to the literal, geographical Bohemia, but in only the second paragraph he is thinking of something altogether separate when Watson reacquaints readers with Sherlock Holmes:

> who loathed every form of society with his whole Bohemian soul [and] remained in our lodgings in Baker Street, buried among his old books, and alternating from week to week between cocaine and ambition, the drowsiness of the drug, and the fierce energy of his own keen nature.

It is in the context of references such as this that the Aesthetes can be seen as the Bohemians of their time. Ignore the specific details and Conan Doyle's description fits Byron, Coleridge or de Quincey better in many respects than it does Dylan Thomas or Augustus John. Drug-taking was no more prevalent among the Aesthetes than any other section of late nineteenth-century society (although not unknown and still less forbidden), but that is a minor point. Far more important is the fact that, though they may not have 'loathed' it as much as Holmes, the Aesthetes were also detaching themselves from their parent society by adopting a private artistic morality. They not only saw themselves as different, they were also perceived as different by everyone else.

7

They were only a temporary phenomenon but their worshipping of, or at least their deep concern for, Beauty makes them the natural inheritors of a 'Bohemianism' which had been in the air certainly since the eighteenth century. More specifically, it establishes their credentials as the heirs to the altogether more modern and more immediately recognisable Bohemianism which, as we will see, had evolved in Paris half a century previously. It too was distinguished by a private cosmology and a casual but none the less perceivable group solidarity – by what a contemporary critic has described as 'a belligerent attitude toward the world and a genuine sympathy for each other'.

Thus – for the want of any better term – the Aesthetes can now be seen as the Bohemians of the moment. And indeed at that moment there can have been few among them who would have more than politely objected to the description. (The syllogism, though, is less than perfect and should not be too rigorously pressed: if every Aesthete was to some extent a Bohemian, it is wholly wrong to suggest that every Bohemian then and still less later was an Aesthete.)

Too often dismissed in the nineties with a mixture of flippancy and impatience, in this – international – context the Aesthetes now deserve to be taken more seriously. For, beneath their velvet knee-breeches, behind their lilies, sunflowers and much-derided devotion to blue china, the Aesthetes were more than an exotic but ultimately irrelevant adornment to the social and cultural life of Britain in the late nineteenth century. Their cry of 'Art for Art's Sake' might have been all-but meaningless, but under it lay an argument for the very existence of Art in a brash new industrial society, an argument which had preoccupied critics of both literature and the visual arts since the middle of the century.

In 1821 Shelley had claimed in his *Defence of Poetry* that 'poets are the unacknowledged legislators of the world', but by 1850 his glib Romanticism was beginning to sound hollow. By 1860 it was palpably risible; industrialisation had taken no heed of Blake and a whole new world was rising in England's pleasant pastures green. King's Cross Station in London opened in 1851, Paddington in 1852. Bessemer developed a process for converting molten pig-iron into steel in 1856; and Darwin published *On the Origin of Species by Means of Natural Selection* in 1859. England was assuming its modern character and, effectively stripped of their self-appointed roles as legislators, poets and artists themselves seemed to be facing the prospect of Darwinian extinction.

Aestheticism, then, can be seen as the manifestation of their fight for survival. There was no lisping, simpering silliness about that; rather it was an aggressive counter-attack to try to recapture the lost ground of Romanticism.

The origins of the movement are obscure. Well before its espousal by free-thinking Oxbridge students of the seventies, a vaguer Aestheticism had arisen from the dying embers of Pre-Raphaelitism and the demands for 'a fuller Nature' which Holman Hunt, Dante Gabriel Rossetti, John Everett Millais and the other members of the original Pre-Raphaelite Brotherhood had made in 1848. But, with its underlying preoccupation with the role of the artist, it only achieved coherence with the arrival on the scene of Walter Pater, one of the principal creators of what we now recognise as the late Victorian sensibility.

Pater was a don at Brasenose College, Oxford for much of his life; a man with an almost clerical detachment from society, but possessing an 'Aesthetic' streak which manifested itself in, among other things, his devotion to yellow kid gloves. For a quarter of a century he patiently spelt out a rather humourless philosophy which held that aesthetic considerations were wholly independent of any morality – the tendentious doctrine which lay behind the Art for Art's Sake slogan – and which itself owed much to the earlier French writer Théophile Gautier. In the preface to his novel *Mademoiselle de Maupin* (1835) Gautier had, after all, suggested that all art was 'amoral, useless and unnatural'.

Pater's views had first been expounded in his *Studies in the History of the Renaissance* (1873), a book which deeply influenced Wilde during his first term at Oxford. Twelve years later he further developed them in his idiosyncratic novel *Marius the Epicurian*, a bloodless and relentlessly high-minded account of life in Rome during the second century AD. As far as the general public was concerned, however, the Bohemian image of Aestheticism lay not so much in theories as in the personalities of its key exponents.

Now, it seems, irrevocably out of fashion, Algernon Charles Swinburne is remembered, if at all, as a boozy, cantankerous pervert, the author of a few extracts in the more comprehensive anthologies of nineteenth-century verse. His range was always limited – rarely straying beyond 'the sea, regret, kissing, delirium, fire, weariness, roses, pain, cliffs, loss, stars, downs, the sun, wine, thunder, blood, pleasure, death, swallows in the foam, Mary Queen of Scots [and] the wind', as Robert Nye has pointed out[2] – but his output was considerable. The standard edition of his complete works runs to no less than twenty volumes.

Before he had turned twenty-five, two of Swinburne's verse plays, both intended for parlour perusal rather than public performance, had been published, albeit at his family's expense. Then, in 1865, they were joined by *Atalanta in Calydon* an ambitious and technically triumphant attempt to re-create in English something of the tone of Ancient Greek tragedy. Swinburne's name was made. Even Tennyson wrote to praise the play's rhythmic virtuosity, and the twenty-eight-year-old poet basked in the sunshine of popular acclaim. He sat to George Frederic Watts that same year for the rather wispy, wistful portrait which now hangs in the National Portrait Gallery; his image adorned postcards which found a ready sale in London. He was caricatured in a novel by George Meredith, while even Matthew Arnold, who had once dismissed him as 'a sort of pseudo-Shelley',[3] noted that he had become 'the favourite poet of the young men at Oxford and Cambridge'.[4]

Capitalising on all this, through a shrewd manipulation of contemporary fashion, Swinburne created for himself a role as the popular epitome of the ultra-sensitive, highly strung and carelessly Bohemian poet. It was extremely successful. While his biographer Edmund Gosse recalled with perhaps just a trace of no-nonsense masculine impatience that 'in the streets he had the movement of a somnambulist',[5] like many other women of the time, Georgina, wife of the painter Edward Burne-Jones, found him simply irresistible. They were near neighbours and she saw a great deal of him:

> Sometimes twice or three times a day he would come in, bringing his poems hot from his heart and certain of welcome and a hearing at any hour. His appearance was very unusual and in some ways beautiful, for his hair was glorious in abundance and colour and his eyes indescribably fine. When repeating poetry he had a perfectly natural way of lifting them

in a rapt, unconscious gaze, and their clear green colour softened by thick brown lashes was unforgettable: 'Looks commercing with the skies' [Milton, '*Il Penseroso*', 39] expresses it without exaggeration. He was restless beyond words, scarcely standing still at all and almost dancing as he walked, while even in sitting he moved continually, seeming to keep time by a soft movement of the hands at the wrists, and sometimes of the feet also, with some inner rhythm of excitement. He was courteous and affectionate and unsuspicious, and faithful beyond most people to those he really loved.[6]

As we now know, there was a great deal more to Swinburne than that; but a combination of the loyalty of his friends and the tight-lipped reticence of the age ensured that the less attractive aspects of his nature did nothing to dull the brilliance of the image he had so painstakingly created and was so effectively projecting. His singular sexual appetites and preoccupation with masochistic pornography were already well established. But, like his pro-digious drinking and the numerous accounts of his 'lunging' for a bottle of sherry while visiting friends or falling insensible from a cab outside his Chelsea lodgings, they were little known outside an immediate London circle.

His 'differentness' made him a natural Bohemian; and that, far more than his early association with the Pre-Raphaelites and close friendship with Rossetti, was the key to his popularity. But behind even Swinburne's frivolous persona was a deeply serious pre-occupation with art and his responsibility as an artist. In 1866 he published his collected *Poems and Ballads* in an attempt to capitalise on the critical success and wide popularity of *Atalanta*. He was not quite thirty, and the book brought together the majority of the shorter lyric and narrative poetry he had written. Unfortunately, however, it was not reviewed by the young men of Oxford and Cambridge nor the adoring women of London, who on at least one occasion had gone as far as crowning him with laurels. It was dispatched by a different brand of reader: the stern critics of the periodical press whose tastes and literary sensibilities had been set by the more decorous work of Tennyson and Browning.

They were not impressed. An anonymous contributor to the 'London Charivari' caught the tone well when he wrote: 'Having read Mr Swinburne's defence of his prurient poetics, *Punch* hereby gives him royal licence to change his name to what is evidently its true form – SWINEBORN.'[7] That was just the start. Week after week the book was pilloried in the press, and its author threatened with legal action over what were perceived as thinly veiled incestuous, lesbian and sadistic references in such poems as 'Phaedra' and the 'unintelligible' 'Anactoria'. The whole volume was 'filthy', screamed the critics. It was 'vile' and full of 'unspeakable foulnesses'.

Swinburne was distraught. But although the book did not immediately promote him to the pantheon as he had hoped it would, the events surrounding its appearance certainly did no harm to what, a century on, would have been called his underground cult following. Nor did his involvement, a few years later, in one of the most celebrated episodes of tribal warfare to trouble the never particularly calm nineteenth-century literary scene. Indirectly, that too had its origins in the furore which had accompanied the publication of *Poems and Ballads*.

In October 1871, five years after the book's appearance, one Robert Buchanan, who had already savaged it in the *Athenaeum*, returned to the offensive with a pseudonymous article in the *Contemporary Review*. Entitled 'The Fleshly School of Poetry', it was chiefly an attack on the literary work of Rossetti, but inevitably it also took a few sideswipes at Swinburne. His poetry was 'the veriest garbage', Buchanan wrote, in which 'the Bacchanal screams, the sterile Dolores sweats, serpents dance, men and women wench, wriggle and foam in an endless alliteration of heated and meaningless words'.

There ensued one of the two most sensational literary rows of the decade. Many more heated and, to those outside the rival camps, frequently meaningless words were exchanged as Swinburne, Rossetti and the latter's younger brother, William Michael, first sought to discover the real identity of their critic and then launched a vigorous counter-attack. With Swinburne apt to refer to Buchanan as 'the pole-cat' or 'dung-dropping', the periodical-reading public found the protracted wrangle endlessly entertaining. But it was more than mere mud-slinging. Behind the personal abuse lay the perennial argument about the role of the artist in society. Should he follow his own conscience, as the Aesthetes believed, and plough a lonely furrow; or should he serve more utilitarian ends and, in short, give the public what it wanted?

Much the same concerns lay behind the second row, which erupted only five years later. In 1877 James Abbott McNeill Whistler exhibited a series of impressionist *Nocturnes* at the Grosvenor Gallery exhibition. An American by birth, he had come to Europe in 1855 and, by means of a studied, almost theatrical flamboyance, had soon created a public personality which vied with Swinburne's in its outrageousness. According to one school of thought, he was a wit, a dandy and, through his painting, which enshrined a pure but entirely different form of naturalism to that of the Pre-Raphaelites, an exemplary Aesthete. According to another, headed by no less a figure than the art critic John Ruskin, he was nothing more than a coxcomb.

Ruskin in fact called him exactly that in his review of the Grosvenor Gallery show, adding for good measure the now famous phrase that he had 'flung a pot of paint into the public's face'. Whistler sued for libel, with the result that the arcane aesthetics which lay behind contemporary culture were once again publicly rehearsed, this time in a court of law rather than the columns of minority magazines. Whistler won a *succès d'estime*, being awarded the sum of one farthing in damages; but, as in Swinburne's battle with his critics and the later Queensbury case, the trial itself was the thing.

Indeed, in retrospect it is tempting to point out the parallels between all three: the clash between realism and decency on the one hand, and the commitment to a personal truth on the other being, in many ways, only the other side of the coin to the opposition of public law and morality to the private (albeit criminal) peccadilloes of the individual. But if each case was of consuming interest to those actually involved, a scandal in Bohemia directly threatening their very existence, to the public at large they were only further examples of the extent to which Aestheticism and its strutting, posturing schools of poets and artists had become a rich source of comedy and middle-brow entertainment. For, far from finding themselves cast as a new generation of world legislators, by the late 1870s Whistler, Wilde and other prominent Aesthetes were beginning to see themselves parodied on stage and made fun of in print. Worse, the public seemed to draw no distinction between them and a whole gallery of fictional counterparts.

There was Walter Hamlin in *Miss Brown*, a pseudonymous

novel first published in 1884. There was Esmé Amarinth and his constant companion Lord Reginald Hastings (sharply drawn caricatures of Wilde and Lord Alfred Douglas), who featured in the anonymously published novel *The Green Carnation* (1894). Most enduring of all, there were Jellaby Postlethwaite, 'the great poet', and the painters Pilcox and Maudle.

Originally conceived as exemplars of a type rather than caricatures of specific individuals, all three were the creations of George du Maurier, then a *Punch* cartoonist. The very fact that they appeared in *Punch* gave a peculiar, semi-official imprimatur to all the parodists. For, as du Maurier's granddaughter, the novelist Daphne du Maurier, has written, in the late nineteenth century the magazine had a reputation for far more than waiting-room jokiness:

> It stood alone, the only weekly paper of its kind. A gibe at the government from *Punch* in 1870, and worried members of Parliament would be discussing the fact in the lobbies the same day. A cool criticism of a picture or a poem, and the luckless author hung his head in shame. Only the best draughtsmen of the day contributed to *Punch* and with them the wittiest writers, the ablest critics.[8]

Postlethwaite, Pilcox and Maudle first appeared, simpering and lisping their way through the 'Aesthetic' salons and reception-rooms of hostesses like Mrs Cimabue Brown, in drawings published in 1879. They obviously struck a chord, for their adventures continued in further sketches which appeared at irregular intervals until the summer of 1881, their satire becoming more savage, their targets more immediately identifiable. In February 1880 in an early drawing entitled *Nincompoopiana*, Mrs Brown had pointed out Postlethwaite to a stranger:

> Oh, look at his Grand Head and Poetic Face, with those Flowerlike Eyes, and that Exquisite Sad Smile! Look at his Slender Willowy Frame, as yielding and fragile as a Woman's! That's young Maudle, standing just behind him – the great Painter, you know. He has just painted Me as 'Héloise', and my husband as 'Abélard'. *Is* not he *Divine*?[9]

A year later Maudle – despite his monocle, by then an

unmistakable caricature of Wilde (see Plate 4) – was being questioned on 'The Choice of a Profession', and the tone was a great deal less friendly:

MAUDLE: How *consummately* lovely your Son is, Mrs Brown!
MRS BROWN (*A Philistine from the country*): What? He's a *nice, manly* Boy, if you mean *that*, Mr Maudle. He has just left School, you know, and wishes to be an Artist.
MAUDLE: *Why* should he be an Artist?
MRS BROWN: Well, he must be *something!*
MAUDLE: Why should he *Be* anything? Why not let him remain for ever content to *Exist Beautifully!*
(*Mrs Brown determines that at all events her Son shall not study Art under Maudle.*)[10]

Nor was the press alone in its exploitation of Aestheticism. The London stage was equally quick to turn the movement to its own advantage, and soon acquired its own galaxy of Aesthetes, all of whom seemed to owe at least something to Wilde. Before the mid-eighties no less than four plays satirising the Aesthetic movement had been produced in the West End. They did much to establish Wilde as a public figure; and, flattered by the attention, he did not object to his identification with the central character of a play called *The Charlatan*; with Herbert Beerbohm Tree's portrayal of Scott Ramsey in a comedy called *Where's the Cat?*; and with the foolish, duplicitious Lambert Streyke (also played by Tree) in F. C. Burnand's long-running play *The Colonel*.

Even the success of *The Colonel* paled in comparison with the 578 performances notched up by *Patience*, W. S. Gilbert and Arthur Sullivan's Aesthetic opera which opened at the Opéra Comique on 23 April 1881. Originally conceived as a satire on the Tractarian movement in the Church of England featuring two rival curates, Gilbert quickly adapted it into an affable send-up of Aestheticism centring around two warring poets.

Like du Maurier, he seems to have been more concerned with types than individuals in his creation of the 'Fleshly' Reginald Bunthorne and the 'Idyllic' Archibald Grosvenor. But establishing their pedigrees quickly became an obsession with audiences; and it has remained critical sport ever since, for cases are still being made for Wilde, Swinburne, Whistler, Burne-Jones and Rossetti. Ultimately, however, it does not matter. The success of *Patience* lay in its effortless, knowing and affectionate mockery of the whole movement. The libretto teems with allusions and references: to primary colours and a paler 'greenery-yallery'; to the South Kensington School of Design and the Grosvenor Gallery; to Early English architecture, lilies, asphodels, blue-and-white pottery and every other Aesthetic prop and predilection. Bunthorne, of course, embodies them all; his Act One patter song is perhaps the most famous statement ever made of the meaning of Aestheticism:

> *If you're anxious to shine in the high aesthetic line as a*
>   *man of culture rare,*
> *You must get up all the germs of the transcendental*
>   *terms, and plant them everywhere.*
> *You must lie upon the daisies and discourse in novel*
>   *phrases of your complicated state of mind.*
> *The meaning doesn't matter in it's only idle chatter of a*
>   *transcendental kind.*
>   *And everyone will say,*
>   *As you walk your mystic way,*
> *'If this young man expresses himself in terms too deep*
>   *for me,*
> *Why what a very singularly deep young man this deep*
>   *young man must be!'* . . .
>
> *Then a sentimental passion of a vegetable fashion must*
>   *excite your languid spleen,*
> *An attachment à la Plato for a bashful young potato, or a*
>   *not-too-French French bean!*
> *Though the Philistines may jostle, you will rank as an*
>   *apostle in the aesthetic band,*
> *If you walk down Piccadilly with a poppy or a lily in*
>   *your mediaeval hand.*
>   *And everyone will say,*
>   *As you walk your flowery way,*
> *'If he's content with a vegetable love which would*
>   *certainly not suit me,*
> *Why what a most particularly pure young man this pure*
>   *young man must be!'*[11]

Oscar Wilde was, of course, among the audience at the first night of *Patience*; it would have been inconceivable for him to have missed it. By all accounts he enjoyed the production hugely, and allowed himself to become completely caught up in the *Patience* fever which swept London in the wake of the production. He did nothing to distance himself from Bunthorne – quite the reverse, in fact – and enthusiastically accepted the suggestion of the opera's producer, Richard D'Oyly Carte, that he should make a lecture-tour of America to publicise the New York production which was due to open at the end of the year.

His keenness to go is perhaps only partially explained by his urgent need of money at that time (and of course his permanent craving for publicity). His choice of subject at least suggests that at a deeper level he still felt some need to explain and justify Aestheticism, albeit to bewildered American audiences. Wearing his 'Aesthetic lecturing costume', comprising velvet knee-breeches and a quilted velvet jacket – which, as Richard Ellmann has pointed out, was not actually Aesthetic at all since it was merely the dress of Oxford University's Apollo Lodge of Freemasons, into which Wilde had been received in February 1875 – he took as his topic 'The English Renaissance'.

It was a predominantly serious lecture with distant echoes of Pater's book, but it must have sounded like nothing so much as a last-ditch stand. Despite its own high-flown hopes, far from being the harbinger of a new order, truly Bohemian in its rejection of conventional morality in favour of a private, artistic credo, Aestheticism had become a huge international joke.

The clerk of the court at the Old Bailey was used to common criminals with common names: the Alfred Taylors of this world and the sorry procession of domestic poisoners whose cases were followed with appalled fascination by readers of the Victorian popular press. Oscar Fingal O'Flahertie Wills Wilde took some getting round. So it was fortunate that, although Esmé Amarinth and Lambert Streyke, Reginald Bunthorne, Archibald Grosvenor and all the rest, to say nothing of James Abbott McNeill Whistler and Algernon Charles Swinburne, were assumed to be standing invisibly behind the prisoner at the bar in May 1895, their names were not listed on the charge sheet too. In their own ideal, artistic world they would have been, for they were all guilty in the broadest sense. And, by the time the court rose in good time for dinner on Saturday, 25 May 1895, they had all disappeared as completely as Wilde.

Taunted by shouts of 'Oscar' whenever they set foot in the streets, the long-haired boys had bowed to the inevitable, had their hair cut reg'lar and temporarily deserted Kettner's and the Café Royal. Dante Gabriel Rossetti had died in 1882. Swinburne, though still alive, was sequestered at The Pines in Streatham with Theodore Watts-Dunton, a lonely relic of a bygone age. And, as the cock crowed, even Wilde's closest friends and associates deserted him. There had been demands during the trial that Bosie too should be charged. He wasn't for, at Wilde's insistence, he had left the country before proceedings began; holing up, just beyond the reach of English law, at the Hotel Terminus in Calais. Others did not wait so long or stay so near: Robbie Ross, Wilde's confidant and greatest friend, took the boat-train to the continent, along with Lord Ronald Gower and what Hesketh Pearson picturesquely describes as a 'holiday rush' of other artists and understandably frightened society homosexuals.

Wilde himself lost everything. At a very early stage his library, manuscripts and personal effects had been auctioned off for a fraction of their real value. He was adjudged bankrupt, and separated from his wife Constance and their two sons Cyril and Vyvyan. Worst of all, perhaps, his work was wilfully forgotten. Anonymously, and with the minimum of fuss, both *An Ideal Husband* and *The Importance of Being Earnest* had been withdrawn in the summer of 1895; and when George Saintsbury, Professor of English at Edinburgh University, came to publish his popular *History of Nineteenth Century Literature* the following year, Wilde was not so much as mentioned.

'The dramatic work of those who have not excelled in other kinds of literature is not literature at all,' Saintsbury proclaims at the end of an altogether scanty chapter on drama. He has little time for frivolity, preferring the stronger meat of tragedy, but even if that explains his otherwise inexplicable passing over of both Dion Boucicault and Arthur Wing Pinero, two of the most popular playwrights of the late Victorian period, the sniffy high-mindedness of his pronouncement still reads like a gratuitous snipe at Wilde.

Swinburne originally fared as badly. Not until the third edition of the book appeared in 1906 did Saintsbury decide to relax what, in 1896, must have been a convenient rule that he would exclude living authors. 'Mr Meredith' and 'Mr Swinburne' thus make belated and brief appearances, Swinburne being accorded just five of the volume's 489 pages.

The events of May 1895 cast a long shadow. To those who stood at the heart of the darkness it must have seemed impenetrable. For as the last of the curious reluctantly left their places outside the Old Bailey and the very tardiest exiles watched the coast of England fade behind their boat-trains or hired packets, for a month or two it really did appear that 'a dash of wholesome dignity' had finally cleansed the stables and that English Bohemianism had been tamed and trampled into submission by the overwhelming might of conformity.

The boats sailed on, but in reality nothing of the kind had happened.

CHAPTER TWO

La Vie de Bohème

ON a warm spring afternoon in 1904 a young man, 'mad to be a Villon', piled his books, a railway rug, a large chair and a few other personal belongings onto the back of a hired grocer's van and set out to discover Bohemia.

Arthur Ransome, the author of *Swallows and Amazons* and several more of the most enduringly popular children's books written this century, was born in Leeds in 1884. The eldest child of the Professor of History at what later became the University of Leeds, he had enjoyed a conventional upper-middle-class child-hood, passed through a local prep school and then carved an undistinguished name for himself at Rugby. He had not gone on to university, and by the beginning of 1904 was living with his mother at Balham in south London, working as a publisher's errand-boy. He was determined to be a writer, however, and he knew very well that *real* writers did not spend their time dodging carts and horse-buses as they ran other authors' proof-copies and galley-sheets from office to office. Still less did they have to face a nightly return to noisy, over-crowded homes among the streets and avenues of suburbia. Something had to give. 'My wishes told my conscience twenty times a day that my work (my work!) could but ill progress in a house where several bustling lives were vividly lived in directions opposite to my own desires,'[1] he later recalled.

His chance of escape came a few months later. The publishing house for which he had been working went out of business, and in the space of one morning Arthur Ransome became a Bohemian. 'Prowling round Chelsea', he 'found an empty room with four windows all in good condition and a water supply two floors below, at a rent of a few shillings a week'.[2] He had just turned twenty and in more sober moments had to admit that the room, 'a large square place' with bare floorboards and dull grey-green walls, was neither cheerful nor comfortable. Nevertheless, he paid a week's rent in advance and went home, ordering the grocer's van to call after lunch.

It was, apparently, a quixotic, virtually spur of the moment decision, but in 1904, for a young man of Ransome's temperament, almost inevitable. He had been eleven at the time of the Wilde trial, immured in his Yorkshire prep school and too young for the sensation surrounding the Old Bailey hearing to have made any serious impression. But he was a voracious reader – Carlyle's *Sartor Resartus* was his Bible – and his adolescence exactly coincided with the period during which accounts of a new, Parisian and distinctly un-Wildean Bohemianism were beginning to appear, accounts in which Bohemia itself was plated with a pinchbeck glamour it has never wholly lost.

Giacomo Puccini's fourth opera, *La Bohème*, was first seen in England in 1897, a mere eighteen months after its Italian première. The Carl Rosa Opera Company originally presented it in an English translation at the Theatre Royal, Manchester on 22 April. Such was its success that this English version transferred to the Royal Opera House, Covent Garden less than six months later, on 2 October.

Along with George du Maurier's novel *Trilby*, first published three years previously, it offered a public which had only recently tired of the feyness, artificiality and frivolity of Aestheticism, an attractive and apparently realistic account of the creative process. *Trilby* has now been relegated to the back shelves of literary history. *La Bohème* on the other hand – despite a review of that first London production which suggested that the score was 'not stimulating enough to be heard often', and a later critic's comment that the whole piece was 'foul in subject, and fulminant but futile in its music' – has found a central place in the operatic repertoire. Indeed, it is hardly an exaggeration to claim that popular twentieth-century notions of Bohemianism are largely derived from the work: in just the first two of its four acts, it does after all indelibly fix the two contrasting sides of the *vie de bohème*.

Nominally, and, as we shall see, inevitably, it is set in the Paris of 1830, but the libretto might just as well have been headed 'Anywhere, anytime'.

The obverse is the extroverted, gregarious and inevitably boozy life of the Café Momus. Puccini and his librettists people it with 'a vast, motley crowd; citizens, soldiers, serving-girls, children, students, seamstresses, gendarmes, etc.'. None is the least bit disconcerted by the arrival in their midst of a painter, a poet, a philosopher and a musician; indeed in the general hubbub it goes almost unnoticed. Waiters rush to and fro, laying tables and delivering trays of drink. Actresses drop in for after-show suppers. Nobody objects to Marcello's flirting with all the *jeunes filles* . . . and absolutely everyone agrees that it is a good wheeze for Alcindoro, the elderly state councillor, to be left to pick up the tab.

In direct contrast is the sordid, solitary life of the garret, in the midst of which the opera opens. There is not so much as an overture; Act One immediately confronts the audience with the attic studio shared by the artist Marcello and his friend Rodolpho. It is Christmas Eve and bitterly cold. The 'spacious window' looks out over 'an expanse of snow-clad roofs', and the room is sparsely furnished. Stage directions call merely for a stove, a table, a small cupboard, a little bookcase, four chairs, an easel and a bed, items which would come to have a symbolic, iconographic significance in the Bohemian life, as would the 'few books' and 'many packs of cards' which are also mentioned.

It is only when Marcello and Rodolpho start singing that the final part of the jigsaw falls into place. Within a matter of minutes the names of both Musetta and Mimi have been mentioned; for love, of a hot-blooded, heterosexual, but invariably virtuous kind, was never far from the centre of things in this new Bohemia or, come to that, in Marcello and Rodolpho's attic. Even as they complain of hunger and, in an attempt to keep warm, burn the manuscript of a three-act drama on which Rodolpho, 'the great poet', has been working, it dominates the conversation. Poverty, hunger, creativity, a close bonhomie in the face of all adversities, and love . . . the picture is at last complete.

Even in the late nineties, however, it was far from original. George du Maurier, the one-time *Punch* cartoonist, had assembled virtually the same ingredients in his novel *Trilby* which was first published in serial form by *Harper's Monthly Magazine*. 'Part First' appeared in the January 1894 issue, and the story immediately caught the public imagination. Even if he was not familiar with *Bohème*, it is inconceivable that Arthur Ransome could have grown up in ignorance of *Trilby*; for, as Daphne du Maurier has written, 'the *Trilby* "boom" was one of the most sensational literary events that ever happened; people went mad about the book in England and America.'[3] Within months Trilby shoes and Trilby sweets had appeared on the market. Du Maurier was asked to endorse Trilby songs and a Trilby kitchen range. Baby girls were christened Trilby. Trilby parties were held, at which true devotees could display their intimate knowledge of the novel, and for no obvious reason a particular style of soft felt hat was for ever renamed.

Yet, despite its title, du Maurier's novel is not just the story of Trilby O'Ferrall, the young Irish girl who lived in Paris, working as a *blanchisseuse de fin* when she was not modelling in the 'altogether'. Indeed, the account of her infatuation with the mesmeric musician Svengali and her short-lived concert career occupies only about a quarter of the text. Most of the remainder is given over to a knowing, sentimental account of exactly the same Parisian *vie de bohème* which inspired Puccini. Du Maurier had himself been an art student in Paris in the 1850s and his memories of the time provided an important source of inspiration when he came to write *Trilby*. Many of the characters are based on his student contemporaries at the *atelier* Gleyre, some so obviously that their real identities were easily discovered by the book's first readers.

In his depiction of Joe Sibley, however, du Maurier went beyond mere portraiture. In several of the 120 illustrations which he himself provided, and in his description of Sibley, 'the idle apprentice, the king of bohemia, *le roi des truands*', du Maurier was consciously parodying the Aesthete and artist Whistler, whom he had known since they were both students in Paris:

> Always in debt, like Svengali; like Svengali, vain, witty, and a most exquisite and original artist; and also eccentric in his attire (though clean), so that people would stare at him as he walked along – which he adored! But (unlike Svengali) he was genial, caressing, sympathetic, charming; the most irresistible friend in the world as long as his friendship lasted – but that was not for ever!

The moment his friendship left off, his emnity began at once . . .

He is now perched on such a topping pinnacle (of fame and notoriety combined) that people can stare at him from two hemispheres at once; and so famous as a wit that when he jokes (and he is always joking) people laugh first, and then ask what it was he was joking about. And you can even make your own mild funniments raise a roar by merely prefacing them, 'As Joe Sibley once said'. The present scribe has often done so.[4]

Whistler was not amused, and he launched a complex libel action. Hardly less celebrated than the similar suit he had filed against John Ruskin in 1877, it was rather more successful. *Harper*'s apologised unreservedly, and the character of Joe Sibley had disappeared by the time that *Trilby* was published in book form.

It would be wrong to see *Trilby* as no more than a *roman à clef*; it is not that kind of novel. Indeed, to modern eyes, it is not even a particularly good one. Like many works originally produced for the serial market, it is patchily written. Critics have pointed to well-realised episodes in virtually every chapter, but generally agree that its opening, introducing the life of the studios, is immeasurably superior to the conventionally melodramatic account of Trilby's life and inevitable death which occupies the latter half of the text.

The fullest account of Bohemian life to have been published in English at the time, the book's first four chapters paint a fascinating, if idealised, picture of the Parisian Latin Quarter during the mid-nineteenth century. Drawing once again on his personal experience, du Maurier introduces three English art students – his 'three musketeers of the brush' – and their studio in the Place St Anatole des Arts. The good-looking Taffy, Sandy 'the Laird of Cockpen' and the young William Bagot, 'Little Billee', have come to Paris to be Bohemians and do all those things which Bohemians were popularly imagined to do:

If it was decently fine, the most of them went off to dine at the Restaurant de la Couronne, kept by Père Trin (in the Rue de Monsieur), who gave you of his best to eat and drink for twenty-sols Parisis, or one franc in the coin of the empire. Good distending soups, omelets that were only too savory, lentils, red and white beans, meat so dressed and sauced and seasoned that you didn't know whether it was beef or mutton – flesh, fowl, or good red herring – or even bad, for that matter – nor very greatly cared . . .

And you hobnobbed with models, male and female, students of law and medicine, painters and sculptors, workmen and *blanchisseuses* and grisettes, and found them very good company, and most improving to your French, if your French was of the usual British kind, and even to some of your manners, if these were very British indeed. And the evening was innocently wound up with billiards, cards or dominoes at the Café du Luxembourg opposite; or at the Théâtre du Luxembourg in the Rue de Madame, to see funny farces with screamingly droll Englishmen in them; or, still better, at the Jardin Bullier (la Closerie des Lilas), to see the students dance the cancan, or try and dance it yourself, which is not so easy as it seems; or, best of all, at the Théâtre de l'Odéon to see some piece of the classical *répertoire*.[5]

The comparisons with Puccini's Rodolpho, Marcello, Schaunard and Colline, and in particular with their carousing among the shop-girls, seamstresses, actresses and urchins at the Café Momus, is inescapable and no mere coincidence. For, despite du Maurier's first-hand knowledge of the subject, *Trilby* and *La Bohème* share the same original source. Puccini and his librettists, Giuseppe Giacosa and Luigi Illica, made no bones about it and admitted on the title page of their score that *Bohème* was based on a French play of the late 1840s entitled *La Vie de Bohème*. A collaboration between the young dramatist Théodore Barrière and an even younger writer called Henry Mürger, it had in turn been based on a collection of stories by the latter, *Scènes de la Vie du Bohème*, which were originally published in *La Corsaire* between 1845 and 1849.

It is not difficult to imagine the appeal the stories would have had for Puccini. Often photographed with a cigarette set rakishly between his lips, he was himself a Bohemian by temperament, happier throughout his life drinking and playing cards rather than working. Even while writing *Bohème* he had bought a share in what his biographer Mosco Carner has described as 'a kind of roadhouse, a shed rather than an inn' in Torre del Lago. At the composer's suggestion it was opened as the Club la Bohème and had among its house rules semi-serious injunctions against silence, wisdom and the playing of any game permitted by law.[6]

Du Maurier appears to have been more reticent about his sources. While critics and the more perceptive of his readers noted that several characters and incidents in *Trilby* had been borrowed from *La Dame aux Camélias* by Alexandre Dumas *fils*, the relative unfamiliarity of Mürger's stories meant that the book's immeasurably greater debt to them passed unnoticed. Du Maurier himself admitted this in a letter, writing that he owed 'so much to *Scènes de la Vie de Bohème*, only the British public does not know that'.[7]

Nor, sadly, did Henry Mürger. Worn out by the poverty and deprivation of a real-life Bohemia which had no place on the operatic stages of the world or between the covers of nineteenth-century romantic fiction, he had died in 1861 at the age of thirty-eight. After selling all rights to his stories, he had retired from 'the Quartier', symbolically moving from the Left Bank to an apartment in a more conservative quarter of Paris. But despite this bourgeois gesture, it is as the chronicler – or, more accurately, to all intents and purposes the creator – of the Parisian *bohème dorée* that he will always be remembered. Quite justifiably he has been called the first Bohemian, although Bohemia had in fact existed long before he was born and he was far from the first writer to have visited it.

Théophile Gautier and others had previously depicted the Bohemian inhabitants of the impasse du Doyenné and reminisced about the wild *bals des truands* which had been held there. Balzac had borrowed the word Bohemia in 1830 to describe the setting of his novel *Un Grande Homme de Province à Paris*, and in *Voyage au Pays de Bohème* Alphonse de Calonne had portrayed it as a 'sad country . . . bordered on the north by need, on the south by misery, on the east by illusion and on the west by the infirmary'. Taking much the same line, a writer in *La Silhouette* of the same period had pointed out that it 'was bordered on the north by the cold, on the west by hunger, on the south by love, and the east by hope'.

What he lacked in originality, however, Mürger more than made up for with personal experience. Written as fiction, his *Scènes* are nevertheless only thinly disguised accounts of incidents from his own adolescence and youth. In his description of Rodolphe, 'the great poet' and the prototype for Puccini's Rodolpho, he went as far as drawing a romanticised but recognisable self-portait. Bald, sunken-eyed, shabbily dressed and prematurely lined at the age of thirty, Mürger stares myopically from one of the pioneer photographer Felix Nadar's daguerreotypes which are now housed in the Cabinet d'Estampes of the French Bibliothèque Nationale (see Plate 5). Seven years earlier he had written that Rodolphe was:

> a young man whose face was hidden behind an enormous, bushy, multi-coloured beard. In contrast to this abundance of facial hair, premature baldness had left the top of his head as bare as a kneecap, although a few stray hairs, so few that you could almost count them, tried to hide its nakedness. He was wearing a black jacket, out at the elbows, which displayed a highly original form of armpit-ventilation whenever he raised his arms too high. His trousers had once been black, and his boots – which had never been new – looked as if they had already tramped round the world several times on the feet of the Wandering Jew.[8]

Nor did Mürger have to look far for the originals of his Colline, Schaunard and Marcel, respectively 'the great philosopher', 'the great musician' and 'the great artist' who, with Rodolphe, comprised the 'Four Musketeers' of his stories and survived intact in Puccini's opera. From an early age he had been brought up in the company of such quintessentially Bohemian figures as writers, artists and actors. And as a young man, he frequented the real-life Café Momus at 15 rue des Prêtres-Saint-Germain-l'Auxerrois in Paris, where coffee was only 5 sous a cup.

A tall, narrow, rather ramshackle establishment, to judge from a contemporary engraving, with fly-posted advertisements peeling from the walls, Mürger erroneously claims that it had been named after 'the god of Jokes and Laughter'. More prosaically, the *Oxford Companion to Classical Literature* lists Momus as 'the personification of criticism and fault-finding' in Greek mythology. But the cheapness of its coffee, the '*4 billards*' and even the prospect of '*Toiles blanches et jaunes*' advertised on crudely painted signs, were far from the Momus's only attractions. Everyone went there: foreigners, prostitutes, the aristocracy, the *nouveau riche* and the young denizens of Bohemia. 'One can go round the world, and then meet up again at the Momus', it was said at the time. In the mid-1840s the novelist and critic Jules Champfleury, once dubbed the King of Bohemia, held court at the Café Momus in a circle which also included Mürger, Nadar, the artist Gustave Courbet, the writers Charles Barbara, Charles Baudelaire, Gautier and the *poète maudit* Gérard de Nerval, this last an arch Bohemian if only through his habit of taking a live lobster for walks in the gardens of the Palais-Royal.

They were all well acquainted with the stark realities of Bohemian life which had been hinted at by Alphonse de Calonne. 'We are aching with hunger. We are at the end of our tether. We must find ourselves a niche, or blow our brains out,' Mürger once confessed in a letter. He belonged to a group calling itself the *Buveurs d'Eau*, or Water-Drinkers, which did exactly that because its members were unable to afford even the cheapest wine. But although the Goncourt brothers were to describe his *Scènes de la Vie de Bohème* as 'socialism dominating literature and firing broadsides at the literary capital',[9] the stories inevitably glossed over the more desperate aspects of the artistic life and painted a somewhat rosier, more romantic picture.

Maintaining a skilful blend of comedy and tragedy, the twenty-three tales portray the *vie de bohème* as 'a gay life but a terrible one'; boisterous, decadent but fundamentally decent. Their Four Musketeers never fall to the level of water-drinking and, indeed, are regular visitors at the Café Momus. Mürger writes that its proprietor was heartily sick of them. Understandably so, for Rodolphe used to comandeer all his newspapers and then play backgammon with Colline from ten in the morning until midnight. Marcel had installed his easel and paint-box in the café, and Schaunard was talking of bringing his piano. Not only that, they behaved as if they owned the place:

> They had chosen to meet in a room which could have held forty people very comfortably; but they were always by themselves there, because in time none of the other customers dared to go in.
>   Anyone who did immediately became the butt of their jokes, and usually fled without finishing either his paper or his coffee – in which the cream had anyway been turned sour by the four's outrageous comments on art, feeling and political economy. Even their conversation was so wild that the waiter who served them had gone mad at the prime of life.[10]

Nowadays, Mürger's stories are most often read by French

students, ironically enough, the inheritors of the battered mantle
of Parisian Bohemianism who live and work in the same Left Bank
streets and throng the same cafés that once fed Mürger. If they are
cited at all, it is most frequently in relation to Puccini's opera.
Their role in the creation of a seductive, artistic never-never land,
loosely based on the Bohemian Paris of the 1830s and 1840s which,
half a century later, would so bewitch Ransome and a whole
generation of English writers, has been virtually forgotten.

To the English poet, francophile and would-be Bohemian
Arthur Symons, however, it was all important. 'To be five-and-
twenty, poor and in love: that is enough', he once wrote. 'At that
age, and in those circumstances, you will find that Mürger has
said everything.'

Arthur Ransome was twenty, had money in his pockets and no
thoughts other than for himself when he set out for Bohemia in
1904. His decision to go had been prompted by his impatience
with the small-minded propriety of Balham, 'the ugliest and most
abominable of London's unpleasing suburbs'. He had taken all he
could of its 'suburban daughters who criticise musical comedies
seriously, and remind you twice in an afternoon that they are
quite unconventional'. They had made Bohemia into 'an
abominable word', he was later to complain; whereas he was sure
he knew its true meaning.

There is a touching naivety in the certainty with which he
maintains this for, still the suburban bookworm, he had no more
to go on than what he had gleaned from Mürger's stories and
entries in 'the best dictionaries'. There, he had found Bohemia
defined as:

'(1) A certain small country; (2) The gypsy life; (3) Any disreputable life; (4) The life of writers and painters' – in an order of
descent that is really quite pleasant. And on consulting a classic
work to find synonyms for a Bohemian, I find the following:
'Peregrinator, wanderer, rover, straggler, rambler, bird of
passage, gadabout, vagrant, scatterling, landloper, waif and
stray, wastrel, loafer, tramp, vagabound, nomad, gypsy, emi-
grant, and peripatetic somnambulist'. If we think of the word in
the atmosphere of all those others, it is not so abominable after
all, and I cannot find a better.[11]

He wanted it all, the Mürgeresque bonhomie as well as the gypsy life. Whatever the suburban daughters of Balham may have thought, he was intent on discovering and savouring to the full an absinthe-sipping, late-rising, freeloading, larky, youthful kingdom that was a lot more than 'unconventional'. But as he said goodbye to all his relations, clambered up onto the tailboard of the grocer's cart, lit a clay pipe and gave his hired driver the order to start, his determination to find it seems to have led him to ignore two facts.

If he had read even the sentimental Mürger more closely he might not have been so glib in dismissing the Frenchman's ultimate conclusion – that Bohemia led only to the academy, the hospital or the morgue – as an overly 'melancholy verdict'. More crucially, Mürger's assertion that the true Bohemian could only live in Paris should have given him food for thought. For if that had been true in the late 1840s, it was still the case in the early 1900s . . . the young Arthur Ransome might well have bided his time if he had only known that there were not – yet – any *true* Bohemians in London.

—— · CHAPTER THREE · ——

Bohemia in London

——————

THE five- or six-mile journey from Balham to Chelsea never-theless marked a significant rite of passage in the life of the young Arthur Ransome. The grocer's cart drove up through the familiar south London suburbs where red brick houses, ugly flats and 'ugly villas, as like to each other as the sheets from a printing press', lined the roads. Then, crossing the Albert Bridge, with Ransome swinging his legs over the tailboard and thumbing through Congreve's *Love for Love*, it struck out for the King's Road and followed that far more interesting thoroughfare almost as far as the appropriately named World's End.

In *Bohemia in London*, Ransome's partly autobiographical, partly fictional account of the following two years, and by his own admission his 'first real book', the trip is duly invested with all the epic qualities of a journey into both freedom and adulthood:

I was as Columbus setting forth to a New World, a gypsy striking his tent for unknown woods; I felt as if I had been a wanderer in a caravan from my childhood as I loosened my coat, opened one or two more buttons in the flannel shirt that I wore open at the neck, and saw the red brick houses slipping slowly away behind me. The pride of it, to be sitting behind a van that I had hired myself; to carry my own belongings to a place of my own choosing; to be absolutely a free man, whose most distant desires seemed instantly attainable. I have never known another afternoon like that . . . For was I not now a free Bohemian, on my way to the haunts of Savage, and Goldsmith, and Rossetti, and Lamb, and Whistler, and Steele, and Carlyle, and all the others whose names and histories I knew far better than their works . . .[1]

31

No, Ransome answers, rather surprisingly. Then he goes on to explain that, although he had known Lamb's 'Elia' essays since his schooldays – even then they had been of far greater interest than Caesar's histories – he knew little about either the life of their author or that of his other hero, Carlyle. Nevertheless, the true answer is a resounding Yes for, as readers of *Bohemia in London* soon discover, that overblown, rhetorical question exactly defines the real nature of his flight from Balham.

Despite the clay pipe and his loosening of a couple of shirt buttons, Ransome was never a true Bohemian, at least not in the way in which Henry Mürger would have understood the term. (Nor did he ever appear to be one. When they first met, in about 1908, Nina Hamnett encountered 'a man in knickerbockers, with a very large moustache'[2] – a young farmer rather than an artist.) If he had been, the notion of going to London would not have occurred to him. He would have set out for France and somehow found his way to Paris, exactly as several other Britons were to do in the next few years.

For, ultimately, Ransome's 'Bohemia' was an historical construct, and such a Xanadu had not flourished in England since the early nineteenth century, or, less charitably, since the day when Dick Whittington heard the sound of Bow Bells from the top of Highgate Hill. In his determination to escape the Philistine suburbs, he was not even fleeing to Mürger's storybook Bohemia but into the roistering, reassuring company of the dead: Savage, Steele, Goldsmith and all the other poets, poetasters and critics who would not contradict his nostalgic yearnings and still less demand the money for a drink.

As a direct result, when he did eventually encounter the realities of the present – something approaching the 'free' Bohemia he had after all set out to discover – all too often he shied away, disappointed and bewildered. Despite the verve and gusto which mark sections of *Bohemia in London*, notably his descriptions of places visited, Balham's middle-class propriety, together with Ransome's own youth and the ingrained values of his childhood, held him back from any real immersion in the world he was seeking.

There is, for instance, more than mere juvenile priggishness in his description of a visit to the Bloomsbury home of 'a well-known writer'. His head filled with memories of William Hazlitt, Pierce

Egan, Sir Richard Steele and the 'pimple-nosed, strong-headed' Ben Jonson – the 'Dick' and 'Ben' with whom he enjoys a mystical, first-naming communion over a last pipe one evening – he expects the writer to inhabit 'a very sumptuous flat', and is more than disappointed to find him holed up in nothing more than a lodging house. Ransome's middle-class prejudices reassert themselves:

> I knocked and went into the most dishevelled room it is possible to imagine. There was a big bed in it, unmade, the bed-clothes tumbled anyhow, several broken chairs, and a wash-stand with a basin out of which someone had taken a bite. The novelist, in a dressing-gown open at the neck, and showing plainly that there was nothing but skin beneath it, was writing at a desk, throwing off his sheets as fast as he covered them . . .
> We drank out of a couple of glasses my great man brought from a box in the corner. Then he talked of literature, and so well that the untidy bed, the unclean room, the wife and the baby were as if they had never been. In spite of his unwashed hands, in spite of the dressing-gown, he won his way back to greatness.[3]

Even so, Ransome cannot help noticing through the window that the novelist's wife, dismissed at the moment of his arrival, is lingering in the street below, having 'not troubled to put on a hat'.

It is a telling passage, which says more about Ransome himself than the characteristically unnamed novelist. Coming near the end of the book, it also retrospectively colours much that has gone before. All too clearly it reveals just how thin is the veneer of Bohemian sang-froid which Ransome adopts, and how much he remains the innocent abroad. However 'Bohemian' they might have been, unmade beds, domestic squalor and the very idea of working before one was dressed were plainly notions undreamt of in his philosophy.

None the less, for all its faults, *Bohemia in London* paints a uniquely detailed picture of artistic life in the capital at the start of this century. For, despite his standoffishness, Ransome is a uniquely well-qualified observer. Even when confronted by the formidable Gypsy, his hostess at a Chelsea party, he shows himself quite prepared to try anything once:

'Who is for opal hush?' she cried, and all, except the American girl and the picture dealer, who preferred whisky, declared their throats were dry for nothing else. Wondering what the strange-named drink might be, I too asked for opal hush, and she read the puzzlement in my face. 'You make it like this,' she said, and squirted lemonade from a syphon into a glass of red claret, so that a beautiful amethystine foam rose shimmering to the brim. 'The Irish poets over in Dublin called it so; and once, so they say, they went all round the town, and asked at every public-house for two tall cymbals and an opal hush.' It was very good, and as I drank I thought of those Irish poets, whose verses had meant much to me, and sipped the stuff with reverence as if it had been nectar from Olympus.[4]

Ransome's room was located somewhere between the Fulham Road and the lower end of the King's Road. The exact address is uncertain, but his biographer Hugh Brogan suggests that he probably lived in either Limerston Street or Lamont Road, behind St Stephen's Hospital. Whichever, it was hardly at the centre of things; and, furnished with no more than his rug, his chair and 3s.-worth of old packing-cases he had acquired from a nearby grocer, it presented Ransome with every incentive to get out. And get out he did. In 1904 and 1905 he quartered literary and artistic London. One foot always in Chelsea, he visited artists in their studios and editors in Fleet Street offices; he penetrated the clubs and coffee-houses of Soho, and hobnobbed with the latter-day Aesthetes of Hampstead. He drank with poets and columnists and, as far as he could, submerged himself in the business of being a Bohemian.

It is difficult to say when this ended and a more conscious quarrying for literary copy began. Brogan is silent on the point, but it is clear that when *Bohemia in London* appeared in the autumn of 1907 Ransome regarded himself not only as an expert on the subject, but as someone who had thoroughly researched it. He wrote dismissively in his introductory chapter of 'a dozen flippant, merry treatises on Bohemia in London, that talk of the Savage Club, and the Vagabond dinners, and all the other consciously unconventional things that like to consider themselves Bohemian'. But they were merely 'unconventional' – that word again – and not 'the real things' that he was after:

. . . no young poet or artist fresh to London, with all his hopes unrealised, all his capacity for original living unspent, has anything to do with them. They bear no more vital relation to the Bohemian life that is actually lived than masquerades or fancy dress balls bear to more ordinary existence. Members of the Savage Club, guests of the Vagabonds have either grown out of the life that should be in my book, or else have never lived in it. They are respectable citizens, dine comfortably, sleep in feather-beds, and find hot water waiting for them in the mornings.[5]

In *Bohemia in London*, then, Ransome is attempting a systematic description of the *demi-monde* in which the idealistic, out-of-town poet or artist like himself could expect to move. And since it is the most characteristic, he begins by describing the existence of painters and life models in their studios and on off-duty evenings at the 'sketch clubs', evoking a scene more strongly reminiscent of the opening of *La Bohème* than of the first few chapters of *Trilby*. For, whereas Little Billee, Taffy and the Laird of Cockpen shared a studio in the Place St Anatole des Arts, which was a cross between the study and a gentleman's club, cluttered with 'a panoply of foils, masks, and boxing-gloves', its dull red walls 'relieved by plaster casts of arms and legs and hands and feet; and Dante's mask, and Michael Angelo's alto-rilievo of Leda and the swan'[6] as well as copies of Titians, Rembrandts, Velasquezes, Rubenses and Tintorettos; that visited by Ransome was a spare, spartan affair.

He gives no clue as to its location, but his description of the studio does have the ring of truth. It is eerily similar to a hundred other studios described in letters and memoirs by Augustus and Gwen John, Walter Sickert, Nina Hamnett and other artists of the period.[7] Ransome neglects to mention only the numbing cold:

A large room, with no furniture but a divan or a camp-bed, a couple of chairs, an easel, and a model-stand made of a big box that holds a few coats and hats and coloured silks that do duty in a dozen pictures; a big window slanting up across the roof, with blinds to temper its light; canvases and old paintings without frames leaning against the walls; the artist, his coat off ready for work, strolling up and down with a cigarette between his lips . . .[8]

But if Ransome is as reticent over the whereabouts of the studio as he is about the identity of the 'well-known writer', when he turns to the cafés, coffee-houses and restaurants of Soho, he becomes positively fulsome, and *Bohemia in London* is at its Baedeker best. He knows his subject, and freely admits that 'the Boulogne, the Mont Blanc, Pinoli's, the France, and many another little restaurant knew us in those days; there was scarcely one, from Brice's and the Gourmet's in the south, to the Venice, at the Oxford Street end of Soho Street, that had not suffered our merry dinner parties.'[9]

He is still in the thrall of history; his account of Bohemian Soho has a lengthy litero-historical introduction revealing, among other things, that 'in Gerard Street, Dryden lived at No. 43, and doubtless found it very convenient for walking down of an afternoon to the coffee-houses about Covent Garden. Burke lived for a time at No. 37, and the greatest of all clubs, The Club, of Johnson, Goldsmith and Reynolds, met at the Turk's Head Tavern in the same street.' But for once it does not get the better of him. He breaks up his text with a row of asterisks and turns to the restaurants. Three are singled out for special mention.

Although for some reason it did not inspire the same affection with which Fitzrovian Bohemians of the twenties and thirties would remember the Restaurant de la Tour Eiffel, the 'Eiffel Tower' in Percy Street, Roche's or the Roche (and later Béguinot's) at the Charing Cross Road end of Old Compton Street was in many ways similarly central to the lives of the pre-1914 London artists, if for no other reason than its location. Old Compton Street had been the spiritual centre and principal shopping street of Soho since the early eighteenth century. It had a history of hospitality to foreigners, Bohemians and eccentrics of all kinds. As early as 1710 more than a quarter of its householders were French. John Leland, the author of *Fanny Hill*, had lived there, so too had Richard Wagner. Closer to Ransome's own time and inclinations, Paul Verlaine and Arthur Rimbaud had drunk Pernod and recited their poetry in a bar at No. 5. In 1900 around half of those living in Old Compton Street were foreign nationals, and socialist and anarchist publications were freely available.[10]

The Roche was more than simply a precursor of the Eiffel Tower and a home from home for the foreign and artistic communities. One contemporary source refers to it as having 'a reputation which is almost world-wide'[11] for the quality of the meals it offered at a price of around 2s. (or 10p.)

'This is Bohemia; what do you think of it?' Ransome was asked on his first visit. He does not say; but his description makes it clear that the Roche at least was everything and more than he was hoping to find when he left Balham on that spring afternoon. Like many another Soho restaurant, it was in effect not one but many; a maze of separate, small diners, one leading off another. There was a front room, an inner room beyond, and a flight of stairs leading to 'a hot little inferno' beneath.

On subsequent visits Ransome would occupy a seat in the inner room; but for his first meal, taken in the company of 'a lean painter', he contented himself with a place at the long, scrubbed table in the front room and watched his fellow-diners:

> All down our long table there were not two faces that did not seem to me to bear the imprint of some peculiar genius. Some were assuredly painters, others journalists, some very obviously poets, and there were several, too, of those amateur irregulars, who are always either exasperating or charming. The painter pointed out man after man by name. There was So-and-So, the musical critic; there was somebody else, who painted like Watteau: 'ridiculous ass,' commented my realistic friend; there was So-and-So, the editor of an art magazine; there was a fellow who had given up art for a place in his father's business, but yet kept up his old acquaintanceships with the men more faithful to their ideals.[12]

The Dieppe was a rather cheaper restaurant at the Piccadilly Circus end of Old Compton Street and offered *table d'hôte* meals at 1/6d. (7½p.) instead of the Roche's 2s. Ransome notes, somewhat wryly, that it was patronised more for its decor than its French menu. Its walls were covered with 'the dearest funny pictures', murals in the style of Botticelli's *Primavera* in which all the figures were incongruously clothed in mid-nineteenth-century costume.

The third of the restaurants which Ransome describes is Brice's, a whitewashed establishment run by Monsieur Brice, once again in Old Compton Street. Ransome was apparently something of a regular there; certainly 'the best of waiters' kept a corner table for him and his friends in the discreet back room where their endless smoking and talking, over bottles of German beer, was good-humouredly tolerated. So were their more boisterous moments. Ransome describes a wedding-party for which the small dining-tables were pushed together. The bride was an artist's model; the groom an artist himself, 'probably, we agreed, a very inferior craftsman, but certainly an excellent fellow'. Songs were sung – everything from 'Auld Lang Syne' to the Soldiers' Chorus from Gounod's *Faust* – doubtless to the accompaniment of Ransome playing the penny whistle which was never very far from his hand, and after an early supper the entire company escorted the couple to Victoria Station, in good time for them to catch the evening boat-train for a honeymoon in Dieppe.

Of the meals served in these restaurants Ransome has surprisingly little to say, beyond the fact that, wherever they were taken, they were generally excellent and very cheap, spoilt only by the frequently disappointing quality of the over-priced house wines. 'The wise drink beer,' he adds.

Robert Machray, the author of *The Night Side of London*, a chatty, informal guide to the nocturnal life of the city which was first published in 1902, was also familiar with many of the restaurants so enthusiastically patronised by Ransome and his friends. A journalist rather than a Bohemian, he nevertheless exhorts his readers to spend evenings, 'say once a fortnight', exploring Soho; not just for the food but also to 'study types of men and women you will hardly behold outside of this district'. His book specifically mentions several establishments which are also described by Ransome.

The Gourmet's at the southern boundary of Ransome's patch had an *à la carte* menu beginning with a 2*d. potage bonne femme*. A sketch depicts the interior of the Café Boulogne, apparently a large establishment with floor-to-ceiling engraved glass mirrors, starched cloths on every table and a waiter in evening dress (see Plate 6). Machray also describes a typical Soho menu of the period:

It begins with *hors d'oeuvres variés* – sardines, smoked herring, anchovies, olives, tomato-salad. Then, your choice of clear or thick soups – and the soups (Heaven only knows what's in them!) of Soho are simply, marvellously excellent. Now follows the fish-course, and here, alas! the Soho restaurant does not always shine, and this, it may be guessed, is because fish is never cheap in London. Then an entrée, after which comes the 'Farinasse', which is usually maccaroni in one form or another. In some restaurants, notably Guermani's, the maccaroni is worth the whole price of the dinner. And next there is a slice off the fillet or a piece of chicken, or rather *poulet rôti*, which du

Maurier always declared was quite a different thing from roast-chicken. Finally sweets, cheese, fruit. And all for two shillings or eighteen pence![13]

Such meals were not daily fare, however. Although artists were generally well able to afford the entry fees to café society at least until the end of the First World War – and indeed mixed on almost equal terms with the aristocracy at the Café Royal among other places – Ransome stresses that visits to the Gourmet's or the Roche were 'a tremulous extravagance', to be undertaken only when justified by 'the sale of a picture, or a longer article than usual'. His more usual haunts were the less formal bars and coffee-houses of Soho and Chelsea.

Downstairs at the Algerian in Dean Street, under the watchful eye of a large red dog, and not infrequently a grim police inspector, away from the French and Italians who filled the shop above, one could find late-night conversation. It was 'a gay, companionable place', somewhere else that echoed to the sound of Ransome's penny whistle; a place to bring girlfriends, drink coffee, smoke cigarettes and argue.

To some extent it still is. For although the Roche, the Dieppe and the other eating-houses have long gone, the Algerian has survived on the same site at No. 52 since 1887 and still trades as the Algerian Coffee Stores. The downstairs coffee-shop is no more, the wooden façade is now maroon where once it was green; but gold lettering still spells out the nature of the business and even its pre-STD telephone number, GERard 2480. Inside is an overpowering smell of fresh coffee, a wall of red bins containing eleven separate types of bean behind the counter and a display of dusty wine bottles, for the Algerian is also a wine merchant's. On shelves reaching to the ceiling are all manner of jugs, pots and percolators in addition to the more esoteric apparatus necessary to the production of espresso and *cappuccino*.

The Moorish Café at the top end of Soho Street was less predictable than the turn-of-the-century Algerian; its life as 'thick and dark and sweet' as the coffee ground and prepared behind its steamy, green-framed windows. Gaudy pictures of Istanbul, serpents and Ottoman warships decorated the walls. Its crowded, small tables were occupied by customers with dark hair, dark eyes and sallow skins, Ransome writes, with here and there the odd 'low caste Englishman'. Only occasionally did one encounter a fellow-Bohemian at the Moorish, rather out of place but immediately recognisable by his corduroy suit and porcelain pipe.

It was apparently the same with public houses. In direct contrast to the compulsive booziness which would characterise Fitzrovian life a quarter of a century later, pubs have little place in Ransome's story. Inevitably perhaps, for some things never change, those few that he does mention are in and around Fleet Street. There is the 'admirable' Cock, a chop-house in which 'you are still fed in high-backed pews and served by English waiters' and an unnamed and now long-vanished tavern in one of the alleys then leading to Salisbury Court in which the 'Antient Society of Cogers' held their meetings.

Further down, on the opposite side of the road, with an entrance in the narrow Wine Office Court opposite the then premises of the Press Club, Ransome celebrates the existence of the Cheshire Cheese, 'still the dirty-fronted, low-browed tavern, with stone flasks in the window, that it was even before Johnson's time':

> Here many of the best known journalists make a practice of dining, and doubtless get some sauce of amusement with their meat from the young men and girls, literary and pictorial, destined to work for the cheap magazines and fashion papers, who always begin their professional career by visiting the Cheshire Cheese for inspiration.

There is an ironic ambivalence in Ransome's description of the Cheshire Cheese, an uneasiness of tone which might be no more than the eternal freelance-Bohemian plaint against the staff journalist. He is distant in his perfunctorily brief description of the pub, and nothing less than offhand when he mentions that 'up a winding, crooked, dark staircase there are other rooms, with long tables in them stained with wine and ale, and in one of them the Rhymers' Club used to meet, to drink from tankards, smoke clay pipes, and recite their own poetry.'[14]

'Used to meet . . .' Maybe it is no more than that. In 1904–5 The Rhymers had only recently ceased to be an active force in British letters. Their regular meetings at the Cheshire Cheese had been one of the features of the London literary scene until a time which even the twenty-year-old Ransome could remember. His coldness towards them might, therefore, spring from the realisation that, once again, he had arrived on the scene too late. A latter-day disciple of Johnson, Johnson, Swift and Hazlitt, he had missed The Club which used to meet at the Turk's Head Tavern in Gerrard Street; now by hardly more than a matter of months he had just missed 'the Irish poets', whose work meant so much to him, and their circle, at the Cheshire Cheese.

There could, however, be another explanation. At the farther end of Fleet Street, the pub was well beyond the artistic ambit; and the young men and girls destined to do no more than 'work for the cheap magazines and fashion papers' and even the well-known journalists who patronised it were themselves hardly Bohemian. Reading between the lines, it is not difficult to see Ransome dismissing them all as merely 'unconventional', and rather sniffily writing off even the Rhymers as no better than the members of the Savage Club and those other, 'consciously unconventional' guests of the Vagabonds.

CHAPTER FOUR

'Give up Verse, My Boy'

IN the 1987 London telephone directory it is listed as 'Ye Olde Cheshire Cheese'; but apart from the touristically archaic change of name, the inn and chop-house at 145 Fleet Street is little altered from the one Arthur Ransome knew.

Like the old Roche, it is still a warren of small bars and eating-rooms spreading over three floors of a building which dates from the seventeenth century. There is the Chop Room, William's Room and Johnson's Bar, the latter commemorating the great lexicographer who lived in Gough Square, just round the corner, for ten years from 1749. Waiters still run up and down the 'winding, crooked, dark staircase' in white shirts and black ties, carrying trays of pork chops and greasy lamb cutlets. Nowadays there is fresh sawdust rather than sand on the uneven floorboards and the cellar's equally worn flagstones. Serviceable wood panelling lines the walls of the main rooms to shoulder height. Above it, pale green distemper is covered by a wealth of framed paintings, photographs and nineteenth-century 'Spy' prints caricaturing the 'Men of the Day'. In one of the bars a glass case displays relics of the pub's literary past; quill pens, clay pipes, bottles and a selection of pewter pots and measures.

The customers too have changed very little since Ransome's day. Hardly Bohemian and predominantly young, they fill every bar. Several clutch copies of the *UK Press Gazette*. Journalists, advertising executives and media people, their conversations are slightly too loud, the key words headlined in oral italics.

Rebuilt on the site of an earlier establishment in 1667, the Cheshire Cheese has been a still point in the changing world of literary affection almost since that time. Although there is no hard evidence that Dr Johnson ever set foot inside the place, it can boast clear and documented connections with Goldsmith, Sir Joshua Reynolds, Thackeray, Dickens and Wilkie Collins. More recently Max Beerbohm, Mark Twain, Sir Arthur Conan Doyle and G. K. Chesterton all sought it out, continuing an artistic pedigree that sets it apart from any other London pub or restaurant. It must have been for these associations rather than for reasons of propinquity or convenience that the Rhymers' Club selected the Cheshire Cheese as their headquarters.

The club was founded in 1891 by William Butler Yeats, then aged twenty-six and still finding his feet in London, together with a predominantly young group of the poets, writers and editors of the day. Its primary function was to serve as a forum at which members' work could be read aloud, discussed and criticised – 'too politely for the criticism to have much value'[1] – and a moderate amount of wine consumed. It seems to have been fairly formally constituted and to have met regularly in one of the upstairs rooms; 'weekly or was it fortnightly', according to Yeats's *Memoirs;*[2] 'every night' if we are to believe his earlier biographical essay, *The Trembling of the Veil,*[3] – although, given the vagaries of poetic inspiration, that seems unlikely. It took itself seriously and even published anthologies of its members' work: *The Book of the Rhymers' Club* and then *The Second Book of the Rhymers' Club.*

It boasted a regular membership of about a dozen, including the now largely forgotten poets Ernest Dowson, Lionel Johnson, Richard Le Gallienne and Ernest Rhys, all of whom were commemorated by one or at the most two lyrics in Sir Arthur Quiller-Couch's 1939 revision of the *Oxford Book of English Verse.* They rubbed shoulders with Arthur Symons, John Davidson – 'older than the rest of us and seeking to hide it with a wig'[4] – and, on occasions, with that ubiquity of the nineties, Aubrey Beardsley. In addition there was an almost equal number of less frequent attenders (among whom Selwyn Image and T. W. Rolleston are also represented by single poems in 'Q' 's anthology) and an outer circle of interested and broadly sympathetic visitors:

William Watson joined but never came and Francis Thompson came once but never joined; and sometimes if we met in a private house, which we did occasionally, Oscar Wilde came. It had been useless to invite him to the Cheshire Cheese, for he hated Bohemia. 'Olive Schreiner,' he said once to me, 'is staying in the East End because that is the only place where people do not wear masks upon their faces, but I have told her that I live in the West End because nothing in life interests me but the mask.'[5]

Together they comprised the group whom Yeats, who outlived nearly all of them, was to characterise as the 'tragic generation'. But although both Dowson and Johnson died before they were forty, the latter having 'developed into a solitary drunkard',[6] and Symons was incapacitated by madness towards the end of his life, taken as a group the Rhymers hardly fit the bill as *poètes maudits*.

As writers, they called themselves the 'new generation' and even during the early nineties went around, as individuals and club members, proclaiming their opposition to everything they considered Victorian: 'irrelevant descriptions of nature, the scientific and moral discursiveness of [Tennyson's] *In Memoriam* – "When he should have been broken-hearted," said Verlaine, "he had many reminiscences" – the political eloquence of Swinburne, the psychological curiosity of Browning, and the poetical diction of everybody.'[7] But, judged by modern standards, theirs was a very polite opposition. Yeats's two principal accounts of their activities, that which he included in the Introduction to his 1936 edition of the *Oxford Book of Modern Verse* and another given in *Letters to the New Island* (1934), references in the various drafts of his autobiography as well as the very nature of the work he and the other poets were producing at the time, make that very clear.

This was, perhaps, inevitable because – although a sort of wistful harking back to the days of the Poet-as-Legislator seems to seep between the lines of Yeats's later writings about the club – at the time the Rhymers never intended to change the world. All they were interested in was poetry. In that small province at least, they were to some extent successful. Beating T. S. Eliot off the mark, they made strenuous attempts to 'purify the dialect of the tribe' which did result in some clarification of both the tangled syntax and archaic diction of Swinburnean eloquence. Ultimately, however, even that was a pyrrhic victory. Their own work never showed anything like the startling innovation present in, for example, that of either of the French Bohemians, Paul Verlaine and Arthur Rimbaud, who were their exact contemporaries.

It was equally inevitable, of course, that even the Rhymers' little, local victories were largely due to Yeats, for he was far and away the most talented of the members of the club. His first published collection, *The Wanderings of Oisin* had appeared in 1889. Principally consisting of dramatic monologues strongly influenced by the myths and legends of his native Ireland, it had demanded rather than invited attention. Even Oscar Wilde had been unable to ignore its arrival. In a characteristic but unsigned review in the *Pall Mall Gazette*, he had hailed 'Three New Poets', Edward Fitzgerald, Richard Le Gallienne and Yeats, of whom he noted: 'Mr Yeats does not try to "out-baby" Wordsworth, we are glad to say, but he occasionally succeeds in "out-glittering" Keats . . . He is very naive, and very primitive, and he speaks of his giants with the awe of a child.'[8]

More perceptively, a reviewer in *The Academy* recognised the 'New Poet' 's nascent anti-Swinburneanism and called *Oisin* 'a remarkable volume [in which] Mr Yeats is seen at his best in his shorter pieces, which have that spontaneous singing quality so rare in our self-conscious modern verse.'[9]

In the early days at least, Yeats's was an active as well as a passive literary influence. His correspondence reveals that he was a stern critic of any back-sliding he perceived in the work of his fellow-Rhymers. In a letter describing the contents of *The Second Book of the Rhymers' Club* he noted that 'everybody is tolerably good except the Trinity College men, Rolleston, Hillier, Todhunter and Green, who are intolerably bad as was to be expected.'[10]

Later, however, his own interests began to overflow the narrow confines of the poetic coterie and embrace the wider world beyond (his 1910 collection *The Green Helmet and Other Poems* not only contained the lyric 'Upon a House Shaken by the Land Agitation' but also a squib which began 'All things can tempt me from this craft of verse . . .') and he seemed to lose interest in the club. His later, numerous and frequently contradictory autobiographical writings play down and, on occasions, needlessly belittle the activities and achievements of the group which had once been so important to him. Indeed, reading them all, one is left with a feeling of tetchiness. Arthur Symons, with his enthusiasm for the new Symbolist poetry of Villiers de L'Isle-Adam and others, as well as the music-halls and *follies* of Paris, should have injected something of their French vitality into the club's meetings, Yeats seems to be saying. The old Cheshire Cheese itself should have lent them an atmosphere of eighteenth-century parlour conviviality . . .

There are other indications too that quite early on he had begun to despair of the Rhymers. Among the uncollected *Memoirs* he left was a recollection that at the club 'we read our verses and criticised one another, but the talk had little vitality; and Symons, who knew Paris and its excellent talkers, gradually ceased to come . . . I once heard Johnson say after a particularly heavy evening, "Ah, yes, it is very dull, but it is interesting." '[11] And in *The Trembling of the Veil* he remembered that:

> Our clothes were for the most part unadventurous like our conversation, though I indeed wore a brown velveteen coat, a loose tie, and a very old Inverness cape, discarded by my father twenty years before and preserved by my Sligo-born mother whose actions were unreasoning and habitual like the seasons. But no other member of the club, except Le Gallienne, who wore a loose tie, and Symons, who had an Inverness cape that was quite new and almost fashionable, would have shown himself for the world in any costume but 'that of an English gentleman'. 'One should be quite unnoticeable,' Johnson explained to me.[12]

Perhaps most telling of all, however, is Yeats's account of the impact on the club of the trial and imprisonment of Oscar Wilde in 1895:

> The condemnation of Wilde had brought ruin upon a whole movement in art and letters. *The Rhymers were not affected*; we had all written for the smaller public that has knowledge and is undisturbed by popular feeling. We were a little more unpopular with those [who] did not read us; it was necessary to avoid a little more carefully than before young men studying for the army and the imperfectly educated generally, but our new books would still sell out their editions of perhaps three hundred copies.[13]

Born and bred a Bohemian, in the widest sense of that word, by his father, the artist John Butler Yeats, at the end of his life W. B. Yeats was inclined to write off the Rhymers Club as a failure. But that was unduly pessimistic. Later critics have been far more charitable. With more of an eye to its social than its literary aspirations, one has even gone as far as describing its foundation as 'an attempt to combine French literary café life with Johnsonian conviviality'.[14]

It is in this spirit, and not in the light of the recriminatory, muddled recollections of Yeats's own *Autobiographies* and *Memoirs*, that we should now consider it. For the Rhymers do have better claims than most to the title of founders of a modern London Bohemianism. Had he been around, the young Arthur Ransome would have found little of the real, unbuttoned Bohemianism he sought at their meetings in the late nineties. But the shortcoming was his, not theirs. Even before he set out in 1904 – and even in Paris – Henry Mürger's escapist Bohemia had been replaced by something far more practical.

Had Ransome only kept his ear to the ground, he would have known that, in the words of a critical study of the completely new French avant-garde which had arrived in Paris a generation after the original *Buveurs d'Eau*:

> The lucid frenzy of Gérard de Nerval and the sentimental Bohemia of Mürger [had] crystallised into a determined group of artists who maintained a belligerent attitude toward the world and a genuine sympathy for each other.[15]

'A belligerent attitude toward the world and a genuine sympathy for each other . . .' That one phrase sums up the essence of all latter-day Bohemianism, setting the perceived 'differentness' of the Aesthetes and the embattled defensiveness of the post-Romantics into a proper social context.

Neither is it an altogether inappropriate epitaph for the Rhymers. Their belligerence might have been refined and targeted against a very small world, but at least they fought. They might not all have been major talents, but in public at least, in collections such as *The Book of the Rhymers' Club*, they stuck together. Despite Symons's 'almost fashionable' Inverness cape and Lionel Johnson's belief that they should 'be quite unnoticeable', almost despite themselves indeed, they were the precursors of a native British Bohemianism which was to have a brief but not inglorious life in the following half century. Fraternal sympathy and a willingness to fight for one's corner would be its hallmarks, although in the late 1890s in the immediate aftermath of the Wilde trial, its literary heroes at least were more preoccupied with a fight for their very survival.

Aestheticism had always been a fragile bloom and never recovered from its exposure to the chill winds of public censure which blew around the Old Bailey during the trial of Oscar Wilde. Within half a decade it had been all but forgotten, and on the surface at least things seemed to have returned to normal, just as the newspapers said they would. Indeed, it was none other than W. B. Yeats who wrote that 'in 1900 everybody got down off his stilts; henceforth nobody drank absinthe with his black coffee; nobody went mad; nobody committed suicide; nobody joined the Catholic church; or if they did I have forgotten.'[16]

Actually, it was not quite as simple as that. Arthur Symons did go mad and John Davidson, after all, did kill himself in 1909. Although Aubrey Beardsley was dismissed as art editor of *The Yellow Book* in 1895 and the book itself slipped from its position among the avant-garde to become a much more conservative periodical, the next year saw the (brief) appearance of another magazine, *The Savoy*, which more than equalled its predecessor in reflecting the mood of the *fin de siècle*. And, for those who knew where to acquire such things, absinthe continued to be drunk in London long after 1900. In Soho, the artist Nina Hamnett was able to acquire a bottle within hours, as late as 1924.

In general terms though Yeats was right. Aestheticism had been permanently discredited, as Harold Acton was to discover as late as 1948 when he came to publish his autobiography:

> Half my friends disapprove of the title I have chosen for this book without having read it. 'What! an aesthete? One of those scruffy long-haired fellows in peculiar garb, lisping about art for art's sake? No, no. You'll prejudice all your readers in advance. Old Oscar screwed the last nail in the aesthete's coffin.'[17]

And it wasn't just Aestheticism. Though it at least recovered well before 1948, the avant-garde in every field of the arts also suddenly found itself out in the cold in the years immediately following 1895, its *amirals* having been duly 'encouraged' by what had happened to 'Old Oscar'. Thus, in the first decade of the new century the pervasive mood was summed up not so much by the Wildean epigrams, the black-and-white eroticism and etiolated young men of Aubrey Beardsley's drawings, which had so decorated the nineties, as by a rash of tuneful but vapid musical comedies which were filling the theatres of London.

The sharp satire of Gilbert and Sullivan's *Patience* and *Iolanthe* had been replaced by an endless succession of more mindless shows with titles such as *The Shop Girl*, *The Circus Girl*, *A Runaway Girl*, and, more exotically, *The Girls of Gottenburg*. But it was Lionel Monckton's operetta, *The Arcadians*, which best expressed the new, fearful conservatism of Edwardian popular taste. It opened at the Shaftesbury Theatre in 1909, its sentimental evocation of a faraway, Spenserian never-never land challenging the popularity of Franz Lehar's *The Merry Widow* which had been playing to packed houses at Daly's Theatre since the previous year:

> *With a melody enthralling,*
> *Loud the woodland echoes ring.*
> *Hark! the pipes of Pan are calling*
> *With a merry lilt and swing.*
> *Hear their joyous carolling,*
> *Flowing, growing, rising, falling,*
> *Youth and joy must have their fling*
> *When the pipes of Pan are calling – Ah!*
> *The pipes of Pan.*
>
> *So follow, follow, follow,*
> *The merry, merry pipes of Pan . . .*

Its appeal was phenomenal but it was not just London theatre-goers who were follow-follow-following the merry, merry pipes of Pan into less challenging realms. *The Arcadians* was symptomatic of the general state of the arts in England during the first decade of the twentieth century. For, after a period of excited creativity, they had lapsed back into a comfortable, reassuring solidity. This was especially true of literature. Ezra Pound had published *Personae* (1909) and *Ripostes* (1912), his Imagistes and the Modernists were gathering in the wings but, for all the agitating of Yeats and the Rhymers, a more conservative group of writers stubbornly remained at the centre of the stage.

Henry James produced his last great novels, *The Wings of the*

49

Dove, The Ambassadors and *The Golden Bowl*, in the first five years of the new century but, even more than the main corpus of his work which had appeared in the previous two decades, the costive complexity of their style as much as the themes they explored put him outside the common run. More typical of the time were the lesser writers whom Virginia Woolf was later to characterise as 'Edwardian' in their preoccupations as much as their chronological placing.

In a lecture, reprinted in essay form[18] in 1924, she singled out the 'prominent and successful' John Galsworthy, H. G. Wells and Arnold Bennett as particularly eminent Edwardians. They were all competent, even considerable writers; but although one could 'admire and enjoy their books', that was not enough. 'In or about December, 1910, human character changed', Mrs Woolf averred. After that date for the new generation of 'Georgians' (notably Forster, Lawrence and Joyce) to look to the Edwardians for help in writing a novel was 'precisely like going to a bootmaker and asking him to teach you how to make a watch'.

The lecture is an intricately argued polemic, advocating a sophisticated, Bloomsbury Modernism; but in her choice of Galsworthy, Wells and Bennett Virginia Woolf shrewdly characterised the post-Victorian literary scene. Wells and Bennett particularly were enjoying enormous popular success at that time. In the years before 1914 Bennett published *Anna of the Five Towns* (1902), *The Old Wives' Tale* (1908), *Clayhanger* (1910), its sequel *Hilda Lessways* and *The Card* (both 1911). H. G. Wells was almost as fecund, producing *Kipps* (1905), *Tono-Bungay* (1909) and *The History of Mr Polly* (1910). They were not alone. What, at its least offensive, comes over as their comfortable, small-town conservatism, and at its worst as complacent middle-class Philistinism, is also apparent in the work of many of the other established novelists of the period. G. K. Chesterton's *The Napoleon of Notting Hill* appeared in 1904, two years before Kipling's nostalgic *Puck of Pook's Hill*. The immensely professional Hugh Walpole was beginning to make his name. And, although Virginia Woolf specifically excluded E. M. Forster from the ranks of the Edwardians, there are strains of the same complacent introspection in his first two novels, *Where Angels Fear to Tread* (1905) and *A Room with a View* (1908).

The other writer singled out in Virgina Woolf's essay is John

Galsworthy. In a sense he was almost too easy a target since *The Man of Property* (1906), the first and best of his nine Forsyte novels, is in itself a satire on exactly the values implicit in the work of the Edwardians. The Forsytes, exemplified by Soames, the thin-lipped young solicitor, personify the Edwardians' concern with property, convention and propriety:

> In the bravery of light gloves, buff waistcoats, feathers, and frocks, the family were present – even Aunt Ann, who now but seldom left the corner of her brother Timothy's green drawing room, where, under the aegis of a plume of dyed pampas grass in a light blue vase, she sat all day reading and knitting, surrounded by the effigies of three generations of Forsytes. Even Aunt Ann was there; her inflexible back and the dignity of her calm old face personifying the rigid possessiveness of the family idea.
>
> When a Forsyte was engaged, or born, the Forsytes were present. When a Forsyte dies – but no Forsyte had as yet died; they did not die; death being contrary to their principles, they took precautions against it, the instinctive precautions of highly vitalized persons who resent encroachments on their property.[19]

Set amid the high Victorianism of London's West End in the 1880s (later books would follow the fortunes of the baroquely extended family as far as the 1930s), *The Man of Property* is, on the surface, the story of the collapse of Soames's marriage. But at a deeper level it shows the Forsytes as ruthless defenders of the status quo. Instinctively they close ranks against the raffish young architect who has become engaged to one of their number. It is a defensive gesture, for by any standards he is an outsider and consequently a threat:

> Philip Bosinney was known to be a young man without a fortune, but Forsyte girls had become engaged to such before, and had actually married them. It was not altogether for this reason, therefore, that the minds of the Forsytes misgave them. They could not have explained the origin of a misgiving obscured by the mist of family gossip. A story was undoubtedly told that he had paid his duty call to Aunts Ann, Juley, and Hester in a soft grey hat – a soft grey hat, not even a new one – a dusty thing with a shapeless crown. 'So extraordinary, my dear – so odd!' Aunt Hester, passing through the little, dark hall (she was rather short-sighted), had tried to 'shoo' it off a chair, taking

it for a strange, disreputable cat – Tommy had such disgraceful friends! She was disturbed when it did not move.[20]

Bosinney is something of a Bohemian by his very profession and hence 'dangerous – ah, dangerous!' He is described by the family as a 'very singular-looking man' and referred to as 'The Buccaneer'. More tellingly, after it is discovered that he is in love with Soames's wife Irene, he is destroyed through litigation initiated by Soames and the hand of a suspiciously conniving fate when he is knocked down by an omnibus amid rumours of suicide.

In a very literal sense, the proprietorial ruthlessness of the Forsytes was also shared by the Edwardian writers. Indeed, Arnold Bennett seemed to revel in Philistinism. 'I write for as much money as I can get', he is reported to have said, and the comment encapsulates both his and their commitment to the very un-Bohemian values of the marketplace. In the most direct sense they were professional writers, their buttoned, waistcoated and, somehow very English, notions of discipline and work worlds apart from the more easy-going, open-necked, 'Parisian' attitudes of the Bohemians.

All was not lost, however. Although Bennett and his ilk held the post-Aesthetic high ground, well before Virginia Woolf rose to deliver her lecture, Ezra Pound and the younger generation had begun an impatient skirmishing in the foothills. The young Midwestern poet in particular was an indefatigable propagandist. At the beginning of 1912 he treated the readers of *Poetry*, a Chicago-based literary monthly for which he acted as 'foreign correspondent', to a violently partisan survey of the English literary scene. Thomas Hardy, Robert Bridges, Laurence Binyon, Henry Newbolt, their fellow 'Georgians', who then represented the public face of British poetry, and not least their readers, would have been shocked by his conclusions:

> I find Mr Yeats the only poet worthy of serious study. Mr Yeats's work is already a recognized classic and is part of the required reading in the Sorbonne. There is no need of proclaiming him to the American public. As to his English contemporaries, they are good, sometimes very good, food for anthologies. There are a number of men who have written a poem, or several poems, worth knowing and remembering, but

they do not much concern the young artist studying the art of poetry . . .[21]

A punchy if not particularly elegant prose writer, Pound had arrived in England after a six-month European sojourn in the summer of 1908, and soon showed himself as dogmatic in his life as he was in his work. The previous year, while a lecturer at the straight-laced, Presbyterian Wabash College in the small town of Crawfordsville, Indiana, he had nailed his artistic colours to the mast, adopting a sub-Wildean wardrobe of velvet jackets, wide-brimmed hats and loose bow-ties, and actively sought out the company of actors and artists. 'Exhibitionist, egotistic, self-centred and self-indulgent', as one of his Wabash students later recalled, he was to treat London to a full-dress version of the same. With a clipped red beard and piercing green eyes, his talent for self-advertisement was highly developed – there is a story that, in a curious parody of Wilde's passion for that bloom, he once ate a tulip in public – and he had soon gained the attention of the great and the good in the Edwardian literary world.

Within three months he had broken into print with *A Quinzaine for This Yule*, a collection of prose and poetry, and been accepted as a part-time lecturer at the Regent Street Polytechnic. Within six he had made the acquaintance of Laurence Binyon, George Bernard Shaw and the Poet's Club; and after less than a year he was dining with the likes of Henry James, Ford Madox Hueffer (who, with the outbreak of war in 1914, would become Ford Madox Ford) and Arnold Bennett. It was satisfactory progress and momentarily pleasing. But Pound was neither softened nor seduced by the blandishments of the 'Edwardians'. After an initial warmth, his friendship with Bennett, in particular, cooled into boredom and irritable impatience.

Hugh Selwyn Mauberley (Life and Contacts), first published in 1920, is Pound's impressionistic memoir of that period of his life and the general disruption wrought by the First World War. It is a bitter, disillusioned collection of lyrics and fragments. Ford, 'the stylist', he pictures sheltering from 'the world's welter' under a sagging roof, unpaid and uncelebrated. European culture is nothing but 'two gross of broken statues . . . a few thousand battered books'. And, rising above it all, is Arnold Bennett, viciously lampooned in the character of Mr Nixon:

In the cream gilded cabin of his steam yacht
Mr Nixon advised me kindly, to advance with fewer
Dangers of delay. 'Consider
    Carefully the reviewer.

'I was as poor as you are;
When I began I got, of course,
Advance on royalties, fifty at first,' said Mr Nixon,
'Follow me, and take a column,
Even if you have to work for free.

'Butter reviewers. From fifty to three hundred
I rose in eighteen months;
The hardest nut I had to crack
Was Dr Dundas.

'I never mentioned a man but with the view
Of selling my own works.
The tip's a good one, as for literature
It gives no man a sinecure.

'And no one knows, at sight, a masterpiece.
And give up verse, my boy,
There's nothing in it.'

Likewise a friend of Blougram's once advised me:
Don't kick against the pricks,
Accept opinion. The 'Nineties' tried your game
And died, there's nothing in it.[22]

Superficially at least, there did not appear to be much more in the visual arts. Although at first sight the boisterous, proletarian world which Ransome found in 'the studios' appears to exemplify rebellion and the rejection of all normal values in favour of everything that was Bohemian and unconventional, on closer examination it is nothing of the kind. The life Ransome discovered among the artists and writers of Chelsea and Soho, that he went on to sentimentalise in *Bohemia in London*, was only a pale imitation of the Parisian *vie de bohème* celebrated in Mürger's *Scènes de la Vie de Bohème* and further refined in *Trilby* and *La Bohème*. Clearly, it existed, and must have been lived in very much the communal, hugger-mugger style which Ransome describes. But it was a second-hand lifestyle, alien, atypical and, unlike the Rhymers', all very temporary. Mürger had pointed out that

Bohemia was merely a phase in the artistic life, and in his Conclusion to *Bohemia in London* Ransome had grudgingly to agree:

> Bohemia is only a stage in a man's life, except in the case of fools and a very few others. It is not a profession . . . for the young man grows older, and perhaps earns money, and takes upon himself responsibilities to another goddess than the white Venus of the arts.[23]

For all the high hopes he had entertained while seated on the tailboard of that grocer's cart, and the dream that, like a latter-day Columbus, he was about to discover a whole New World, all Ransome penetrated was an early precursor of the student underworld which has existed in London since the late 1950s. Too much in the thrall of Mürger, Carlyle, Johnson and the eighteenth-century coffee-house essayists, he had set off in quite the wrong direction. If we are to believe other writers of the period, Ransome's tireless explorations hardly ever brought him into contact with the real artistic life of London. He should have known better, of course; for as early as 1894, no less a figure than George du Maurier had graphically shown how this native, English *beau monde* was radically different from the Mürgeresque *demi-monde* of Paris.

Halfway through *Trilby*, he interrupts the story with an Interlude. Five years have gone by since Taffy, the Laird and Little Billee were students in Paris. Taffy and the Laird have remained in the Place St Anatole des Arts, but Little Billee has long since returned to London. On a whim, his erstwhile companions of the brush decide to visit him; but whereas they have remained Parisians, and between them cannot manage to buy tickets to hear Trilby sing nor even raise the price of a meal, they find Little Billee totally reformed. A Londoner, the model of probity, and a respected pillar of society, nobody even calls him Billee any more. He is William Bagot, the fashionable artist about town:

> He had a fine studio and a handsome suite of rooms in Fitzroy Square. Beautiful specimens of his unfinished work, endless studies, hung on his studio walls. Everything else was as nice as it could be – the furniture, the bibelots and bric-à-brac, the artistic foreign and Eastern knick-knacks and draperies and

hangings and curtains and rugs – the semi-grand piano by Collard and Collard.

That immortal canvas, the 'Moon-Dial' (just begun, and already commissioned by Moses Lyon, the famous picture-dealer), lay on his easel.

No man worked harder and with teeth more clenched than Little Billee when he was at work – none rested or played more discreetly when it was time to rest or play. The glass on his mantel-piece was full of cards of invitation, reminders, pretty mauve and pink and lilac scented notes; nor were coronets wanting on many of these hospitable little missives.[24]

In the non-fiction writing of the period too – and notably in two of what must have been those 'dozen flippant, merry treatises on Bohemia in London' which so irritated Ransome – this artistic respectability is also repeatedly commented upon. As far back as 1879 Charles Dickens the younger (a son of the novelist) had attempted to define Bohemia in his encyclopedically wide-ranging *Dictionary of London*. He was an indefatigable researcher, but even he failed to discover anything remotely resembling Mürger's Paris – quite the reverse, in fact.

In London it was no longer necessary to be 'drunken, disorderly, dirty and dissipated' to be a Bohemian, he reported. They were the characteristics of 'the class *bümmler* of Germany, and the "loafer" of New York'. But further than that he was unable, or unwilling, to venture, contenting himself with what must have seemed a reassuring observation: 'Cleanliness, order, a respect for the outward observances of society, combined with an absolute disregard of every moral law and obligation has [*sic*] been held up in many recent novels as the qualifiations of a genuine Bohemian.' Even that was only part of the story. Having described both the drunken, dissipated *bümmler* and the clean-living amoralists of contemporary fiction, Dickens went on:

> Both these monsters, who have usually been described as belonging to the literary, artistic, or dramatic professions, are far from representing the truth. Bohemianism may be said to be confined to no district, to no profession, and to no class. The hallmark of your true Bohemian is that he declines to own himself a subject of Mrs Grundy. He has emancipated himself from conventionalities and shams, and done his own work in his own way . . .[25]

Despite the brief flowering of Aestheticism, it appears that little had changed a quarter of a century later.

'Shakespeare gave "Bohemia" a sea-coast; it would be nearly as incorrect to say that London nowadays has within it a Bohemia,' proclaimed Robert Machray in his 1902 handbook to the 'night side' of London. Its chapter on 'La Vie de Bohème' even stated in so many words that 'the English artist never was of the Mürger type'. Like Little Billee, he 'has become a member of the "respectable" classes; he is in "society" – if he wishes to be in it, and he generally chooses to be so'. He enjoys 'larks, frolics, jokes, some of them of the practical variety, tricks, and general buffooneries'. But he also belongs to a club or two and, judging from the book's illustrations, habitually wears a suit and tie.

In previous chapters Machray had guided his readers through 'Piccadilly Circus (11 p.m. to 1 a.m.)', society balls, an East End music-hall and a 'shilling hop', but for any who were expecting something more raffish or even frankly decadent, his Chapter Fourteen, which deals with 'La Vie de Bohème', would have come as a great disappointment. There are no garrets and certainly no starving artists. To be Bohemian in the London of 1902, it suggested, it was sufficient to belong to a sketch club.

The chapter invites the reader 'to take a look at two of these clubs, the Langham and the London Sketch Club [since] what may be styled their Night Side is one of the most attractive phases of London'. Arthur Ransome too found these clubs, but even he could not pretend that the larky goings-on at the Langham were possessed of anything like the truly Bohemian *joie de vivre* which had existed in such abundance at the Café Momus:

> Artists meet there regularly, and draw and make pictures all in a room together, with a time limit set for the performance. At intervals they exhibit the harvest of their evenings on the walls. They have also merry parties, for men only, when the doors are opened by fantastical figures, and scratch entertainments go on all the time, and there are songs and jovial recitations. Nights there are as merry as any, and the rooms are full of celebrated men, and men about to be celebrated; for the club does not tolerate bunglers.[26]

'Making pictures together' also filled winter evenings at the London Sketch Club, an offshoot of the Langham, which had rooms at the Modern Gallery in Bond Street. 'The artists begin work ("to slop colour", in the words of the candid friend) at seven o'clock; at nine the whistle is blown, and the brushes are thrown down. There then succeeds a quarter of an hour of frank but friendly criticism.'[27]

Twice a year, in May and October, the London Sketch Club held an exhibition of its members' work – 'a pleasant, not to say festive meeting' which concluded with a 'smoker'. Members did turns, 'good, rollicking, rumbustious ditties' were sung, those guests unwise enough to have turned up in dress shirts had them drawn or scribbled over and 'the celebrated Bousa Band' played. But that was all, and even the biannual smokers came to a decent and early end. 'It is significant of that "respectability" to which reference has already been made that midnight is now considered quite late enough for the termination of these festivities,' Machray noted, adding that, 'many of the artists live at some distance away, and they want to get home by the last train or the last 'bus, as it may be.'

Here as elsewhere, through their suburban preoccupations the sketch club Bohemians seem to resemble Marcello and Rodolpho, Mürger, his cronies at the Café Momus and the high-living Puccini far less than they do George and Weedon Grossmith's Mr Pooter. But in the context of references such as these, Yeats and the Rhymers, with their modern determination to 'be quite unnotice-able', again emerge as the true London Bohemians of their period.

Despite their close association with the opal-hush-drinking Irish poets, they moved in a very different world from the youthful, impoverished *demi-monde* which Ransome describes. (Theirs was actually a territory he would have stood more chance of penetrating had he remained in his job in publishing.) They had little or nothing in common with Rodolpho and, despite Arthur Symons, still less with the rackety lifestyles of 'Parisian' Frenchmen like Henry Mürger. By inclination if not always by nationality, like the artists, they were as English, as middle class and, barring the odd night of drunkenness, basically as decent as du Maurier's Little Billee.

Most of them were fairly recently down from Oxford or Cambridge. They were not rich but they had money. Their meetings were conducted with a mannered politeness very different from the loud abusiveness of the Café Momus, where dinner was eaten to the accompaniment of the clicking of billiard balls, and even the boisterous extravagance of suppers at Brice's or the Roche. They were, in fact, among the natural inheritors of the easy, convenient liaison between talent and society from which Wilde had gained so much in the 1880s. Despite some temporary inconvenience, that too had survived the scandals of 1895 virtually intact. The public effusiveness of Wilde, Lord Ronald Gower and the society homosexuals of the nineties was long gone, but otherwise very little had changed.

The writers' only problem was the fact that their whole existence was predicated on a social system which itself was changing. They could not have known it at the time, but the Rhymers' weekly meetings at the Cheshire Cheese in the mid-1890s took place in a twilight which was spreading over more than the Celtic world. The new century would see the ground cut from under their feet by innovations in a field of the visual arts which owed nothing to the sketch clubs. Ironically enough, the new dawn would reveal something far closer to that mythical, primary-coloured Bohemian world which Arthur Ransome had set out to discover, but so signally failed to find.

CHAPTER FIVE

Augustus and the Demi-Johns

———————————

THERE had been artists before Augustus John; but from the day he erupted out of the Slade School of Art in 1898, he seemed to redefine the term. As Voltaire had noted of a higher deity, if he had not existed it would have been necessary to invent him.

It was not just that he was Bohemian. Through his clothes, high-profile litigiousness and general theatricality, Whistler had been that as early as the 1880s. Through a studied sartorial eccentricity and a natural talent for unpredictability, Walter Sickert was still doing his best to uphold the tradition in the late 1930s. Nor was it solely that John was possessed of prodigious technical skill, although the fact that he was quickly became apparent. While still a student, he had been described by the American portrait artist John Singer Sargent as the greatest draughtsman since the Italian Renaissance.

There was another aspect of John's character which played a far from inconsiderable part in his extraordinary, and extraordinarily rapid, canonisation. Even as a very young man he displayed a unique personal magnetism which made him attractive to men and women alike:

> He looked like a young fawn; he had beautiful eyes, almond-shaped and with lids defined like those Leonardo drew, a short nose, broad cheek-bones, while over a fine forehead fell thick brown hair, parted in the middle. He wore a light curling beard (he had never shaved) and his figure was lithe and elegant. I was at once attracted to John.[1]

The impression he made on the artist William Rothenstein, a few years his senior, was typical. There are many similar accounts of his physical grace, mercurial temperament and boundless talent which date from this period. Among the most enduring is the story, romanticised but with a basis in fact, that, on holiday in Wales, he had 'hit his head on a rock whilst diving, and emerged from the water a genius'. Even his Christian name was seized upon by some as evidence of his Petronian nature;[2] others preferred to believe that he was some kind of changeling or gypsy-child, and acting accordingly. The more astute of his fellow-students were said to have taken to rescuing his discarded sketches from wastepaper bins at the Slade as early as 1897.

Every scrap, tatter and rumour contributed to what can only be called the legend of Augustus John. Uneasy though he was within this gaudy public carapace, then as later by his very behaviour the artist himself did little to diminish its currency. In 1895 he was already cutting a wild, irresistible figure in the cafés and studios of London. Since his last year at the Slade, he had cultivated what his biographer Michael Holroyd describes as 'a kind of inverted Dandyism'. He wore his hair long; uncut if not entirely unkempt. His shoes were unpolished, his suits unpressed and his ears adorned with rings of gold or brass. He never wore a collar or tie, preferring a flowing scarf fastened with an intaglio pin or secondhand brooch; and he topped the whole ensemble with a battered, fedora-style hat whenever he ventured out.

Like that of his slightly younger contemporary, Ezra Pound – still at that time affecting velveteen jackets and floppy ties à la Yeats – the whole outlandish and, it must be admitted, calculatedly Bohemian costume seems to have been donned with one eye at least on achieving a harmless but professionally advantageous notoriety. Like Pound's again, it was outstandingly successful. Commissions flowed in, and less than ten years after he had left the Slade, a younger generation of students had become accustomed to standing up whenever John entered the Café Royal, and to conversing in whispers if he happened to fall asleep over his crème de menthe frappée. Within another decade he had become the most famous artist in the country and, in exactly the same way as Wilde, the popular epitome of Bohemianism. He was included (as No. 31) in a set of fifty cards depicting famous people which was given away with packets of Brooke Bond tea. Later, in 1937, Wyndham Lewis was to dismiss him somewhat sourly in his autobiography *Blasting and Bombardiering* as 'that standard celebrity',[3] but it seemed rather different at the time. By the early twenties, Soho restaurants were naming dishes after him – 'Entrecôte à la John' was the speciality of more than one chef – and neither the public nor a wide range of writers needed to look any further than John for the perfect image of an artist. He was immediately recognisable, and had been parodied in revue as early as 1917:

> *John! John!*
> *How he's got on!*
> *He owes it, he knows it, to me!*
> *Brass earrings I wear,*
> *And I don't do my hair,*
> *And my feet are as bare as can be;*
> *When I walk down the street,*
> *All the people I meet*
> *They stare at the things I have on!*
> *When Battersea-Parking*
> *You'll hear folks remarking:*
> *'There goes an Augustus John!'*

Thinly disguised, other Augustus Johns stalked through the pages of contemporary fiction. There was Struthers in D. H. Lawrence's *Aaron's Rod* and the painter John Bidlake, 'a great worker, a great eater, drinker, and taker of virginities' in Aldous Huxley's *Point Counter Point*. There was Albert Sanger, the musician in Margaret Kennedy's *The Constant Nymph*, and Owen, the sculptor in *The Diary of a Drug Fiend*, a suitably diabolic novel by Aleister Crowley, the poet and satanist who called himself The Beast 666 but was dubbed 'the wickedest man in the world' by the London press when stories began to circulate about sexual depravity and the drinking of a cat's blood at ceremonies associated with his Order of the Silver Star. Later, and more memorably, there was the painter Gulley Jimson in Joyce Cary's *The Horse's Mouth* (first published in 1944), a character who might or might not have been largely based on the artist Stanley Spencer, but whose engaging fecklessness still seemed strongly reminiscent of the middle-aged John. Each in its own way added to the reputation of the real John; but none, however colourful, was a patch on the original. No novelist, not even a Lawrence, could have come up with anything approaching the John of popular legend.

For, apart from anything else, even at the end of the nineteenth century he was presenting himself as everything the twenty love-sick maidens who sang the opening chorus in Gilbert and Sullivan's *Patience* had been looking for. From 1898 until at least the end of the First World War, he really was what they had called the 'very cynosure of our eyes and hearts'. The only difference was that, unlike the 'fleshly poet' Reginald Bunthorne, the original cynosure, the young Augustus John was not 'icily insensible' at all, certainly not to the attentions of a new generation of love-sick young women. Like John Bidlake, he was widely known as 'a taker of virginities'; it was not for nothing that an anonymous *Virgin's Prayer* had achieved wide currency in the years before the First World War:

> *Ezra Pound*
> *And Augustus John*
> *Bless the bed*
> *That I lie on.*[4]

Iris Tree, Lady Tredegar, Sybil Hart-Davis, the society heiress Sylvia Gough, chorus-girls, ballerinas, models, artists and increasing numbers of adoring female students did undoubtedly succumb to his charms, lie back on a grubby studio couch and prepare to enjoy what must have seemed like a liaison with the true Bohemianism of Paris. (The experience itself, however, frequently failed to live up to expectations. Michael Holroyd reports that one model, surprised by John in 1921 while she was posing naked, remembered only his 'being so old [in 1921 he would have been forty-three], the coarse beard, smell of whisky and tobacco, no words, just grunting and snorting'.[5])

Such behaviour, of course, did no harm at all to the Augustus John of popular legend. Quite the reverse; it merely added another layer to his wild Bohemian image – and the commissions kept on coming. As a young painter in London in the early years of this century, he was at the height of his powers. He drank and smoked and womanised, but still found the time to paint some of the leading figures of the day: actors and actresses, military and political leaders in the immediate aftermath of the First World

War, musicians, writers like W. B. Yeats, and an endless succession of those fashionable society women who have always provided the staple income of any equally fashionable portrait artist. 'When I think of him,' Lytton Strachey wrote in 1907, tongue-in-cheek but with ill-concealed envy,

> I often feel that the only thing to do is to chuck up everything and make a dash for some such safe secluded office stool as is pressed by dear Maynard [Keynes]'s bottom. The dangers of freedom are appalling! In the meantime it seems to me that one had better buy up every drawing by him that's on the market. For surely he's bound to fizzle out; and then the prices![6]

At times it seemed that Augustus John really was, as his society sitters would have had it, the *only* artist. In actual fact, however, that was very far from the truth.

Behind (or quite possibly because of) the reddish-brown beard and a battered, wide-brimmed hat he holds on his knee, there is an air of Bohemian bravura about the full-length portrait of Augustus John which now hangs in the National Portrait Gallery in London (see Plate 9). Huddled in a thick grey overcoat, the artist-subject is slumped in a hard wooden chair, apparently in one corner of a dingy studio. His boots and the details of his overcoat are almost lost in its thick, crepuscular gloom. Only his face and hands (hyper-realised, the knuckles are knotty as those of a Michelangelo sculpture) stand out in Rembrandtesque clarity. His face, in particular, compels attention. White-pale above the curling beard, knowing and even arrogant in its hooded stare, beyond anything else it is the face of a hero.

Inviting, almost demanding, comparison with Whistler's *Thomas Carlyle*, the portrait, like its subject, exudes supreme confidence. Assured, technically accomplished and worthy of John himself, it is actually the work of his exact contemporary, William (later Sir William) Orpen. Completed in 1900, when both artist and subject were just twenty-two and at the very start of their careers, it is nevertheless much more than a 'prentice piece'; far more than the product of idle days. Though John himself disliked it, and in particular its implication of bold romanticism, in 1900 it was one of a number of calling-cards left by a rising generation of younger

British artists who, by their work as much as their lives, would do more than most to add colour to the literary and artistic map of London for the next quarter century. *'Hier stehe ich'*, it might have been called, with both John and Orpen aptly parroting the words of Martin Luther.

Yet for all that, it is a curiously dated piece, its very academic correctness harking back to Sargent rather than forward towards the new century. Orpen might have depicted John as the hero, an *éminence grise* slouching in the wings, but even in 1900 those in the know were beginning to ask whose mantle he would assume and which lands he would conquer.

Like Macbeth, John appeared to have it all: the respect of his peers, the beginnings of a reputation, and promise. Above all he had promise. Everybody said it. Sargent had started the ball rolling; Strachey, George Moore and virtually every critic would keep it in constant motion for the next twenty years. The problem was that nobody knew how it would be fulfilled. Neither did John; and the fact that, ultimately and at the highest level, it never really was became the tragedy of his life. It should have been, but the cruel fact was that he had been born out of his time, too late to have taken his place among the successful traditionalists of the eighties and nineties, and slightly too early to have been a real part of the revolution which swept through English painting in the first two decades of this century. In a very literal sense, even as he sat for Opren, he was becoming a rebel without a cause, a genius who poured his talent into himself simply because there was no other vessel available and large enough to contain it.

He was born in 1878 in Tenby in South Wales, and had arrived at the Slade in 1894, more by accident than design. Its pleasing remoteness from his family and the claustrophobia of small-town life were more of a draw than any aesthetic or academic leaning. Yet if he had pored over the prospectuses of every art school in the country, the young Augustus could not have found an establishment better geared to the development of his talent.

Endowed by one Felix Slade as the University of London's 'Faculty of Fine Arts', the school had opened in 1871 in premises adjoining University College in Gower Street. Right from the start its syllabus had stressed the importance of sound technique. By the time John arrived its acquisition had become the primary requirement of every student. 'Observe the construction of the forms and explain it,' he was told as he started his apprenticeship.[7] To begin with this involved sitting with 'a stick of charcoal, a sheet of "Michelet" paper and a chunk of bread for rubbing out'[8] before casts of Greek, Roman and Renaissance statuary. Only later were students introduced to the palette and the life class.

Even then they endured a laborious, hardly glamorous life, more akin to that of an English public school than the *vie de bohème* shared by Sandy, Taffy, Little Billee and Trilby O'Ferrall in the studios of Paris. Male and female students were strictly segregated, fraternising with models was severely frowned upon; final-year students looked with the lofty disdain of prefects on the work of their juniors; while members of the teaching staff, and particularly the forthright one-time surgeon Henry Tonks, were held in considerable awe.

Unlikely as it now seems, despite an initial period of loneliness (alleviated by the arrival at the Slade of his sister Gwen in the autumn of 1895) John positively thrived under such a regime. Working from early morning until late at night, spending long hours crouching before casts in the Antique Rooms, and cultivating the habit of never setting out from his lodgings without a sketch-book, brought out his talent. Within two years of leaving the Slade he had had work accepted for the New English Art Club's 1900 exhibition and gone some way towards establishing his popular reputation with a successful one-man show at the Carfax Gallery in St James's, from which he emerged with a very respectable profit of £30.

There were other benefits too. While still a student he had 'formed an attachment to' a fellow-student, Ida Nettleship, whom he was later to marry. Ida was the daughter of Jack Nettleship, a one-time Pre-Raphaelite and for a while the associate of both Jack Yeats and Robert Browning, although by the time John knew Nettleship his horizons had so contracted that he painted little more than what he called 'pot-boilers', chiefly studies of wild animals. (Somewhat embittered by the hand he had been dealt by Fate, he had also turned to religion, and once assured John that, 'God was nearer to him than the door'.[9]) Nevertheless, he maintained a certain style in the family home in Wigmore Street. Calling on Ida there, John recalled, he first met such personalities of the nineties as W. B. Yeats, Ellen Terry and Mrs Patrick Campbell as well as Max Beerbohm and William Rothenstein. It was an easy introduction to the society in which he would soon be moving for at the end of the 1890s the Slade was as much an artistic finishing school as it was an academy. Like a public school again, it saw its role as one of preparing its students for the world – or, at any rate, for one particular world – beyond its doors.

Then, even more than now, however, the artistic world-within-a-world into which the Slade pitched its graduates was riven by argument and aesthetic discontent. Impressionism had revolutionised artistic life across the Channel and even made some inroads in America, but English painting was at low ebb. Schools opened and closed, and groups and factions formed, re-formed and dissolved on an almost monthly basis as its practitioners, leaderless after what by then could be seen as the false dawn of Pre-Raphaelitism, sought their own equivalent of Parisian Impressionism.

Reacting against what they perceived as the Royal Academy's dated orthodoxy – despite the collapse of Pre-Raphaelitism into maudlin decadence, the committee was hanging nothing else – as early as 1886 a group of fifteen painters had joined together to establish what, at one stage, they even considered calling The Society of Anglo-French Painters. Rejecting that title, even though, like George du Maurier and his 'three musketeers of the brush', they had all studied in the Paris *ateliers* of Julian, Bonnat or Jean Paul Laurens, the rebels eventually presented themselves to the public as the New English Art Club (NEAC). A flurry of manifestos and press statements stressed that their purpose was 'to vindicate the soundness of engrafting English feeling and sentiment upon what is known as French technique'.[10] In other words, although their subject-matter would remain conventionally 'English' – their first few exhibitions contained numerous canvases reminiscent of the busy social realism of Holman Hunt, Ford Madox Brown and the later Pre-Raphaelites – their working patterns would be unequivocally 'French'. They colonised new premises such as the Bolton Studios in Redcliffe Road and the Wentworth Studios in Manresa Road, both in Chelsea. As far as the English climate allowed, they adopted the French ideal of *plein air* working, and they lived, ate and drank together in frank emulation of their Parisian *confrères*.

Ten years on, even that was deemed insufficient, and one faction of the NEAC at least had ventured even further down the Francophile path. Following the resignation in 1892 of a group of rather sentimental Scottish artists known as 'The Glasgow Boys', by the mid-nineties the club was heavily under the influence of Wilson Steer (a founder member), Walter Sickert and the egregious Whistler. Reflecting their interests, the crowded *verismo* of Hunt and Brown, which was the prevalent NEAC house style, found itself under attack by a more austere, French-influenced 'London Impressionism'. The term was derived from the title of a rebel exhibition mounted by Wilson Steer, Sickert and disaffected NEAC members at the Goupil Gallery in 1889. Not without a certain boardroom appeal even today, for a quarter of a century and more it was to have an immense influence on London painting and be instrumental in binging about the eclipse of the rapidly ossifying NEAC mainstream.

Only a generation previously, the NEAC had acted as one and embodied all that was current in English art. But by the turn of the century the neat conventionalism of its older members, as well its hanging committee's very Sladean insistence on the importance of just that 'English' technique and 'finish' which John embodied, was being pushed further and further up the beach by a wave of new, 'foreign' Impressionism and the tireless proselytising of Walter Sickert.

The son and grandson of artists, Sickert was nearly twenty years older than John. Yet in the early years of the twentieth century, as he entered his early forties, it was he and not the ever-promising John who was to emerge as the real apostle of the new. He had had a brief career on the stage before entering the Slade, a generation ahead of John and Orpen, in 1881. Heavily influenced in his younger days by Whistler, he had purged this and any remaining 'Englishness' from his work during a period of self-exile in France, returning with a wholly original style of his own. It quickly came to manifest itself both on and off the canvas, particularly off; through a stream of witty and percipient critical essays he wrote for periodicals including *The New Age*, as much as the strength of his personality. John, who had first met him, along with 'old William Michael Rossetti', on one of his visits to Ida, recalled 'his manners and style of dress combining old world elegance with the licence of artistic tradition'.[11] A noted wit, he was also an inveterate dandy. One day he would present himself attired in the black frock coat and top hat of London society, the next he would have affected the Parisian artist's smock and beret. Despite such personal iridescence, his painting had the consistency of a master, and in its impatience with the formality and tradition of the NEAC it came to lie behind many of the later developments in English art.

'Do present-day art-students bring their sketch-books with them to the cinema, night-clubs or wherever they go in the evenings?' Augustus John asked in his autobiography *Chiaroscuro*,[12] first published in 1952. Answering his own question, he added: 'I think not.' He did, of course; but he was not the first artist to have done so. Long before him, Sickert had seen the need for precise, documentary observation and crammed a pad into his jacket pocket.

Nearly half a century earlier, at precisely the time when John was beginning to make a mark in the fashionable world of society portraits and accepting a commission to decorate the walls of the wealthy connoisseur Sir Hugh Lane's home in Cheyne Walk (a job which would occupy him on and off for more than five years), Sickert's work was already celebrating and immortalising a much more basic proletarian existence. In style as much as subject-matter, it was a whole world away from the sub-Corotean landscapes and polite, Sargentesque society portraits which still filled many of the walls at NEAC exhibitions.

Sickert's previous career on the stage – as much as his admiration of Degas – perhaps explains his continuing fascination with the music-hall; and canvases such as *Noctes Ambrosianae* (1906) and *The Brighton Pierrots* (dating from as late as 1915 but harking back to similar works like *Minnie Cunningham at the Old Bedford* which the NEAC had accepted for its show in the winter of 1892) revelled in its vibrancy, artificiality and seedy glamour.[13]

Together with a series of canvases painted at Dieppe during his French sojourn, they soon attracted notice – there was little to do with Sickert which did not – and within months of his return students, younger artists, sympathetic critics and would-be patrons as well as the merely curious were seeking him out in a studio he had taken at 8 Fitzroy Street, a quiet, decaying road at the northern end of what was then vaguely known as Soho. Once occupied by his mentor Whistler, it has been described by a friend of its new tenant as:

a huge room at the back of the first floor of that vast rambling rockery of a house; one reached it by winding passages and steps turning odd corners that seemed to double on themselves; strangers seldom managed to find their way through the labyrinth without assistance. But when one did finally arrive, the picture was unexpected. One was transplanted suddenly from the mundane present to the heart of the eighteenth century . . .

I doubt if there was another room with more echoes of the Georgian era in London. Spacious, beautifully proportioned, rather dark with long windows looming through the dusk and misty looking glasses on the high walls, it held secrets that were all its own.[14]

Sickert was flattered by all the attention which his return to London attracted and, characteristically, he capitalised on it. Noting that among the more frequent of his visitors were the painters William Rothenstein and his younger brother Albert (who was to change his name to Rutherston in 1914), Walter Russell, Spencer Gore and Harold Gilman, he suggested that between them they could make something more formal – 'a Salon d'automne milieu' – out of the casual visits, cups of tea, considerations of work in progress and conversations about the relative merits of Seurat, Signac and Degas which had become such an important part of life at No. 8. Accordingly, the six (who were soon joined by Ethel Sands and Nan Hudson) took the lease of two first-floor rooms in a house at 19 Fitzroy Street and elected themselves members of a formally constituted Fitzroy Street Group.

It was a straight, commercial undertaking. The artists paid equal annual rental fees (initially between £6 and £7) to cover the cost of the rooms, provided their own easels and acted as their own dealers when, 'week in, week out' the group was 'At Home' on Saturday afternoons to anyone who cared to come. (As the original women members, Ethel Sands and Nan Hudson were also expected to act as hostesses, serving cake and handing around cups of tea on these occasions.)

The studio was exactly that, a room with bare floorboards and no pretensions, more like a dusty provincial auction-room than a chic Mayfair salon. An interior painted in about 1913 by Malcolm Drummond, one of the lesser members of the group, shows it to have been simply furnished with racks full of unframed canvases covering one wall and other works displayed on easels or simply stacked against the walls (see Plate 11). But it did not matter. Very soon the Saturday At Homes became an institutionalised part of the London art scene and a recognised centre for the avant-garde. There was no gallery commission and so prices were low. Pictures sold for anything from £5 to £15 ('less than a supper at the Savoy', Sickert noted) and rooting through them week by week became an article of faith for critics and a source of bargains for enlightened collectors such as Sir Hugh Lane.

Students, and in particular a greater than usual number of young women, began to call, leading Sickert to remark that he was some new kind of matinée idol, 'the Lewis Waller of the Art Schools'. Indeed, although women were never to play a particularly important role in London Bohemian life, such a position as they had was established by these early Fitzroy Street pioneers. Ethel Sands and Nan Hudson were soon joined as members of the group by Sylvia Gosse (the daughter of Sir Edmund), Nina Hamnett, Stanislawa de Karlowska, Thérèse Lessore and others, including, for a long time, the young Enid Bagnold, who recalled in her *Autobiography* that it was not so much the aesthetics of it all which appealed to many of them, as the character of Sickert himself:

> I didn't fall in love with him. Or hardly. We were all enslaved, enchanted. The day glittered because of him. But he had a doctor's morality about his students. Women on the whole were kittle-cattle to him. Like Tonks (then Head of the Slade) he would sigh and say – 'So brilliant girls are! And then the damn fools marry.'[15]

Inevitably it was not long before the press was talking about Fitzroy Street art. But for once the label was more than journalistic shorthand. There was a discernible Fitzroy Street style. Taking their cue from Sickert, Gore, Gilman and Charles Ginner in particular also submerged themselves in the minutiae of ordinary domestic life and evolved a technique by which to celebrate even its bleakest moments. The thick and rather bleary opacity of their canvases depicting such subjects as a *Mornington Crescent Nude* (Sickert), *Sunset, Letchworth, with Man and a Dog* (Gore), *An Eating*

71

House or *Tea in the Bedsitter* (both by Gilman) brought a new and recognisable 'realism' to English painting. The cold blues of so many of their interiors – relieved here by the dull, brassy glint of a bed frame or fender, there by the awkward, lardy whiteness of a model's thigh – suggested a world at once squalid and romantically attractive. In the same way that, a generation earlier, the 'English Impressionists' Alfred Sisley and Camille Pissarro (the father of another Fitzroy Street painter, Lucien Pissarro) had celebrated London suburbia in canvases such as the latter's *Lower Norwood under Snow*, the Fitzroy Street Group rejoiced in the crowded mantelpieces, grimy rumpled sheets and cramped and cluttered back gardens of the proletarian inner city.

It offered a range of subjects of which they never tired. The style survived a realignment in 1911 which gave rise to the more celebrated Camden Town Group – a men-only association in which Sickert, Gore, Gilman, Ginner and Pissarro were again the leading lights – and even that group's submersion in a wider London Group, which was established in 1913 and was to have an influence on the agenda of English art for the following half century. It was even able to take on board the radical airiness introduced by Gore and Gilman in about 1912 with a series of sunlit, suburban-Fauvist canvases influenced by the latter's discovery of the new-town delights of Letchworth in Hertfordshire.

In the annals of art history the decade leading up to the outbreak of the First World War is not so much celebrated for the brief maturity of the short-lived Fitzroy Street Group as it is for the opening of the first of Roger Fry's 'Post-Impressionist' exhibitions in 1910. In reality, however, the two events were closely connected. Indeed, the arrival of the Fitzroy Street Group was as much a symptom of the change in human nature, which Virginia Woolf was later to date to the November of that year (when the exhibition opened), as the notorious show at the Grafton Gallery.

Actually mounted under the title 'Manet and the Post-Impressionists', Fry's exhibition was more a self-conscious manifestation of chic Bloomsbury Modernism than a mere show of work. Fry himself, a one-time disciple of Sickert as well as an habitué of the drawing-rooms of Gordon Square, was as adept as his master when it came to self-promotion. Coining the term

'Post-Impressionism' and arranging the exhibition had been ploys *pour épater le bourgeois*, and as such both were outstandingly successful. The Grafton Gallery was crowded with critics and hordes of curious visitors, all anxious to see and pronounce upon the works of Cézanne, Van Gogh, Matisse, Renoir, Degas, Manet himself and the other foreigners which filled its walls. Inevitably, with a very few exceptions, it is the opinions of the former which have come down to us. The reviewer of *The Times* saw the whole show as a prelude to anarchy. In tones which were reminiscent of Ruskin's criticism of Whistler, others found it variously filthy, pornographic, degrading, or merely a practical joke in very dubious taste. The contributing artists were written off as lunatics, while even artists such as John were unsure quite how to take it. 'A bloody show!' he had fumed after his first visit; although he did at least return and admit an admiration for Van Gogh, a couple of Gauguins and, above all, for Cézanne.

John's outraged exclamation was a telling sign of how far things had gone – for him and for the English art world. With the benefit of hindsight, critics have seen it as the first indication of the erstwhile Bohemian's capitulation; the first step on the long road back to respectability which would end with his being elected a Royal Academician in 1928. It was not perhaps as simple as that. By 1910 he had four children to support and financial obligations well beyond the comprehension of most people. For all his admiration of Van Gogh, he simply could not afford to turn his back on 'the market': there was no escaping the fact that the sheer unconventionality of the Dutchman's work had led to his famously having sold only one painting in the course of his life.

In addition, in the winter of 1909 the continuing struggle to decorate Sir Hugh Lane's walls had induced a period of profound self-doubt. Writing to Lady Ottoline Morrell, John announced:

> it seems my fate to be hasty but I have serious thoughts of quitting this island and going somewhere where life is more stable and beautiful and primitive and where one is not bound to be in a hurry. I want absolutely to grasp things plastically and not merely glance at their charms, and for that one needs time.[16]

A putative, latter-day Gauguin or Robert Louis Stevenson, in his own eyes at least he was still rather more than the slick society colourist: that self-pitying letter was a real cry from the heart. But things were not quite so easy; despite frequent attempts, John could never truly up and go.

Four years earlier he had tried. Lured by the prospect of a salary in the region of £400 he had beaten a temporary retreat from London and accepted a one-year post as Professor at the school of art attached to University College, Liverpool. It was, however, an acceptance on his own terms: every morning during term-time he had been observed striding 'across the drab quad to the studios in his grey fishermen's jersey and with golden rings in his ears'. But although John claimed to have found the actual business of teaching 'amusing', Liverpool was Liverpool and throughout his stay he seems to have been even more a fish out of water than he was in London, where he at least enjoyed a certain eccentric celebrity.

Two pictures – one a photograph, the other a painting – accurately summarise his predicament. The first is a snapshot which, with all the care of a Delacroix, depicts the hanging committee of the New English Art Club in 1904. Henry Tonks, Philip Wilson Steer, William Rothenstein, D. S. MacColl, the art critic of the *Spectator* (who had been instrumental in securing John's post at Liverpool) and even Roger Fry are all there, neatly turned out and wearing the high-necked collars and ties of the day. The way in which the photograph has been composed, however, relegates them all to the status of bit-part players. At the centre of everything is a heavily bearded Augustus John, his jacket open, his jersey rumpled, a hat on his head, a pipe between his teeth and his hands jammed into his trouser pockets.

But even more than the others, John is posing. The outré costume and rather arrogant self-consciousness of his stance inadequately hides the fact that as early as 1904 he was playing a part while all those around him were doing things for real. Even as the photographer was fiddling with his plates for the NEAC committee portrait, his fellow-subjects at the rather dusty-looking Dudley Gallery (the NEAC never quite managed to acquire galleries of its own) were emerging as the *true* artistic avant-garde – and unlike him they were secure enough in their convictions not to need to flirt with a theatrical Bohemianism.

That this was indeed the case comes over even more strongly in William Orpen's slick and very finished canvas *Homage to Manet* (now opened by the City of Manchester). Completed in 1909, the year before Fry's first Post-Impressionist exhibition opened, it is deliberately formal; a mannered 'conversation piece' in which we are once again confronted by the uniformly well-dressed figures of Wilson Steer, MacColl and Tonks. Grouped beneath a recognisable Manet nude, they are depicted with three more real apostles of the new, Walter Sickert, Sir Hugh Lane and George Moore.

But the point of the picture lies not so much in its *dramatis personae* – interesting though they are – as in the idea of these balding, ostensibly-conservative, middle-aged men paying homage to the then outrageously-provocative Manet – and being publicly depicted in doing so. For, retrospectively and almost incidentally, that depth-charges the Augustus John of the legend. He might just as well not have bothered, it seems to be saying, since the quiet assurance of Sickert and his fellows (and on another level the sheer conventionality of Orpen's portrayal of it) was just as effective when it came to breaking the mould.

The picture's sheer clubbiness – *'Ravishing, eh, Sickert?' 'Oh, yes indeed, Sir Hugh'* – compels attention. But more than that it is a testament to the existence of a quiet and peculiarly English Bohemianism which John had no part in. He was a member of the Café Royal crowd – and, as Sir Herbert Beerbohm Tree once observed, 'If you want to see English people at their most English go to the Café Royal where they are trying their hardest to be French.' The point was that the real English Bohemians of the time did not feel the need to be anything except themselves. They did not need to hide behind props like pipes, fisherman's jerseys, beards or even earrings – and, sadly, they did not need Augustus John either.

It would be an exaggeration to claim that his non-inclusion in the canvas was a deliberate snub, but it still speaks volumes. By 1909 it seems that even his friend William Orpen had realised that John's theatrical Bohemianism was superficial – commercially advantageous but in the final analysis a blind alley. Despite it all, Orpen seems to be saying, the self-same polite frock-coated English Bohemianism which W. B. Yeats had – at one and the same time – both embodied and despaired of, a Bohemianism which still looked to its 'betters' for both sartorial and intellectual guidance, remained the most likely passport to the future.

Events were to prove him right. Although Orpen himself was

never one of them (and was temporarily to out-John even John with a commercial success which London art dealers still remember for 'the Rolls Royces nose-to-tail outside his studio'); and although the John camp was to continue with its vituperative but private campaign against society and the establishment at large – 'Oh God, not that old bitch!' cried Nina Hamnett when the hostess Lady Ottoline Morrell loomed on her horizon a few years later – it was to be the dark-coated Manet-worshippers who made the running.

Indeed, the opening of the 'Manet and the Post-Impressionists' exhibition (and, for that matter, the very existence of a second Post-Impressionist show in 1912) was to prove a watershed for the younger artists of the day, then occasionally known as the 'demi-Johns'. In exactly the same way that the rhythmic modernism of Igor Stravinsky and Sergei Diaghilev's Ballets Russes (whose first London season the following year excited comparable controversy) was to split the musical world, the reaction of any artist to Post-Impressionism became a litmus-test of his own 'Modernism'. And this time it is *not* an exaggeration to say that battle-lines were drawn around the Grafton Gallery. On one side the conservatives at the New English Art Club retreated still further into traditionalism. (Tellingly, Augustus John remained 'consistently loyal' to the Club, and it to him; his work continued to adorn its shows until about 1925.) While on the other a predominantly younger set of painters and critics elected Sickert and the Fitzroy Street Group – who had, after all, anticipated events in their recognition of Manet, Degas and Seurat – the heroes of the hour.

Even if they wished it otherwise, the Fitzrovians had little option but to accept the role. After 1910 they found the doors of the NEAC closed in their faces, and heard that there would no longer be room for their work in its annual exhibitions. They had crossed a Rubicon and could only press on with their bedsteads and back-garden views, painting the only way they knew how.

And so could John. Beached out of his time, he too had no option but to go on, lonely and increasingly isolated – and in this context it is probably no accident that, whereas the Fitzroy and Camden Town groups were well represented in the major 1987 Royal Academy retrospective exhibition *British Art in the Twentieth Century: The Modern Movement* the eternally 'promising' Augustus

John was not even included. But, ever the desperate Bohemian, he still had one role to play.

In company with the critic Tommy Earp and Nina Hamnett, it was John who decreed one night in 1926 that the Fitzroy Tavern would henceforth be the headquarters of London Bohemia.

CHAPTER SIX

'Welcome, Gentlemen, to Tot'nam Court!'

THERE was one other side-effect of the arrival of the Fitzroy Street Group and the furore surrounding Roger Fry's Post-Impressionist exhibitions. Indirectly, they both led to the isolation of a section of the artistic community in one particular area of London.

To some extent Fry, Virginia Woolf and their fellow 'Blooms-berries' had already achieved this isolation for themselves. Even before 1910 what has become known as the Bloomsbury Group was well established. Those in a position to know recognised it as a branch of high, Aesthetic, *fin de siècle* Cambridge which had been grafted onto what critics have since called the 'intellectual aristocracy' of London. Its whole ethos was founded on a sophisticated, upper-middle-class and decidedly 'above-stairs' culture which its members had smuggled into the then rather dilapidated eighteenth-century squares on the western fringe of the borough of St Pancras. At the time St Pancras was neither a good nor a fashionable address. Property prices were cheap; and it was this more than anything else which first brought the Bloomsberries to Bloomsbury.

The advance guard arrived as early as 1904 when, a few months after his death, the four children of Sir Leslie Stephen gave up the family home in Hyde Park Gate – an address which was both good and fashionable – and moved to 46 Gordon Square. It is difficult now to appreciate the consternation caused by that easterly migration, although the letters and diaries of Sir Leslie's third child Virginia (who became Mrs Woolf in 1912) relate how she, her sister Vanessa, and brothers Thoby and Adrian had to endure 'screams against Bloomsbury' from their friends. Three years later, following Thoby's death and Vanessa's marriage to the critic Clive Bell, Virginia and Adrian faced still worse when they progressed to Fitzroy Square. No matter that the house they had chosen (No. 29) had once been occupied by George Bernard Shaw. Their friends were appalled. 'Beatrice comes round, inarticulate with meaning, & begs me not to take the house because of the neighbourhood,' Virginia wrote to a friend[1] – and was herself only finally convinced of the relative safety of the area after she had made enquiries at the local police station.

In a very physical sense, however, the move to Bloomsbury both bound the young Stephens and their friends together and liberated them from the constraints of Victorianism. It was literally an escape into a Modernism unthinkable under the gloomy, mid-century regime which Sir Leslie had imposed at Hyde Park Gate. There, behind a high stucco frontage, all the formality of the 1860s was preserved as if beneath an aspic glaze in dark and over-furnished rooms. Life was organised around Sir Leslie, first editor of the *Dictionary of National Biography* (who was fifty years of age before even Virginia was born), his ear-trumpet and his mutton-chop lunches. In direct contrast, 46 Gordon Square with its tall windows and well-proportioned rooms, offered both light and air; and they were the two qualities of mind most prized by its young occupants.

Soon the Stephens had attracted a group of sympathetic friends to their sparsely furnished house whose 'modern' interior is not difficult to imagine: the walls a plain white or modishly decorated, the floorboards bare and every chimneybreast adorned with a painting by Vanessa, Clive or Duncan Grant. Thoby threw Thursday-evening At Homes, chiefly for young men like Clive Bell and Saxon Sydney-Turner with whom he had been at Cambridge, intellectuals who were also in full retreat from the dark mahogany values of their parents; and with their arrival, from about 1905 the Bloomsbury Group was established in everything but name.

It never had a fixed membership any more than it was ever formally constituted, but virtually all its hard-core 'members' arrived at this time. Like Thoby, as an undergraduate Clive Bell had joined the Cambridge Midnight Society. At its meetings the two had met Saxon Sydney-Turner, Lytton Strachey and Leonard Woolf, all of them also members of a more secretive society, The

Apostles. They, in their turn, introduced others; the young E. M. Forster and two further members of The Apostles: Desmond MacCarthy and Maynard Keynes.

Critics have often sneeringly suggested that, with its chichi, limp-wristed notions of friendship, the pre-1914 Bloomsbury Group was hardly more than an extended, London-based version of these undergraduate societies; and there is some truth in the accusation. Its severely intellectual tone, marked by late-evening meetings over whisky, buns and cocoa, at which G. E. Moore's *Principia Ethica* might again be discussed, or a new theory of art propounded by Roger Fry, was certainly both earnest and elitist. It was also frank and unbuttoned – or so Vanessa Bell would have us believe. 'We did not hesitate to talk of anything . . . You could say what you liked about art, sex, or religion,' she once recalled.[2] You could, and they did. Any group which numbered her husband, not to mention Lytton Strachey, among its members could not after all have been 'conversationally chaste', as Vanessa and Clive's son, the historian Quentin Bell has pointed out. But, as he has also written, judged by contemporary criteria Bloomsbury's much-vaunted frankness was strictly relative:

> Bloomsbury was never promiscuous either in its normal or its homosexual relationships. By modern standards it was restrained in its language and romantic in its attachments. Carnal adventures were justified only by passion, although passion was licence enough; Bloomsbury, while denying that there was such a thing as an impure act, would certainly have recognised and condemned impure states of mind.[3]

Far more than Bohemian licentiousness then, what cut Bloomsbury off from ordinary people – and made it both literally and intellectually inbred – was its sheer intelligence. The careers and characters of some of its leading figures in the years immediately before the outbreak of the First World War bear this out. It is impossible to imagine either Saxon Sydney-Turner, who pursued an exemplary career in the Foreign Office, or the ascetic, intellectual Leonard Woolf, who had already seen colonial service in Ceylon, engaging in 'carnal adventures'. In their own eyes at least, such capers were far more the domain of Roger Fry and Lytton Strachey. Even they, however, setting out on the quest from opposite ends of the sexual spectrum, seldom went further than a little furtive bottom-patting. Platonism too had its place in the Bloomsbury ethic.

For Sickert and the younger members of the Fitzroy Street Group everything was rather different. In contrast to the Bloomsberries, across the borough boundary in Holborn they enjoyed a professional rather than a personal-cum-social relationship. Instead of houses, they rented studios and were bound together by forces which had more to do with basic economics than the old school, or university, tie. Although, in theory at least, they shared many of the Bloomsberries' Modernist ideas, and lived and worked only a matter of a few hundred yards away from Gordon Square, until the First World War there was little real communication between the two cliques. Even Nina Hamnett, with whom Roger Fry at one stage had an affair, always felt somehow prohibited from the innermost circles of St Pancras.

Marjorie Lilly, a long-time member of the Sickert camp, has given a persuasive, and very logical, reason for this isolationism. 'Bloomsbury was composed of writers, not painters,' she recalled in her memoir Sickert, The Painter and His Circle. On the other hand,

> With the exception of Sickert, Fitzrovia was almost inarticulate. And generally speaking, it did not deplore the deficiency; the visual arts were all that mattered here, considered as more important than literature or any other civilized achievement.[4]

The opening of the Omega Workshops in July 1913 might have presaged some kind of rapprochement between the two groups, since one of the Workshop's principal aims was to give an income to promising young artists of the Modernist persuasion. In the event, even it could do no more than temporarily bridge a culture-gap wider and more difficult to cross than the busy Tottenham Court Road which would later come to separate the rival domains of Bloomsbury and Fitzrovia.

Significantly enough, the workshops were established on the less reputable, Holborn side of that road, in premises at 33 Fitzroy Square, right at the heart of an area which had been associated with furniture-making for more than a century. At its peak in the early 1860s there were 110 separate firms of cabinet-makers, upholsterers and French-polishers in Fitzroy Square and the surrounding streets. Charlotte Street alone boasted thirteen, while another ten had premises in nearby Cleveland Street. But fifty years later Fry had no wish to compete with their highly finished wares, most of which were by then supplied direct to Heal's, Maple's, Catesby's, Shoolbred's, Waring and Gillow's and many of the other department stores which were a feature of London by the end of the nineteenth century. Omega was an attempt to harness some of the energy generated by his two Post-Impressionist exhibitions and introduce a 'spirit of fun' into furniture and fabrics. In a preface to the workshops' catalogue Fry warned that his artists would

> refuse to spoil the expressive quality of their work by sand-papering it down to a shop finish, in the belief that the public has at last seen through the humbug of the machine-made imitation of works of art.[5]

They were fine words, which many interpreted as prophesying the arrival of an Earthly Paradise such as had been described by William Morris. In reality they cloaked a caveat prompted by considerations which were as practical as they were aesthetic. The artists Fry employed – never for more than three half days in any one week so that they should have time for their own work – were just that, painters who knew little or nothing about the construction of a chair or the firing of a pot. As a result, reported Wyndham Lewis (who had broken noisily and vituperatively with Fry shortly after the opening of the workshops), although they did not actually make, but only decorated them, 'the chairs we sold stuck to the seats of people's trousers; when they took up an Omega candlestick, they couldn't put it down again, they held it in an involuntary vice-like grip. It was glued to them and they to it.'[6]

Curiously, such shoddiness did not seem to matter. The workshops attracted attention and were written up, not always favourably, in the press. One picture spread in the *Daily Mirror* had photographs of two Omega interiors with, between them, a portrait of Fry and a caption reading:

> Would you like your house fitted with Post-Impressionist furniture, carpets and hangings? If you would, go to the Omega workshops, Fitzroy Square and Mr Roger Fry will do the rest: (1) the kind of cushions you would have on the armchairs; (3) the kind of room in which you would live, that is if your

nerves could stand it. (2) shows Mr Roger Fry thinking out some new futurist nightmare.[7]

Society's nerves were evidently stronger than those of Fleet Street, for among the Omega Workshop's first and most enthusiastic patrons were the rival hostesses Lady Cunard and Lady Ottoline Morrell. Sickert too was up to the challenge. After looking at the range of Omega goods, entirely typically he chose to buy a painted chamber-pot; while Augustus John, H. G. Wells, George Bernard Shaw and even Arnold Bennett were among the numerous, non-Bloomsbury visitors to the company's ground-floor showrooms.

Few, however, found their way to the upstairs workrooms. There, if one reads between the lines of contemporary accounts, it seems that Fry's ideal of creating a William Morris-like workers' Utopia was only superficially realised. It had early on been decided that all Omega wares – and according to an advertisement they ranged from furniture and textiles to 'hand-dyed dress materials, trays, fans and other objects suitable for Christmas presents' – were to be produced anonymously and marked only with the workshops' Greek-letter symbol. Although the policy succeeded in its stated aim of establishing a uniform style, coordinated across virtually every aspect of the applied arts, it also masked an element of cultural hegemony. Behind the bald Ω-symbol, Bloomsbury still called the tune. Together with a few trusted friends, Fry and his co-director Vanessa Bell were responsible for much of the original design work, and left merely its execution, generally boring and repetitive because of the need to accept large orders, to their part-time staff of artists. 'I seem to remember spending a long time painting the legs of tables . . . and endless candlesticks, for electric lights. When I remember Nina Hamnett at work, it is always a candlestick she has in her hand,' Winifred Gill, one of Fry's most devoted workers, recalled much later.[8]

Nevertheless, Nina Hamnett and others, who had a looser connection with Sickert's group, were only too delighted to give up a day and a half a week to work at 33 Fitzroy Square. Hamnett herself recalled in her autobiography that she made 'two or three pounds a week' from painting batiks (despite the fact that she was 'never very good at decorative work') and 'felt like a millionaire'.

Between 1913 and their dissolution just before the end of the First World War, the workshops attracted a large number of the younger and most promising artists of the day including Mark Gertler, Edward Wadsworth, David Bomberg, William Roberts, Paul Nash and, on occasions, Henri Gaudier-Brzeska. Some, like Wadsworth, Bomberg and Roberts, soon left, transferring their allegiance to the more abstract Vorticists and the apostate Wyndham Lewis. His disagreements with Fry had never healed, and in tones reminiscent of the stridency of the Vorticist manifesto, *Blast*, he was soon denouncing Omega as mere ' "greenery yallery", despite the Post-What-Not fashionableness of its draperies'.[9] But to others the workshops, despite the drudgery of painting endless trays and decorating clumsy jugs which did not even pour, undoubtedly remained a life-line.

In exactly the way in which Fry had hoped it would, the money they received for their work enabled them to continue as artists and to remain together as an increasingly clannish, lumpen parody of Bloomsbury in that district of London long known for its tolerance of the foreigner, the odd and the outsider. For Sickert (and Whistler before him) had not been acting on a whim when they chose to live and work in Fitzroy Street. The area had acquired a certain reputation centuries earlier.

The prologue to what seems to be a lost seventeenth-century city comedy hints at the bawdiness that used to accompany the Tottenham Court Fair, a riotous general wayzgoose which spilled over much of the area then and in the following century when it was all still open farmland:

> Y'are welcome, Gentlemen to Tot'nam Court,
> Where you (perhaps) expect some lusty sport,
> Such as rude custom doth beget in hay,
> When straggling numbers court that jovial day,
> With early riot . . .[10]

The fair was tamed and finally suppressed in 1808, but something of its looseness and vitality remained in the area around 'Tot'nam Court'. Well before 1883 when Emma Lazarus wrote her sonnet 'The New Colossus', ultimately to be inscribed on the pedestal of its subject, the Statue of Liberty in the approach to New York harbour, the district had been offering a haven to some at least of the tired, the poor and the huddled masses of

Oscar Wilde and Lord Alfred Douglas ('Bosie'): The studied insouciance of Wilde's pose belies the fact that this photograph was taken little more than eighteen months before his arrest. Douglas was then just twenty-three; he survived Wilde by more than forty years and died – a literary and social curiosity – in 1945.

Augustus John: One contemporary critic described William Orpen's portrait as 'Mr John in the character of a French Romantic'. Augustus himself was less keen, ultimately concluding that its bravura was 'most regrettable'.

Walter Sickert: 'Certainly an amusing and curious character — aimiable withal,' Augustus John noted. Others went further: Enid Bagnold remembered that all his female students were 'enslaved and enchanted' by the charismatic Walter Sickert.

'19 Fitzroy Street': The Fitzroy Street Group's Saturday 'At Homes' provided a unique link between Bohemia and Society. Malcolm Drummond's painting, completed in the months immediately before the First World War, is the only surviving record of the interior of the rather spartan studio in which they were held.

(Below) *George Gissing:* His face marked by his years in the new Grub Street of the late nineteenth century, the novelist George Gissing brings to the early years of the twentieth a weary and resigned pessimism. This photograph was taken in about 1905.

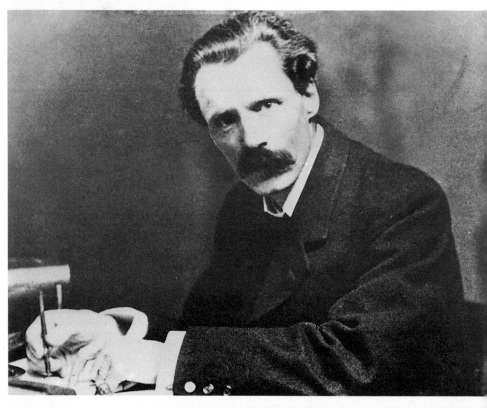

Europe. By the first decade of this century Fitzroy Street and
Fitzroy Square were at the heart of an area of London uniquely
well used to the cosmopolitan lifestyle more commonly associated
with the Latin quarters of other European capitals. Rents were low
and property prices cheap. Later, the district would, for a time,
become synonymous in the public mind with Soho. Later still, it
would flower as 'Fitzrovia', although that term is of very recent
provenance. Writing about the area as late as 1930, E. Beresford
Chancellor could find no better title for his book than *London's Old
Latin Quarter*. Back in 1907 Beatrice Thynne was only expressing
popularly held sentiments when she warned her friend Virginia
Stephen that it was simply a bad neighbourhood.

It was as if something of the spirit of the Tottenham Court Fair had
taken root in the soil. For, almost since the time it was first
developed, Fitzrovia evolved in ways very different to those
envisaged by its original architects.

Even by the middle of the eighteenth century it did not so much
as exist. The manor of Tottenhall, one of four which together
comprised the parish of St Pancras, was a patchwork of small
fields with names like Walnut Tree Field, Crab Tree Field and
Culver Meadow. (And as late as 1800, a sizeable part of what is
now Bloomsbury was still in this undeveloped state. A contemporary map shows Home Field extending over the whole of the
area now occupied by the northern end of Gower Street,
University College and University College Hospital.)

It would be a mistake, however, to imagine some bucolic
Arcadia. In *Barnaby Rudge*, first published in 1841, Charles Dickens
gives a graphic, if imaginative, description of precisely these plots.
One of his two historical novels (the other being *A Tale of Two
Cities*), the book is subtitled 'A Tale of the Riots of '80' and
contains an episode in which a mob, fleeing the aftermath of the
Gordon riots of 1780, seeks refuge in 'the Green Lanes' behind
Tottenham Court Road, Green Lane having been the original
name of Cleveland Street which Dickens (born in 1812) had
known since childhood:

> This was a retired spot, not of the choicest kind, leading into the
> fields. Great heaps of ashes; stagnant pools, overgrown with

rank grass and duckweed; broken turnstiles; and the upright posts of palings long since carried off for firewood, which menaced all heedless walkers with their jagged and rusty nails, were the leading features of the landscape; while here and there a donkey, or a ragged horse, tethered to a stake, and cropping off a wretched meal from the coarse stunted turf, were in keeping with the scene, and would have suggested (if the houses had not done so sufficiently of themselves) how very poor the people were who lived in the crazy huts adjacent, and how foolhardy it might prove for one who carried money, or wore decent clothes, to walk that way alone, unless by daylight.[11]

'The fields' were on the very fringe of London. Metropolitan sprawl had long since overrun the boundaries of the old city, and the capital already covered an area extending from Westminster to the Tower of London. By about 1700 High Holborn and Tyburn Road (now Oxford Street) marked its approximate northern boundary, and a rougher track led on from there, past the gardens and orchards of Tottenham Court, the Elizabethan manor house which gave the road its name, and out to the village of Hampstead.

The area was obviously ripe for development; and no one recognised this more than Charles Fitzroy, who became lord of the manor of Tottenhall on the death of his grandfather in 1757. It only remained for him to acquire its freehold, then held by the Canons of St Paul's Cathedral, whose claims to all 'rights, privileges and emoluments from the prebend' went back at least to the time of Domesday. Under the intricate property laws of eighteenth-century England, the process of acquisition was complex in the extreme. Some ten years were to go by before Fitzroy emerged as the legal owner of his manor. It might have taken even longer had he not been aided in his efforts by his brother, the Duke of Grafton, who became Prime Minister in 1766. Quite what Grafton's influence was remains unclear, but it is indisputable that an Act of Parliament establishing Fitzroy's title to the manor (at a very advantageous price) received the royal assent in 1768.

Even that was not the end of the matter, however; for at that time lessees, like those who held the small fields which comprised much of the manor, enjoyed a freedom in their management of the land akin to that of its actual owner. Most importantly, in some circumstances these tenants were quite at liberty to divide up their plots and sell building leases. Thus, the historic pattern of field boundaries came to have an enduring effect on the future development of the area for, whatever may have been his initial plans, Charles Fitzroy was unable to enforce any real control on the buildings which came to cover Walnut Tree Field, Culver Meadow and the surrounding lands.

Had he been able to, it is clear that Fitzrovia would have acquired a very different character. In late eighteenth-century London there were many freeholders in Fitzroy's position and, for those fortunate enough to control a substantial plot in the right area, the potential profits were enormous. Fitzroy's land (just the northern section of what is now Fitzrovia) was frankly neither large enough nor in the best location, but that did not prohibit his indulging in dreams of grandeur. He had been created Baron Southampton in 1780 and clearly set out to make his mark with a development which could take its place beside the recently completed Bedford Square estate in London, Queen Square in Bath and the contemporaneous Charlotte Square in Edinburgh.

While it was 'classical' in overall conception, in matters of detail his plan conformed exactly with the requirements of the 1774 Building Act. As indeed it had to. The fourth piece of legislation since the Great Fire of London, little more than a century previously, to have been directly concerned with standards of construction, the new Act was in many ways also the most thorough. It established seven rates of housing, no less than four of which applied to the terraces which were rising in the centre of every town and city. In its insistence that standards of space (as calculated by floor area) and height be observed, it came to have a crucial influence on the architecture of the towns and cities of England, an influence which survived in London until the Blitz and the city's wholesale reconstruction in the 1950s and 1960s.

Even today, something of its impact can still be seen in the streets around Bedford Square in Bloomsbury. A largely green-field site on the Duke of Bedford's Southampton Estate in 1774, building work began there barely a year after the Act came into force. Two years later the first occupants were moving into houses in what we would now term a zoned development. There was a central square of tall first-rate houses for the aristocracy, sur-

rounded by streets of smaller, second- and third-rate accommodation for merchants and tradesmen of the emerging middle
class. Like similar developments in other cities, in overall
conception, if not entirely in execution, it owed much to
Renaissance designs for the ideal city.

The development of Fitzroy Square followed some seventeen
years later, in 1792–4. Although the plot was smaller, the scheme
was hardly less grand. Robert and James Adam, who had recently
finished working on Edinburgh's Charlotte Square, were given
responsibility for the square itself, and expressed themselves most
fully on its southern and eastern sides, in each of which it is
known that they had some financial involvement. (Though they
still followed the Adams's pattern, the square's nothern and
western sides were not developed until the end of the 1820s.) The
housing was of the first rate, faced with stucco or Portland stone
and even today it retains something of the grace and style of the
Adam brothers' original designs.

Like Bedford Square again, Fitzroy Square was also conceived
as the apex of a social pyramid, this time one which had as its base
the third- and even fourth-rate terraces in nearby Conway Street,
Grafton Way and Warren Street. The tragedy was that the
pyramid was never broad enough. Charles Fitzroy's plot was
hemmed in on all four sides: by Tottenham Court Road and the
recently constructed Euston Road (then called New Road) respectively on the east and north; by the large Portland estate on the
west; and by the smaller plots created out of what had once been
Culver Meadow and Crab Tree and Walnut Tree fields on the
south.

These were to prove the problem. They had been built over in
the previous twenty years, but the separate, small-scale developments which covered individual fields were all on a more basic
scale. The terraces which defined the roads that would become
Charlotte Street and Goodge Street, Tottenham Street, Rathbone
Place and Percy Street were thrown up with one end in mind, and
that was profit.

According to Eric Partridge, the term 'jerry-building' did not
enter the English language until the 1880s, but there is no other
way of describing the rash of speculative developments which
covered these, and many other, small plots in London at this time.
They were offered by their tenants on ninety-nine-year leases to

whoever believed himself able to capitalise upon them. There were many who thought they could and in the short term some who actually did. Typically, they were speculative builders who undertook to put up houses at their own expense but to the designs of the lessor. These they then had the right to lease out for the remainder of the ninety-year period, after which, of course, the houses reverted to the original lessor.

Any altruism the builders might originally have possessed was short lived. For the first (but not the last) time in its history the character of Fitzrovia changed even as the building boom of the last quarter of the eighteenth century was at its height. Primarily, the area had been designed for the upper classes, but before the stucco on sites such as Fitzroy Square was so much as dry, social changes led to a westerly migration of the aristocracy, to newly desirable addresses in the West End, Mayfair and Belgravia. Back in Fitzrovia this meant that brand-new, first-rate houses were suddenly unlettable and hence uneconomic. Understandably, their builder-landlords became less and less worried about how the premises were used. Division and sub-letting became common-place, and a pattern in which even once-grand houses came to be sub-divided to provide cheap rented accommodation became the norm. The properties were carved up vertically and horizontally into a warren of separate workshops, studios and lodgings with no regard to their original plan. Individual rooms might some-times remain intact, but getting to them entailed negotiating the 'winding passages and steps [and] turning odd corners that seemed to double on themselves', the labyrinth which Marjorie Lilly vividly remembered confronting the casual visitor to the Whistler-Sickert studio at 8 Fitzroy Street in the early 1900s.

Nick Bailey, the author of a modern topographical study of the area, was hardly overstating the situation when he wrote that large tracts of what is now Fitzrovia were converted from virgin meadowland to slums in rather less than a century. His analysis of the census returns for just one street in a sample year shows the scale of decline. In 1841 Goodge Place comprised just 27 four-storey houses with basements. Yet it was the registered address of 485 people, an average of 18 to a house. One house in particular accommodated no less than 32, or rather more than 3 to a room. Bailey adds: 'When it is remembered that many occupants also carried on trades such as dressmaking in the same room, the extent of the squalor and overcrowding can just about be imagined.'[12]

It was precisely this scenario of urban dereliction which gave rise to what we now know as Fitzrovia. Rents in the ravaged, gutted properties were low and individual rooms were large. Even by the middle of the nineteenth century the area was attracting unusual numbers of foreign immigrants. Central European Jews, Huguenots, Belgians and French Catholic priests seeking a freedom of belief denied under the Terror all crowded in. As early as 1710 it was being reported that French nationals alone occupied more than a quarter of the premises in a street in what was then known as 'Soo-Hoo Fields', directly across Oxford Street from the area in which Fitzrova would develop. Within half a century similar numbers, mostly craftsmen, joiners and French-polishers, would also find employment in the workshops which lined Tottenham Court Road and Fitzroy Street.

They did not have the area to themselves, however. In the late eighteenth and early nineteenth centuries, its low rents and the availability of short-term tenancies also made it attractive to a raffish, floating population of native Englishmen. Dodging the debtors' prison, at various times John Dickens brought his family to premises in Margaret Street and at 22 Cleveland Street. The novelist himself returned to the area in his youth and had lodgings at 25 Fitzroy Street.

Nor was he alone. Fitzrovia played host to a legion of writers in the years after Dr Johnson lodged at 6 Great Castle Street in 1738, the address at which he finished his epic poem, *London*. Their tenancies, along with those of vastly greater number of now-forgotten artists, are faithfully listed in Volume XXI of the great *Survey of London*. In the main they were hacks; essayists, water-colourists, playwrights, portrait-painters of little renown and reviewers, the flotsam and jetsam which drifted on the surface of an expanding urban economy. They arrived one month and were gone the next, taking little and giving still less to a neighbourhood which had offered very temporary shelter. The names of some of the more notable, nevertheless give some indication of the area's appeal to the literary and artistic communities of the period.

As the young Arthur Ransome never tired of recalling, William Hazlitt was an early arrival, and lived in Rathbone Place from 1799 until 1803. A few years later, Thomas de Quincey occupied a house in Great Titchfield Street. John Constable lodged at 63 Charlotte Street before moving to a studio at No. 76 in 1822, which he retained until 1837. Samuel Taylor Coleridge had rooms in Berners Street for a period in 1812–13, but left them only months before Percy Bysshe Shelley moved into 56 Margaret Street while arranging a separation from his first wife, Harriet. Rather more importantly for the later history of the area, William Godwin, the father of Shelley's second wife, Mary, was all the while running a radical bookshop less than half a mile away in Hanway Street at the bottom of Tottenham Court Road.

Despite such a plethora of talents, this nineteenth-century Fitzrovia was anything but a kind of urban Grasmere or inner-city Hampstead. Understandably, perhaps, it impinges very little on the works of these temporary inhabitants. Even Dickens makes no direct reference to the cramped and sordid realities of life in Margaret Street and Cleveland Street, although it is beyond doubt that the privations of his childhood had a profound effect on much of his later writing. But the books of a later generation of its denizens give a graphic picture of conditions, which remained the same for virtually the whole of the nineteenth century.

Born in 1857, the novelist George Gissing was more than a generation younger than Dickens and he wrote with an anger and psychological power which ally him to the ineluctably twentieth-century Lawrence rather than to Meredith and Hardy or mid-century novelists such as Disraeli, Charles Reade and Wilkie Collins, with all of whom he has at one time or another been bracketed. Gissing too had come up the hard way. He was imprisoned for theft at the age of twenty, and could never forget that a room in 'Grub Street', where even carpet was a 'luxury undreamt of', remained the inevitable, if not the natural, environment of the serious writer forced to serve a frivolous public.

The real Grub Street of the gazetteers had disappeared long before Gissing arrived in London in 1867 after a year in America. An inconsequential City lane, originally linking what is now Fore Street EC2 with Chiswell Street, it was described by Dr Johnson in the *Dictionary* as 'much inhabited by writers of small histories'. By the mid-nineteenth century it had been renamed Milton Street and its inhabitants were long dispersed. Now even the road has gone: in the 1960s it vanished beneath fountains and pre-cast concrete, a victim of the Barbican redevelopment scheme.

91

Well before 1867, however, the 'new Grub Street' of Holborn and St Pancras had taken its place; and in two of his novels Gissing chronicles life there more precisely than anyone ever did its predecessor. Personal experience had taught him that a new generation of writers, critics and even lexicographers – the 'harmless drudges' whom Johnson had described a century and a half before – had taken over rooms and garrets once occupied by Coleridge, Shelley and the rest in the rotting streets which straddled the Tottenham Court Road. Like the eponymous hero of one of his last novels, the semi-autobiographical *Private Papers of Henry Ryecroft* (1903), he had even been there himself. Shortly after his arrival in London, he had had lodgings in Gower Place before moving to rooms in an 'alley', actually Colville Place off Charlotte Street. Their memory remained with him ever after, to be recalled time and time again and with exactly the vividness with which they would haunt his hero: 'Would I live it over again, that life of the garret and the cellar? Not with the assurance of fifty years' contentment such as I now enjoy to follow upon it!'[13]

Looking back at that time, with all the hindsight of thirty years, Henry Ryecroft, aged 'three-and-fifty' and (in a phrase that was the book's first title) 'an author at grass' in exile in France, is still possessed by the squalor of it all; the poverty, the hunger and 'a slight attack of diphtheria – traceable, I imagine, to the existence of a dust-bin *under the staircase*'.[14] He confesses that he can still

see that alley hidden on the west side of Tottenham Court Road, where, after living in a back bedroom on the top floor, I had to exchange for a front cellar. There was a difference, if I remember rightly, of sixpence a week, and sixpence in those days was a great consideration – why it meant a couple of meals. (I once *found* sixpence in the street, and had an exultation which is vivid in me at this moment.) The front cellar was stone-floored; its furniture was a table, a chair, a wash-stand, and a bed; the window, which of course had never been cleaned since it was put in, received light through a flat grating in the alley above. Here I lived; here *I wrote*. Yes, 'literary work' was done at that filthy deal table . . .[15]

But it is in his best – and best-known – novel, *New Grub Street*, that Gissing says most about the reality of life in the area. His account of the struggles of another writer, Edwin Reardon, to preserve his integrity was largely historical when it first appeared in 1891, but its indisputable power has ensured the book's survival ever since, not least as a primary source for any researcher into the late-nineteenth-century literary scene. Reardon is trapped by the 'procrustean' fashion of the day for bulky three-volume novels, the 'three-deckers' beloved by Mudie's and the other circulating libraries. At the beginning of *New Grub Street* (itself a fine example of the form) he is living in Regent's Park, beyond his means and facing the prospect of a return to the penury of his younger days. The very thought of it obsesses him, much as it had done Gissing himself; and the author's personal experience of such hardship accounts for much of the book's extraordinary power. The writing has none of the excess of the *Ryecroft Papers*, however. In *New Grub Street* Gissing's tone is cold, factual, and deadly:

> From a certain point of Tottenham Court Road there is visible a certain garret window in a certain street which runs parallel with that thoroughfare; for the greater part of these four years the garret in question was Reardon's home. He paid only three-and-sixpence a week for the privilege of living there; his food cost him about a shilling a day; on clothing and other unavoidable expenses he laid out some five pounds yearly. Then he bought books – volumes which cost anything between twopence and two shillings; further than that he durst not go. A strange time, I assure you.[16]

Indeed it was; and in many ways it was stranger than Gissing suggests, for even *New Grub Street* paints only half the picture. In the seventies and eighties literature was just one of the activities with which Tottenham Court Road was synonymous. Indeed, in the public mind those who followed its calling there and in nearby streets really would have seemed harmless drudges, *mere* harmless drudges. For at that time Tottenham Court Road and its environs were well known to be the centre of something far more serious. To Parliament and the popular press they were nothing less than hotbeds of anarchy and insurrection.

In retrospect it is almost inevitable that they should have been. The area's cheap accommodation, the large numbers of skilled manual workers who both lived and worked there, and above all its traditional tolerance of both the foreigner and the disaffected native meant that it was a natural breeding-ground for the anarchist and proto-Communist theories which were sweeping through Europe in the wake of the French Revolution and more particularly the explosive events of 1848.

That London's role in their development and propagation is not better known in Britain is one of the conundrums of nineteenth-century history. Certainly at the time there was none of the cosy, *laissez-faire* 'it-couldn't-happen-here'-ism which used to mark popular histories of the period leading up to Queen Victoria's Golden Jubilee in 1887. The monarch was herself only then emerging from a slough of deep unpopularity dating from her withdrawal from public life in the years following the death of Prince Albert, the Prince Consort, in 1861. In the course of her reign there were to be no less than seven attempts on her life. A pistol was fired at her carriage as early as 1840, while some years later she was actually knocked senseless by an aggrieved ex-lieutenant of the 10th Hussars armed with a heavy walking-stick.

Isolated incidents though these were, they also amounted to signs of the times; and nowhere were those times changing faster than in Fitzrovia. In a sense the district had even been instrumental in starting the whole clock ticking, for one strand of the tangled skein of anarchist and revolutionary thought which stretched across most of Europe led directly back to Shelley's father-in-law, William Godwin, the bookseller of Hanway Street. Ostensibly a dealer in children's books, under the counter he peddled more radical wares, not the least of which were his own expositions of a brand of Utopian socialism which had received its clearest expression in the writings of two French philosophers of the Enlightenment, Pierre Joseph Proudhon and Jean Jacques Rousseau. '*On façonne les plantes par la culture et les hommes par l'education*,'[17] wrote the latter out of an optimistic belief in the innate goodness of the Noble Savage. Godwin was to refine and develop such sentiments into a 'soft' English radicalism which would be further honed by the more practical approach of Robert Owen.

An activist rather than a thinker, Owen had equally close links with Fitzrovia. Forced out of premises in Gray's Inn Road, in 1833 he reopened his National Equitable Labour Exchange at 4 Charlotte Street. It was an ambitious attempt to establish a brotherhood of labour in which individuals contributed time and skill and received in return credits which could be exchanged for the services of others. Ultimately, however, it proved too ambitious, and the exchange closed the following year. Less revolutionary in its aims, but in the long run of far greater significance, was a later project of Owen's. The Scientific and Literary Institute in Whitfield Street opened in 1840 and for the next eighteen years provided a venue for union meetings and political discussion groups. Like its successor, the Communist Working Men's Club (which occupied the basement of 4 Tottenham Street from 1879 to 1902, and then premises at 107 Charlotte Street until it was closed by the police in 1918) the institute became the headquarters of left-wing activity in the area.

But if the tone of the institute was one of earnest, self-improving socialism – and its influence never really searched far beyond the basements of Hanway Street and Charlotte Street – as its name implied, the club was altogether more radical. By the 1880s its very existence had established Fitzrovia as one of the recognised British centres of anarchism and the international Communist movement. Karl Marx and Friedrich Engels were frequent visitors to the Tottenham Street basement during their time in London. So too were many of the founding fathers of Fabianism and British socialism. But the presence there at one time or another of William Morris, George Bernard Shaw, Sidney Webb and Keir Hardie was understandably upstaged in the public imagination and the minds of the police by the clandestine visits to the club of virtually every prominent European anarchist activist.

Every shade of revolutionary thought had its supporters in the area, who were always ready to accommodate their leaders, many of whom were already exiled from their native countries. The moderate Mikhail Bakunin spent three years in London in the early 1860s. A decade and more later a far more radical clique had established itself in the *Épicerie Française* at the other end of Charlotte Street. With their belief in the justification of terrorism and assassination, Errico Malatesta, Johann Most and the Russian nobleman, Prince Peter Kropotkin far more accurately personified the cartoon image of anarchists as bearded, bomb-carrying foreign revolutionaries. The image was not entirely without foundation. There was a police raid on the Charlotte Street premises in 1894 following what was described in the press as an 'anarchist' murder at the Café Royal, while as late as 1910 Malatesta was

95

indirectly involved in the Houndsditch murders and the ensuing Siege of Sidney Street. It is difficult now, however, to see much of a threat to world order in the activities of another of their number, a disaffected Frenchman called Charles Malato.

At about the time of the Café Royal murder, when fear of anarchism was at its height, he wrote a brief guide for fellow-exiles from France. As well as counselling 'if in trouble, call on Victor Richard, at 67 Charlotte Street, W., or on Louise Michel, at 15 Placquett Road, East Dulwich, S.E.', it also included a glossary of useful phrases for the would-be anarchist.[18] Had the police seen this beforehand, it is doubtful whether they would have bothered with the raid on the *Épicerie Française*:

FRANÇAIS	ANGLAIS ÉCRIT	ANGLAIS PARLÉ
Patron!	Governor!	Gueuv'neur!
Ma jolie fille?	My pretty girl?	Maille prêté guele?
Donnez-moi un shilling.	Give me a bob.	G'hive mi é bob.
Je vous tirerai le nez.	I will pull your nose.	Aille ouil poule your nose.
Je vous mettrai mon pied dans le derrière.	I will put my foot on your bottom.	Aille ouil poute maille foute one your botome.
Cochon!	Pig!	Pig!
Fermez ça!	Shut up!	Chatte ap!
Je vous ferai des bleus sur le corps.	I'll make rings about your body.	Aill'le mêke rin'gse abaoute your bodé.
Sacré étranger!	Bloody foreigner!	Bladé forégneur!
Sacré homme!	Bloody man!	Bladé mane!
Sacré femme!	Bloody woman!	Bladé oumane!
Ma femme me bat.	My wife strikes me.	Maille waill'fe straïkse mi.
Parce que vous vous soûlez.	Because you get drunk	Bicause you guette dreun'k.
Oh! mon pauvre ventre.	Oh! my poor belly.	Oh! maille pôr belli.

FRANÇAIS	ANGLAIS ÉCRIT	ANGLAIS PARLÉ
Il est inconvenant de nommer le mâle de la poule, dont le nom est donné a autre chose.	It is improper to name the male of the hen, whose name is also given to another thing.	Ite iz im'propeur tou nême de mêle of de henne, ouse nême iz olso guiven tou enne odeur tin'gue.
Voyou!	Ruffian!	Rofe!
Si vous ne me donnez pas une pièce de six pence, je vous casse le nez.	If you don't give me a sixpence, I'll break your nose.	If you deun't g'hive mi a sixepen'ce, aill'e brêke your nose.
Merdé . . .e!	Sh.t!	Ch.tte!

Foreign anarchists with pains in their bellies, if not always bombs in their pockets; Communists, socialists and Utopians of every hue; exiled Russian princes, and writers starving in garrets – it is hardly surprising that the area which would become Fitzrovia was already attracting attention in the last years of the nineteenth century. There is even a theory that in the early 1880s Queen Victoria's grandson, Prince Albert Victor, was secretly 'apprenticed' to Walter Sickert at a studio the painter then occupied in Cleveland Street.[19] The idea was for the sensitive Prince, known as Eddy and, after his father, the Prince of Wales, in direct line to the throne, to masquerade as Sickert's younger brother Albert and learn something of the realities of life in the kingdom he would one day rule. Apparently he did, to the extent of fathering an illegitimate daughter by one Annie Elizabeth Crook, a girl he also secretly married, but who was then working in a tobacconist's shop almost opposite the artist's studio.

If Prince Eddy's visits to the area are to be believed – and we have little more than the routinely melodramatic Sickert's word to go on – the heir to the throne can be counted as among the very first visitors to Fitzrovia for, like Montmartre, the area was always to attract the curious. The poet John Heath-Stubbs recalls that in the late 1940s 'people used to come as tourists, but they were never accepted'.[20] Half a century earlier it was rather different. The occasional day-tripper from the upper classes was generally as welcome as anyone else at the watering-holes of Bohemia. No matter that he was in all probability only indulging some strain of *nostalgie de la boue*: his wallet was full and his credit generally good in a wide variety of clubs and restaurants. And the brief reign of the luckless Prince Eddy's father, Edward VII, marked the period when café society too began coming to the ball.

CHAPTER SEVEN

Café Society

IT was in the years immediately after the First World War that an ambitious young Armenian, new to London, began to write novels and short stories in a premeditated attempt to make both his name and a fortune (though not necessarily in that order). But Dikran Kouyoumdjian was not the sort of name one made in the post-war England of 1919, and on the advice of his publisher he had changed it by the time his first book appeared in 1920. *The London Venture* was a collection of short stories, ascribed on its title page to Michael Arlen. Simpler and snappier than Dikran Koyoumdjian, it was 'a name he'd made up (and had then checked out through all the available international phone directories in the Post Office Building to make sure there weren't any other Arlens anywhere else; there weren't in 1919')[1].

The adoption of a new, English identity was a shrewd move; for as his son, the novelist Michael J. Arlen, was to write, within five years Arlen had it all: a name, albeit pseudonymous; fame; and, following the appearance of his second novel *The Green Hat* in 1924, a fortune large enough for him to 'buy a long damn canary-yellow Rolls-Royce. And speedboats. And good clothes. Things like that. And he could afford to marry my mother, in the sense that they could take a fairly large nice house in the South of France. Have nice things. Invest in the stock market in 1928.'[2] It had all paid off; but then his whole life, as Arlen himself once told a reporter, was a struggle *'Per ardua ad astrakhan'*.

He had the *astrakhan* soon enough. After his death his widow presented one of Arlen's extravagantly collared coats to Evelyn Waugh's elder brother Alec. He was, for a time, the highest-paid short-story writer on either side of the Atlantic and had a contract from *Cosmopolitan* magazine to prove the fact. He had appeared on one of *Time* magazine's first covers. With his fast cars, speedboats and an address book which included everyone from Clark Gable to D. H. Lawrence (who used Arlen as a model for Michaelis in *Lady Chatterley's Lover*) he was certainly one of the earliest members of the twenties 'jazz set', equally at home in New York, Cannes, Paris and Monte Carlo. But his early books at least are firmly set among London's café society. It is the spiritual home of Boy Fenwick and the headstrong and breathlessly modern Iris Storm in *The Green Hat*, while *The London Venture* is an almost embarrassingly autobiographical collection of short stories, written in the first person and recounting the struggles of a young Armenian called Dikran endeavouring to make his way in the capital.

Despite its exotic title, *Piracy*, his second book (but first novel) has much the same theme. Published in 1922 and a prime example of what the writer Denton Welsh would later characterise as the 'smooth' novel, it is an ambitious account of the career of Ivor Pelham Marley from his schooldays, through the First World War (in which he loses an arm) and up to the present. Beginning with Ivor sitting alone over his coffee one evening in the 'Mont Agel' restaurant, a thinly disguised version of the Restaurant de la Tour Eiffel in Percy Street, it quickly flicks back in time to the pre-war London of his youth. A London characterised by a fashionable Deanery Street party, a certain small bar in the Haymarket and romantic suppers in Wilton Place, it is, in the historic present Arlen employs, 'an amazing city':

> . . . not so much because of the numbers of its population, which it simply cannot help, but because of its hospitality, which it can. Take a man, without money – say, £800 a year – without particular wit, without a Lancashire accent, of no stock to speak of and of less education: let him have a slightly constrained manner, as of one who simply *can't* be ingratiating, and a few other properties of a gentleman – and, if he be not by nature too vulgarly disposed, if he steel himself against the lure of the footlight favourite and the guile of the wanton *bourgeoise*, he will find himself, without particular effort, among People.[3]

Effectively sketched by Arlen in the phrase 'a man with no ties and plenty of money', Ivor is soon under the spell of it all; the

Mont Agel, the parties, and most of all the 'People'. Hardly out of his teens, he discovers, just as Arlen himself had discovered, that 'society in London is sociable: its dignity is that of ease.' Everything about it is so very different from Manton, the public school from which he had been expelled for drinking the masters' port. It is wider, freer – and equally intoxicating: 'it burnt him just a little, pleasantly, like a liqueur brandy. (Later, it hit him on the head; but that was later.) And he rolled and wallowed in it . . .'

And so did Arlen. The phrases he added to *Piracy* about a Lancashire accent and lack of 'stock' were not inserted lightly, for his family were small businessmen in Manchester and Liverpool. Nevertheless, in the argot of the time, he too was soon 'taken up'. By all accounts, the figure his son describes as 'this young, slight, short, foreign-looking man, dark hair, long nose, dark face – and intelligent, talkative, nervy and desirous to please in that endearing and awful way of certain foreigners in a strange court'[4] was a familiar enough sight in all the right places long before the end of the First World War. He had a flat in Shepherd Market, an acquaintanceship at least with Arnold Bennett and H. G. Wells and a familiarity approaching Ivor's with all that the West End had to offer. Like Ivor's, his too was

> the London of Whitehall, Chelsea, Mayfair, Cambridge, Blooms-bury, Downing Street, Oxford and the Mont Agel – but of course the Mont Agel! The London of those new young men and women, but mainly young men, who in those few years before the war suddenly confronted and conquered it with a new and vivid charm, now never to be forgotten. They, even more acutely than the Russian Ballet, were the social success of that time, in a new and brilliant way.[5]

It wasn't difficult to find those new young men and women. Hardly original, they had adopted exactly the same cafés, hotels and restaurants which their fathers had used in their salad days. Twenty years on, they too drank champagne in the mornings, brandy and sodas in the clubs of St James's, and glasses of beer in the promenade at the Empire, Leicester Square. They too ate at Kettner's and the Ritz, the Criterion, the Solferino and the St James's Hall Restaurant. And, whenever they could afford it, inevitably they too found themselves heading for the Café Royal.

*   *   *

101

The establishment which, more than any other, came to epitomise the 'above-board' London Bohemia of the nineties – and was to preserve both its memory and more than a few of its leading personalities for another two decades – had opened way back in February 1865. It was the creation of Daniel Nicols, more accurately Daniel Nicolas Thévenon, a Frenchman who had fled to London to escape his creditors earlier in the decade, arriving at Victoria Station with his wife Célestine and no more than five gold sovereigns to his name. (That, at least, was the story he liked to repeat in later life when the spectacular success at the Café had more than recouped his fortune; he died in 1897, leaving an estate of around £600,000.)

Originally the Café-Restaurant Daniel Nicols, a modest establishment in Glasshouse Street which cuts across the curving southern end of Regent Street, it did not begin to acquire its reputation for loucheness and decadence for another quarter century. Indeed, Dickens's 1879 *Dictionary of London* contents itself with a laudatory comment on its singular reputation among diners 'who know how to order their dinners'. The excellence of its cuisine, its service and particularly its cellars, was to continue well into the twentieth century; but even by the end of the nineteenth the Café itself was a different place. It acquired its Regent Street frontage later in 1865 and became the Café Royal in 1867, but by the early nineties that basically modest entrance gave little clue about what lay within. Even the normally blasé Max Beerbohm could hardly believe it. 'This indeed is life!' he recalled telling himself on his first visit,[6] a Ransomesque journey into the unknown, undertaken with the artist William Rothenstein.

A uniformed footman would have been on hand to whistle for cabs for those departing – 'once for a hansom, twice for a four-wheeler'[7] – and hold open one of the three sets of double doors for newcomers who, like Beerbohm, were just arriving. Those doors were, however, only part of a plain wooden façade no more elaborate than that of many pubs and gin palaces of the period. Above the hanging gasoliers was a marbled cartouche surmounted by a crown and bearing the legend 'Café Royal'. That in itself was no larger than another board which advertised the name of the proprietor. (Nicol's or Nicol's Café Royal was the name by which the establishment was formally known, certainly until the end of the nineteenth century; it survives to this day in the decoration of the fanciful blue-and-gold marquee over the entrance to the present Trusthouse Forte restaurant.) The whole pediment rose no higher than the signboards of adjacent shops, at the beginning of this century the premises of Messrs Thierry, boot and shoe makers at No. 70, and the rather dowdy-looking West End Clothiers which occupied No. 66.

Inside, however, it was a different story. By the mid-1890s the Café Royal had swallowed up all the premises between Nos. 9 and 25 on the southern side of Glasshouse Street and all those between Nos. 4 and 16 on the eastern side of Air Street which led down into Regent Street. Nicols thus controlled most of a block only a stone's throw from Piccadilly Circus, a block which was uniquely and very conveniently located within easy walking distance of both the clubs of St James's and the garrets and studios of Fitzrovia.

Like the much smaller restaurants a mile away in Soho, his premises were divided into separate areas. Beyond the swing doors, Beerbohm and Rothenstein would have found themselves in a large lobby, in one corner of which M. Roussel had a bookstall offering English and European newspapers and magazines, as well as a range of stronger literature; but that was kept under the counter and generally reserved for special customers such as Frank Harris.

In the parlance of the day, regular diners headed for the main restaurant or the Grill Room, or climbed the horseshoe-shaped staircase and ate in one of the many private suites upstairs. Frank Harris habitually did so, although it was hardly reticence which led him to ignore the clubbiness of the ground floor and climb all the way up to a suite on the seventh. If we are to believe his own account – with Harris, always a dangerous thing to do – it was up there that the blustering, extravagant and compulsive womaniser who was editor of the *Saturday Review*, and at various times a range of other publications including the *Automobile Review* and the *Lady*, relieved the young Enid Bagnold of her virginity. (On another occasion Harris prevailed on Nicols to send a complete Café Royal meal, consisting of Nijni caviare, salmon trout and cold grouse ('fresh not high'), together with bottles of Chablis, Haut-Brion '78 and Perier-Jouet '75, to his own house in Park Lane where he had an assignation and, between courses apparently, similar success with one Laura Clapton.)

103

But for Beerbohm and Rothenstein, like Wilde, Beardsley and the rest in the nineties, as well as the increasingly syncopated pre-war generation which included Michael Arlen, Nancy Cunard and Augustus John, the Café Royal meant the ground-floor Brasserie or Domino Room. So much so that in virtually every account of the Café before its reconstruction in the 1920s neither the restaurant nor the Grill Room, and still less any of the numerous private dining-room and banqueting suites, gets so much as a mention. Nor does the Royal Masonic temple which Nicols also incorporated into the establishment. They might just as well not have existed, for it is the Domino Room which crops up again and again, under its own name in autobiographies and memoirs, and, under a variety of *noms de guerre*, in novels and stories by writers as disparate as Evelyn Waugh, G. K. Chesterton, Somerset Maugham and Wyndham Lewis.

Even D. H. Lawrence remembered it when he came to create the Café Pompadour in *Women in Love*. Typically, however, his account has none of the sentimental affection displayed by the majority of his contemporaries. Never more than a casual visitor (and for this reason, perhaps, never a trusted one – he was always made to pay in cash) he concentrates on what he calls its 'atmosphere of petty vice and petty jealousy and petty art', and puts all his own feelings of impatience with the room's more regular inhabitants into the mind of Ursula Brangwen. Taken there late one evening by Gerald Critch, she stares sullenly at them, ruminating on how they looked 'like creatures in some menagerie of apish degraded souls. God, what a foul crew they were!'[8]

Exaggerated and somewhat vindictive though Lawrence's comments seem to be, they do contain at least an element of truth. Even in the late eighties it was the eclectic clientele of the Domino Room, far more than Nicols's fine food, starched napery and oenophilia, which accounted for the success of the Café Royal:

> 'Twas rollog; and the minim potes
> Did mime and mimble in the Cafe.
> All footly were the Philerotes
> And Daycadongs outstrafe . . .[9]

By then the 'Daycadongs' or Decadents and 'Boy-Ohs' had long since annexed the Domino Room. Beerbohm and Will Rothenstein found no one else in residence on the evening of their first visit in October 1893, and fifteen years later Beerbohm was to have great fun at their expense in 'Enoch Soames', the first in a collection of imaginary biographical sketches he called *Seven Men*.

It describes how Soames sells himself to the Devil in order to discover posterity's view of 'Fungoids' and his other collections of verse. He is given an afternoon in the British Museum Reading Room as it would be on 3 June 1997. Everything in the Reading Room has remained the same except the language. Consulting a 1992 study of *fin de siècle* English literature, Soames discovers 'some sort of phonetic spelling'. But that is not the end; the index leads him to the sole entry relating to Soames, Enoch:

> Max Beerbohm, hoo woz stil alive in th twentieth senchri, rote a stauri in wich e pautraid an immajnari karrakter kauld 'Enoch Soames' – a thurd-rait poit hoo beleevz imself a grate jeneus an maix a bargin with th Devvl in auder ter no wot posterriti thinx ov im! It iz a sumwot labud sattire but not without vallu az showing hou seriusli the yung men ov th aiteen-ninetiz took themselvz.[10]

A 'sumwot labud sattire' the story may be, but Beerbohm's Soames is the quintessential Domino Room Aesthete; they really did take themselves very 'seriusli'. Beerbohm, however, warms to his 'weak doggedness': 'Neither he nor his work received the slightest encouragement; but he persisted in behaving as a personage: always he kept his dingy little flag flying.'[11] Some months after their first meeting, Beerbohm encounters him again. A glass of absinthe at his elbow, he is engrossed in a book:

> I asked him if he often read here. 'Yes; things of this kind I read here,' he answered, indicating the title of his book – 'The Poems of Shelley'.
> 'Anything that you really' – and I was going to say 'admire?' But I cautiously left my sentence unfinished, and was glad that I had done so, for he said, with unwonted emphasis, 'Anything second-rate.'
> I had read little of Shelley, but, 'Of course,' I murmured, 'he's very uneven.'
> 'I should have thought evenness was just what was wrong with him. A deadly evenness. That's why I read him here. The noise of this place breaks up the rhythm. He's tolerable here.'[12]

Like W. S. Gilbert's Bunthorne, Enoch Soames satirised a type rather than a specific individual, but by 1893 that type comprised a sizeable percentage of the Domino Room's clientele. Oscar Wilde was an habitual lunchtime visitor from as early as 1884; while Lord Alfred Douglas, Whistler, Frank Harris, Ernest Dowson, Arthur Symons, George Moore, Bernard Shaw, Aubrey Beardsley and the etiolated artist Allan Odle, who so confusingly resembled one of Beardsley's own drawings, were hardly less regular in their attendance. Despite the impression Beerbohm gives, however, they did not have the room entirely to themselves. It had also been commandeered as a convenient West End home from home by a whole tribe of the *fin de siècle demi-monde*. There were down-at-heel aristocrats, cells of foreign anarchists on their way to or from Charlotte Street, check-suited bookmakers with names like Box-o'Tricks Palmer and Ball o'Twine Sampson, less than success-ful artists with drawings to sell, criminals, furtive pimps, loitering prostitutes and, most evenings, a goodly number of curious lookers-on. The whole unique ambience of the room that was once called 'the home of lost causeries' is well captured in a series of reconstructed conversations by Guy Deghy and Keith Waterhouse:

> . . . six or four . . .
> . . . You ask me what life is? Life, my dear fellow, is like a Japanese fan. Exactly why escapes me for the moment . . .
> . . .five or a two . . .
> . . . *ce crapaud Rochefort* . . .
> . . . so he makes me sit eight hours in the freezing cold studio and when I ask for a cup of tea he says: 'Goddesses never drink tea. Have the juice of a grape,' he says . . .
> . . . fours . . .[13]

Claret, brandy and beer were the house drinks of the nineties. In the Domino Room Miss Sunderland and Miss Cheswick served them all from a partially glazed dispense bar at one side of the room, while next to them Miss Dewar had charge of a cigar stall. At that time too absinthe was also generally taken; it was certainly not the exclusive thrill of the arch-Aesthetes. The sticky green liqueur, flavoured with wormwood and angelica root, was sipped by Wilde and his friends in imitation of the genuine French *décadents*, who drank it in great quantity before its manufacture and sale were proscribed under French law, but it was also ordered by pimps, prostitutes and bookmakers.

Tastes changed with the turn of the century. The sweeter, greener and sicklier crème de menthe frappée replaced absinthe and was much enjoyed by Augustus John. Champagne was consumed on other than special occasions. Whisky and sodas appeared on the tables. The bookmakers stuck to beer, but for those whose pockets could not stretch even as far as a single brandy and soda, mazagram, a non-alcoholic mixture of coffee and milk, was freely available. Nina Hamnett, who 'went every morning to the Café Royal' during the First World War, did not even venture that far. 'We could stay the whole evening there on a fourpenny coffee in those days,' she recalled in her auto-biography.[14]

For some, however, life went on as it always had, regardless of taste. One of the best-known faces in the Domino Room was that of T. W. H. Crosland who, from the nineties until the early twenties, could be seen going from table to table cadging money on the strength of his visiting-cards which read 'Jobbing Poet, Funerals attended' and downing, in rotation, glasses of lager, sloe gin, whisky and soda, brandy, hock, claret, burgundy and champagne.

In its original form, the old Domino Room has long disappeared. In the course of the refurbishment and partial rebuilding of the Café Royal, necessitated by the realignment of John Nash's Regent Street, it was converted into a smaller, plainer Grill Room. Something at least of its cosmopolitan, boulevard-café atmosphere is preserved, however, in paintings and drawings by Nina Hamnett, Charles Ginner, William Orpen, Dame Laura Knight, Harold Gilman, Adrian Allinson and C. R. W. Nevinson, among others. Nevinson's slight, and rather bleak, canvas *In the Café Royal* is particularly interesting in this respect. It is strongly reminiscent of Edgar Degas's *L'Absinthe*, now in the Louvre but exhibited in London in 1893 under the title *Au Café* but – like Nina Hamnett's Café Royal sketches – almost Lawrentian in its clear-eyed depiction of suppressed desperation.

Gilman's *The Café Royal* and Allinson's better known *The Old Café Royal* give wider, more genial and almost identical views. The former dates from 1912, while Allinson's canvas reveals that nothing had changed four years later, despite the outbreak of the First World War. Both show crowded corners with red velvet chairs and banquettes, white marble-topped tables and a cross-

107

section of the regular clientele. Clearly recognisable amongst the crowd in Allinson's picture are the young Nancy Cunard, her companion Iris Tree (the younger daughter of the actor-manager Sir Herbert Beerbohm-Tree), the tiresome old Etonian practical joker Horace de Vere Cole, Allan Odle and Augustus John, as well as John's wife Dorelia and Allinson himself. In both paintings the diners are dwarfed and effaced by the opulence of their surroundings, the Sickert-like impasto employed by the two artists vividly conveying what to Max Beerbohm's blue eyes on that first visit was an 'exuberant vista of gilding and crimson velvet'.

In contrast to their smudgy opulence, Sir William Orpen's picture *The Café Royal*, now in the Musée d'Art Moderne in Paris, is more exact and indeed almost photographic in its depiction of both the details of the Domino Room's décor and another selection of its more notable habitués. Orpen went to considerable pains to get things right, to the extent of setting up his easel in the Domino Room itself and painting the background from life on Sunday mornings when the Café Royal was closed. Some of the room's eighteen regular waiters were persuaded to stand in for the foreground figures.

The completed canvas shows a heavily bearded, uncollared Augustus John, together with the more formally attired but equally recognisable figures of George Moore and the artist William Nicholson. It is more than a conversation-piece, however, for all three are cowed by what to modern eyes can only be described as the overblown, Louis Philippe vulgarity of their surroundings. Tall mirrors line the walls and are themselves framed by extravagantly French gilded moulding. Above them, garlanded caryatids hold dark blue urns aloft, while swags and rococo ornamentation snake across a turquoise ceiling, supported by matching blue columns entwined with pinchbeck foliage. Perhaps because it was painted on successive Sundays and the Domino Room had been allowed to air, there is no suggestion in Orpen's picture of the clouds of tobacco smoke which many regulars later recalled billowing above their heads and hiding the licentious intricacies of the plaster moulding.

Nevertheless, the brilliantly coloured canvas is eerily redolent of the shabby and, in the lingering aftermath of the Wilde scandal, still ever so slightly shady atmosphere of the Edwardian Café Royal. Looking at the painting today, it is easy to imagine the shock and dismay felt by the Domino Room's regular clientele that day in 1926 as the mirrors were taken down and labourers from the firm of Higgs and Hill at last moved in with scaffolding and sledge-hammers. Nevinson went as far as trying to buy one of the wooden caryatids, but fittingly it was T. W. H. Crosland who had the last word. 'They might as well have told us that the British Empire is to be pulled down and redecorated,' he said . . . and then doubtless ordered another drink to drown his sorrows.

It was among the old Domino Room's dark-red velvet banquettes, even by 1895 stained and worn rather smooth, and beneath the swirling cigarette smoke and nicotine-stained moulding, that the peculiar tone of twentieth-century London Bohemianism was set. It is impossible now to say quite when it happened, but even before the outbreak of the First World War there had been a significant change of style. Victorianism had died with the old century among the avant-garde of the Café Royal, and it is possible to see the beginnings of a new, professional Modernism of spirit with the arrival in the Domino Room of Augustus John and his followers. It went far deeper than not wearing collars and indulging a preference for crème de menthe frappée rather than the Aesthetes' absinthe. Every aspect of John's character was in open and conspicuous revolt against the standards of the old century. Nor was he alone. The same was true of W. B. Yeats who had, of course, been fostering a more decorous, literary form of that revolt at meetings of the Rhymers' Club since the early nineties.

The challenge did not go unnoticed by the old guard, and one day in the Domino Room the comparison was drawn between the long-haired Yeats, attired as always in a velveteen jacket and loose tie, and the veterans' champion of the moment, the immaculately dressed Lord Alfred Douglas, a rather undistinguished poet but one who, by his very intimacy with Wilde, was condemned to a perpetual association with the nineties.

'What a contrast!' someone remarked.

'Yes,' answered a voice from the Douglas camp, 'all the difference between verse – and *poetry*.'

But unfortunately for them, henceforth it was to be verse – and occasionally even doggerel – all the way.

In part these changes of style were only a reflection of greater changes which were making themselves felt in society as a whole. Women, in particular, were beginning to demand, and being grudgingly accorded, greater freedom. Suddenly it had become possible for Gwen John, Nina Hamnett and Iris Tree to enrol at art schools and, later, be accepted as equals in bodies such as the Fitzroy Street Group and the Omega Workshops. At around the same time Nancy Cunard, Iris Tree and the fast set began to wear trousers, go out alone and unchaperoned, and smoke and drink in public. They were important advances and not to be taken lightly.

Indeed, the 'New Woman' was a perceptible phenomenon well before she became a recognisable type in the comedies of George Bernard Shaw and achieved caricature status as the twenties flapper. In *Women in Love* D. H. Lawrence presents pathologically detailed portraits of two such creatures in the characters of Gudrun and Ursula Brangwen. They had originally appeared in his earlier novel *The Rainbow*, but in *Women in Love*, first published in 1921 and the novel Lawrence himself considered his best, they take centre stage. Significantly, Ursula is a teacher. Right from the start, from the opening exchange on the first page of the novel, she is also imbued with this new spirit:

'Ursula,' said Gudrun, 'don't you *really want* to get married?' Ursula laid her embroidery in her lap and looked up. Her face was calm and considerate.
'I don't know,' she replied. 'It depends how you mean.'[15]

A similar spirit affects Magdalen Gray and Virginia Tracy, the principal female characters in Michael Arlen's *Piracy*, published only months after *Women in Love*. As early as 1916, Magdalen is taking advantage of her husband's absence and inviting Ivor Marlay to a late-night supper *à deux*, while Virginia – the daughter of Lady Carnal and one of the earliest literary portraits of Nancy Cunard – is able not only to eat alone at the Mont Agel but to return home unaccompanied in the early hours of the morning. Arlen describes the journey in tones of excited wonder:

Swiftly she would penetrate the black solitudes of Soho in war-time: a rich and fragile figure braving all the dangers of the city by night, an almost fearful figure to arise suddenly in an honest man's homeward path: so tall and golden and proud of carriage, so marvellously indifferent to his astonished stare! Sometimes she would have to walk a long way before she could find a taxi – through Soho to Shaftesbury Avenue, and up that to Piccaddilly Circus. Sometimes men would murmur in passing, sometimes they would say the coarsest things, and once or twice a man caught at her arm as she swiftly passed him; and Virginia looked at him straightly, for a swift second, as though secretly understanding his desire and mocking it; and then she went on her way as though her way had been uninterrupted . . . homewards to Belgrave Square.[16]

Women had begun to make their presence felt at the Café Royal in the early years of the century, although only a few years previously a house rule had forbidden their entering and seating themselves unaccompanied. Most of these early explorers would have euphemistically described themselves as 'models'. A few really were, drawn to the Domino Room by the sensible realisation that, where two or three artists were gathered together, work was to be found. Lillian Shelley was one and Betty May, the Tiger Woman who was to become one of the sights of Fitzrovia in the inter-war years, another. Both were sculpted by Jacob Epstein, Betty May for a bust now in the Tate Gallery. Their vivacity and exuberance did much to brighten the Domino Room, then signally failing to live up to the reputation for style and incandescent wit it had acquired in the nineties. The young Betty May in particular, attired like a gypsy in remnants she had bought from the stalls in Soho's Berwick Street market, was utterly unabashed by the opulence and refined masculinity of her surroundings. In the restaurant she once blithely added spoonful after spoonful of sugar to the extra dry champagne being pressed upon her by an elderly admirer. Back in the Brasserie, enthusiastically egged on by the likes of Epstein and Augustus John, she would clamber onto one of the marble-topped tables and give impromptu demonstrations of her Terpsichorean talent.

But it was the arrival of the tall and almost boyishly elegant Nancy Cunard which pointed the way forward. The only daughter of Sir Bache Cunard, whose grandfather had founded the famous shipping line, and his young wife Maud, a Californian heiress, she was born in 1896 and had grown up amongst the armour, stuffed animals, dark panelling and Victorian gothic of the family home, Nevill Holt in Leicestershire. From her earliest days she had also shown an alarming independence of spirit, proof, some said, that she was not Sir Bache's daughter at all but the fruit of a furtive liaison between her mother and the novelist George Moore.

Lady Maud, who would later transform herself into Emerald – a 'ridiculous little parakeet-faced woman' according to Virginia Woolf but, for all that, the most celebrated hostess of her day – had left Nevill Holt in 1911 and moved to London to devote her undoubted energies to furthering the career of the young Thomas Beecham. Thus, when Nancy returned from spells at French and German finishing schools in time to come out as a débutante at the beginning of the 1914 season, she found herself left very much to her own devices. Lady Diana Cooper recalled her suddenly announcing: 'My mother's having an affair with Sir Thomas Beecham; I can do as I like.'[17] Which she did. Encouraged by George Moore, she began to write poetry. In a desperate attempt to escape the 'revolving guardsmen' she met again and again at parties, she rented a studio in Fitzroy Place with Iris Tree, then still a student at the Slade. She cut her hair short and had as little contact as she reasonably could with Her Ladyship.

In all probability, Nancy first visited the Café Royal in 1914, the diminutive Iris Tree at her side. They must have made a striking impression in the shabby, smoke-filled Domino Room – two 'gels' who were obviously not prostitutes or hopeful models, but free women whose chalk and kohl make-up in the up to the moment Pierrot style and aristocratic bearing suggested that they were out for fun. Why, they even smoked in public! And quite how far that simple act was a measure of female emancipation in 1914 is brought out in W. Seymour Leslie's novel *The Silent Queen*. Not two decades before, in 'the vanished spaciousness of the nineties', he recalls, if women smoked at all it was in secret:

> My mother was writing letters and perhaps *smoking* in her bedroom upstairs. My grandmother returning from the picnic surprised her thus engaged.
> 'May I come in, my dear? I thought I smelt something burning?'
> 'I – I was – it was a cigarette!'
> 'My dear!' laughed my grandmother, 'you must, of course, do whatever you wish – but not, I pray, before the children.'[18]

The occasional presence of George Moore, the 'G. M.' whom Nancy always held in high regard, would have gone some way to relieve the frankly little more than sordid Brasserie ambience; but for someone like Nancy, who was accustomed to the strident, unrepentant Modernism of Stravinsky in the concert hall and New Orleans jazz at more intimate, all-night parties thrown by the American socialite George Gordon Moore, for all its memories, the dusty, increasingly dowdy Café Royal must have been rather disappointing, its relative conservatism relieved only by yet another influx of would-be artists.

In 1914 neither Yeats nor Augustus John could any longer lay serious claim to be in the forefront of avant-garde Bohemianism. The former was to turn fifty the next year, while his friends and numerous mistresses would doubtless have been amazed to discover that even John was fast approaching forty. Both were variously set in their ways, famed for being so and already gods, or, at the very least, grand old men, in the eyes of a new generation.

Born for the most part in the 1880s and early nineties, too young to have been a part of, or even remember, the Aestheticism of the old century, these were the men – and women – who would take Bohemia out of the West End and back to its old haunts. But for the present they were grateful and, dismissing Ransome's false trail, realistic enough to foregether like previous generations in the Domino Room. To list all their names is to do no more than reprint the indices of many of the chronicles and memoirs of this period in English art and letters. Among them, however, were several who would be celebrated in the following two decades.

The composer Cecil Gray had broken away from his Scottish family, made the journey to London and installed himself in a 'miniature' Chelsea flat in September 1915. He first visited the Café Royal some weeks later. Not quite twenty-one, he was easily impressed. Under the insidious influence of the Domino Room, the 'shy, studious, cloistered young paragon of virtue turned overnight into the precise opposite – a wild, riotous, dissipated youth-about-town'.[19] The Café Royal, he admitted, was still 'the chief focus of my initiation into the joys of Life'. But as he also admitted, those joys were not sampled alone. For a time he moved among 'the lowest kind of company, male and female', although it was not long before he had encountered a more fitting set of companions.

113

Philip Heseltine was one of the earliest. Better known as Peter Warlock, the name under which he composed, he too was then barely twenty, but in the fortunate position of having an inheritance large enough to allow him to devote himself almost entirely to pleasure. Bernard van Dieren was more serious-minded; another composer, but hampered in the war years by his Dutch nationality. Furthering his interests appears to have been uppermost in the minds of Gray and the more mercurial and frequently unpredictable Heseltine during 1915 and 1916. The three were often seen together in the Café Royal at that time, frankly lording it in the conscripted or, more rarely, voluntary absence of the likes of John, who had been turned down by tribunal after tribunal and finally acquired for himself the rank of major in the Canadian Overseas Military Forces, Bombadier Wyndham Lewis and a very reluctant Pte. Epstein, J.

Together with Nina Hamnett, Osbert Sitwell, Michael Arlen, the eccentrically neurotic novelist Ronald Firbank and the Jewish artist Mark Gertler, among many others, they comprised the last real Café Royal generation. Writers and painters – notably the clubby egoist and drama critic James Agate – would continue to make the rebuilt Café their West End base until the early forties, and even later, but it could not adapt itself to that quickening of the artistic pulse which immediately preceeded the outbreak of the First World War. Increasingly, the young Turks resorted to the Domino Room not, as their fathers had done, simply because it was the Domino Room, but in the hope of hearing of somewhere better, brighter and more modern. Despite the almost exotic remoteness of Percy Street and Fitzroy Square, like Virginia Gray, the more adventurous were already discovering it among the artists, anarchists and students of 'Fitzrovia'. They began sloping off to the Eiffel Tower Restaurant, even though suitable alternative venues lay much closer to hand. Well before 1920 the West End boasted a sprinkling of night-clubs which came alive only after the Café Royal closed its doors (and during the First World War they were closed very firmly at half-past ten). In their exclusive, expensive darkness the drink never seemed to run out, the new jazz bands played and there was lively conversation until the early hours of the morning.

The first of these venues, the Cabaret Club, had opened in June 1912, less than half a mile away from the Café Royal, in premises beneath a cloth-seller's shop in Heddon Street. Better known as the Cave of the Golden Calf, its main arena celebrated the Old Testament story in which the Israelites 'offered burnt offerings and brought peace offerings; and the people sat down to eat and drink and rose up to play'[20] before the image of just such a calf. It was owned by Frida Strindberg, a journalist and translator by profession and the recently widowed second wife of the Swedish dramatist, August Strindberg. 'The Walking Hell-Bitch of the Western world', as Augustus John was to describe her, she had been stalking both John and Wyndham Lewis for the previous two years, faking suicide attempts and hiring private detectives in her endeavours to lure the former away from Dorelia and the admittedly fragile domestic life he had built at his newly acquired Alderney Manor home.

The Cabaret Club might well have been another attempt. If it was, it failed. 'My attendance was counted upon,' John recollected in his autobiography, 'but I never entered the place. One look at the seething mob outside its doors, on the opening night, was enough for me. I passed on. Another miscalculation!'[2]

In passing on, however, and doing his best to keep away from the planning and decoration of the club, John absented himself from what turned out to be something of a showplace for the work of the new generation of British artists. All traces of the club itself have, sadly, long disappeared; but plans, descriptions and sketches to survive, so that it is possible to re-create something of its unashamedly modern and fittingly hedonistic ambience, a world away from the mirrors and moulding of the Café Royal.

The tone was set by Eric Gill's stone bas-relief of a clearly masculine calf mounted on the wall just inside the entrance. But, no more than 15½ inches by 12, according to measurements appended to the artist's pencil and watercolour drawing now at the Yale Center for British Art, that gave little indication of the scale of things downstairs. There, a group of the more exciting tyros of the day had been brought together to transform a low-ceilinged cellar into what, in the words of its manifesto, was to be 'a place given up to gaiety, to a gaiety stimulating thought, rather than crushing it'. And, unlike the old sketch clubs, the Cabaret was intent on conjuring 'a gaiety that does not have to count with midnight'.

The old Harrovian Spencer Gore was lured away from Fitzroy

Street and Camden Town and put in charge of the decorations. One of the most gifted colourists of his day, among his first decisions had been to involve Charles Ginner, Wyndham Lewis and Jacob Epstein in the project. Ginner was given responsibility for several of the enormous murals which encircled the main arena. Epstein, who had been willing to undertake the monument to Oscar Wilde at the Père Lachaise cemetery in Paris, was rewarded for his daring with a commission to disguise two vast, iron ceiling supports, and responded with suitably hedonistic plaster claddings featuring entwined men and beasts. In addition to overseeing the design and printing of posters, programmes and menus, Lewis was asked for a huge mural which would cover the staircase wall. He came up with *Kermesse*, for which only fragmentary sketches survive. With its strong black lines and figures frozen in an instant of urgent motion it was both a hymn to Vorticism and an apt introduction to the real vortex downstairs.

Mme. Strindburg had always intended the Cabaret Club to be something more than a late-night watering-hole for the monied upper classes. Like many later club owners she was very happy to waive the annual membership fee for anyone she thought 'interesting'. Artists – including the fugitive John – were given honorary membership almost as a matter of course, 'out of deference to their personalities', and led to understand that their drinks would be charged to the bills of wealthier members.

Partly because of such enlightened policies, the club became an established venue within months, and as popular with the *beau monde* as it obviously was with a whole school of pampered artists. Its basement 'arena', the actual cave of the golden calf where 'the people sat down to eat and drink and rose up to play', was a cockpit in which painting, sculpture, good wines, fine food, the performing arts and café society coupled and combined in a manner hitherto unknown. On the tiny stage a gypsy orchestra or the strident tintinabulation of a band of Coppersmiths would be followed by a reading of Modernist poetry; a 'melodramatic' declaration from the inexhaustible Frank Harris by an appearance of Margaret Morris and her Greek Children dancers. Betty May found an equally appreciative audience for her less predictable dancing, and Ford Madox Ford presented, of all things, a series of shadow-plays. Later, as the footsteps of homeward-bound theatre-goers and diners, ejected from more orthodox establishments, echoed on the pavement above, Mme. Strindberg's patrons continued to eat, drink and dance until the small hours in what Osbert Sitwell remembered as 'a super-heated Vorticist garden of gesticulating figures'.[22]

Epstein's two columns, together with a free-standing and much larger version of Gill's calf-motif, formed the centrepieces of the room. But it was the murals covering every wall which gave it its peculiar character. Ginner and Gore obviously worked together on their execution, for they all had exotic hunting themes and shared a palette of vivid primary colours. Ginner contributed *Tiger Hunting*, a strongly expressionist design in which the tiger bares its fangs and monkeys swing through an angular, scarlet-and-blue jungle. Among Gore's work were two slightly more representational hunting murals, in one of which mounted horsemen chase deer beside a bay where two galleons are anchored.

But for all its hectic style and the 5-guinea annual subscription Mme. Strindberg levied on ordinary members, the Cabaret Club was to prove no more successful and indeed a shorter lived phenomenon than many of the more conventional (or conventionally Bohemian) clubs which succeeded it. By the end of 1913, after a police raid, it was in deep financial trouble; there were limits even to the hell-bitch's patience and resources and in February 1914 the club closed its doors for the last time. Mme. Strindberg carried off all that was readily portable and sailed for New York, writing sadly to Augustus John that 'dreams are sweeter than reality. We shall never meet again now . . .'[23]

Everything saleable that remained went under the hammer that month, and the Cave of the Golden Calf disappeared as irrevocably as the biblical idol which had inspired it. Yet its influence had been far more profound than its eighteen-month life would suggest. Its brief flowering had exactly coincided with the arrival of the 'new Bohemians' and, in the words of a modern critic, it 'played a vital part in the prodigious spirit of artistic renewal which galvanized British art in the years leading up to the First World War.'[24]

—— · CHAPTER EIGHT · ——

At the Eiffel Tower

IT would be wrong to imagine Augustus John sulking in his tent during the Cabaret Club's months of triumph. He might well have passed by on the other side, seeing the crowds which gathered in Heddon Street for the opening night, but he had also noticed the way in which things were moving.

His response was in many ways typical: within three months of Mme. Strindberg's return to New York, he had opened a club of his own. Less exclusive than the Cave of the Golden Calf, and by sheer necessity more down-market, the Crabtree Club nevertheless soon became another centre of Bohemian life in wartime London and, for a period at least, one of the homes of that 'prodigious spirit of artistic renewal'. To be strictly accurate John was only its co-founder, part of a consortium which also included William Orpen and Lord Howard de Walden; but among the artists, musicians and writers who made up the club's regular clientele, his very celebrity assured him the status of president.

It was also largely responsible for the club's success. The Crabtree would be the 'real thing', John was telling everyone long before it opened its doors in April 1914. It would be 'amusing and useful at times'. And so it was – for a time. Its cheaply furnished premises above a shop in Greek Street (a far cry from the expensively converted Cave, and in down-at-heel Soho too) were far more to the taste of the real Bohemians. The tables and chairs were of plain wood; there was a small stage, an endless supply of beer, bread and cheese, and an admission charge of 1s. levied on any 'tourist' who was rash enough to turn up in evening dress. Betty May and Lillian Shelley were always around, up on stage singing their way through the repertoire of rather dubious folk-songs they shared with Nina Hamnett, dancing or just shrieking with laughter. There were 'boxing-matches' (and other fights even less subject to the Marquess of Queensbury's rules) and chorus-girls. To John at least the Crabtree was perfection, despite the crabs he suggested he encountered there.

Others were not so sure. Mark Gertler described it as 'just an inferior cabaret',[1] while even the redoubtable Nina Hamnett claimed to have paid it only one visit. The artist Paul Nash can hardly have been a more frequent attender. He reported to Albert Rutherston that the Crabtree was

> a disgusting place . . . where only the very lowest city Jews and the most pinched harlots attend. A place of utter coarseness and dull unrelieved monotony. John alone, a great pathetic muzzy god, a sort of Silenus – but alas no nymphs, satyrs and leopards to complete the picture.[2]

Whatever the details of its ambience and facilities, however, even more than that of the Cabaret, the flourishing of the Crabtree Club and a network of similarly stark but principally daytime cafés and restaurants which opened in London at this time marked a significant change for London's Bohemia. Slowly, gradually, it was becoming aware of its own identity, acquiring the confidence to detach itself from society, and in doing so irrevocably altering the balance of what for centuries had been a perfect symbiotic relationship.

Previously, society had possessed the money, while the artists and writers had literally lived on their wits, selling themselves as much as their wares like any other commodity in a bourgeois economy. They were outsiders – beyond the pale, below the salt – with all the obligations of servants; but they also enjoyed a traditionally privileged and unfettered access to the ear of their masters.

In the modern period Oscar Wilde perhaps exploited this ambivalent role more effectively than anyone else could (or would even have dared to) in his conquest of the salons of Mayfair and Belgravia. Like any number of writers and artists before him, he had early on discovered that the advantages which could be gained from scrubbing one's fingernails and hiding one's pre-judices beneath a starched collar more than made up for the monetary loss of principle. He had no real money of his own before the concurrent successes of his plays in the early 1890s, so it made sound economic sense to sing for his supper at any aristocratic dinner table under which he could get his feet. It was not necessarily a demeaning role, he realised, and he was, anyway, by no means the first to have played it.

> *And my poor fool is dead: no, no, no life?*
> *Why should a dog, a horse, a rat have life,*
> *And thou no breath at all? Thou'lt come no more,*
> *Never, never, never, never, never,*

laments King Lear at the end of Shakespeare's tragedy and, with a passing thought for the dead Cordelia cradled in his arms, he too dies. It is a significant moment. *King Lear* was written in 1603, but no other document so well expresses this mutual interdependence of patron and artist and the lengths to which it could extend. Freed from the normal obligations of class and caste, the licensed Fool had a right of access second to none:

> FOOL: If thou wert my fool, nuncle, I'd have thee beaten for being old before thy time.
> LEAR: How's that?
> FOOL: Though shouldst not have been old till thou hadst been wise.[3]

But if he enjoyed a friendship with his patron – as indeed he usually did – that friendship was based on mutually understood rules. Both parties knew their place.

In his plays, Shakespeare might have talked of 'degree' and seen the relationship as just one small part of a grand cosmological pattern, but he was not above trying to advance his own position with a well-turned phrase. Each of his narrative poems, *Venus and Adonis* and *The Rape of Lucrece*, is fulsomely dedicated 'To the Right Honourable Henry Wriothsley, Earl of Southampton, and Baron of Titchfield', the latter in terms of abject abasement: 'What I have done is yours; what I have to do is yours; being part in all I have, devoted yours.' There is nothing particularly unusual in this; quite the reverse in fact. Shakespeare may have been one of the first writers to benefit from literary patronage, but for 300 years after the first performance of *King Lear* his successors strove to act the Fool to a succession of more or less worthy Lears.

It was not as easy as it sounds, and the tensions inherent in the relationship frequently broke the surface calm. For, however much the writers fripped, tripped and excused themselves, it all came down to the same thing: they were dancing to somebody else's tune. In 1697, for instance, Sir John Vanbrugh seemed to have known that, with his play *The Relapse*, he had come close to biting the hands which were feeding him. His preface is a classic exercise in damage limitation. It veers uneasily between the joshing and the toadying – as well it might since the play had, after all, introduced that archetypal *arriviste* Lord Foppington – but Vanbrugh finally gets around to saying what he really means:

> If I have offended any honest gentlemen of the town, *whose friendship or good word is worth the having*, I am very sorry for it. [My italics]

Other writers managed rather better. In forewords, prefaces, private letters, public declarations and the dedicatory epistles to all manner of plays, poems, novels and treatises, Pope, Macaulay, Fielding and Sheridan, among others, trumpeted the virtues of their various hosts and patrons for most of the following two centuries. Even Dr Johnson managed a typically Augustan tribute to 'the Right Honourable Philip Dormer, Earl of Chesterfield' in the 1747 Plan for his *Dictionary*, signing off as his 'Lordship's most obedient, and most humble servant'.

A century and a half later, Yeats and Augustus John were still doing very much the same thing, using the correct knives and forks as adroitly as any pen or brush. But by the time they appeared on the scene in the years immediately before 1900 there was a difference. We have already seen that, despite his wild, Bohemian image, John was not a servant but a welcome guest in the houses of Lady Gregory, Jack Nettleship, Sir Hugh Lane and the far from negligible personalities whose portraits he painted. Values were changing in society as a whole. The perceived differences between the classes which underlay Victorian society were diminishing in the face of the twentieth century's accelerating egalitarianism. Much the same forces which brought Keir Hardie and John Burns to Westminster as the first Labour Members of Parliament in 1892 (at precisely the time when Wilde was at the pinnacle of his fame as a dinner guest) were engendering a society in which writers and artists like Yeats and John were no longer automatically classed as 'beyond the pale' but – once they had proved themselves – treated as equals and seated above the salt . . . at those tables from which it had not been removed altogether.

As social changes go, this redefinition of the role of the artist happened extraordinarily rapidly, and in an eerily exact parallel with the changes that were recolouring the political map of Britain. Like the arrival of Hardie and Burns in the House of Commons, Wilde's social success can be seen as a bridgehead. Little more than a quarter of a century later, the ensuing battle appeared to have been conclusively won. Within twelve months of Ramsay MacDonald's emergence as Prime Minister and leader of the first Labour Government, Bohemia – the Fools – had been appointed the titular heads of society. Or of one section of it at least.

With what now seems a perverse sense of timing, the Hon. David Tennant and the actress Hermione Baddeley, whom he later married, opened the Gargoyle Club in 1925, the year after MacDonald came to power. It was, however, still unashamedly aimed at the upper-crust and it attracted them, despite (or perhaps because of) a normal membership fee of 7 guineas and entry criteria more arbitrary than those of the most exclusive of today's New York discotheques. In the early thirties the Prince of Wales (later King Edward VIII) was often seen there, and on one famous occasion two princes, three princesses and the King of Romania were all present on the same evening. Evening dress was insisted upon, the dining-room cutlery was solid silver; and yet when the Hon. David Tennant cast around for a president of this plutocratic power-house the first person he thought of asking was Augustus John.

Not unnaturally, John accepted with alacrity. Times had changed since the days when he had refused to so much as visit Mme. Strindberg's Cabaret Club. Sections of the art world had long since despaired of him and his seemingly headlong flight into respectability (although even that had a certain inevitability: Henry Mürger had, after all, noted that Bohemia *could* be a staging-post on the road to the Academy). But it is at least tempting to credit John with more laudable intentions. For, although it is undoubtedly true that he and the considerable number of his fellow-artists who followed him there were originally tempted to the Gargoyle by the reduced membership fees and cheap food and drink with which Tennant, like most club owners then and now, set out to woo an 'interesting' artistic clientele, his appointment as president did seem to confirm Bohemia's new-found equality. Just thirty years after the trial of Oscar Wilde and what seemed like the end of everything, Wilde's direct descendants suddenly found themselves the honoured guests at the ball – and it was a ball like nothing which they or anyone else in London had ever seen before.

Occupying the top three floors of a building on the corner of Dean and Meard Streets in Soho, the Gargoyle had been designed by the unlikely combination of the British Imperial architect Sir Edwin Lutyens and the French *fauviste* painter Henri Matisse; although from later descriptions it seems likely that the latter had the upper hand. Two of his murals decorated the walls of the main rooms and, on his insistence, everywhere else was tiled with tiny mirror squares. There were, it was said, 20,000 of them in all, the shimmering fragments of some 200-year-old mirrors which Matisse had rescued from the salon of a French château.

On the surface it seemed a rout, but the Gargoyle was special in more ways than one. David Tennant was an inspired host, a man who was truly (and not, like Mme. Stindberg, principally financially) interested in Bohemia and the arts. And in precisely the same way in which MacDonald's 1924 Government remained in office only because of Liberal support, Bohemia ruled the roost at the Gargoyle only because of his liberal outlook. Away from Dean Street the battle for acceptance was still being fought, and some of the fiercest skirmishing was yet to take place in a restaurant less than a mile away from the Gargoyle.

It is hardly accidental that, with the exception of goings-on at the Café Royal, life at the Eiffel Tower is better documented than almost any other aspect of the twentieth-century London literary scene. Not only did everyone from Augustus John and Nina Hamnett to the young Anthony Powell frequent the place, the artists preserved their sketches and the writers later polished up their memories. Many of these were to find their way into autobiographies – the restaurant figures prominently in both

Powell's and Hamnett's – but novelists too found 'The Eiffel' an irresistible location. W. Seymour Leslie used it in *The Silent Queen*, first published in 1927. His characters talk about dining at 'The Big Wheel', but the fact that Leslie himself was thinking of the Eiffel Tower is borne out by several sketches of Nina Hamnett's which decorated the original edition: in one in particular, although the lettering on the front window says 'The Big Wheel' the interior is very clearly that of the Tower.

Michael Arlen was equally coy in matters of nomenclature, but just as shameless in his scene-stealing. We have seen that in *Piracy* (which had appeared five years before *The Silent Queen*, in 1922) a thinly veiled Eiffel Tower makes its appearance as the Mont Agel. The disguise fooled no one, if indeed it had ever been intended to. For, never less than tantalising, Arlen not only gives a fairly precise address for his Mont Agel (it was 'on the northern fringe of Soho') in the very first chapter of the novel, with characteristic bravura he takes his reader there for dinner. He leads this suburban sophisticate down Percy Street ('a not ill-favoured little street') towards the restaurant's 'wide and well-lit windows' and then, in tones rather too sententious for modern taste (another characteristic of his writing) describes the building in infinite detail:

> On the left of these spacious windows, at the head of a few steps, is the door of the restaurant, pleasantly inviting your pressure, if indeed it is not widely open to show the elegant interior; and on the right is the door of the hotel, a door of a very different air to the other, a sealed and reticent looking door, in fact, with the secret air of having very important business of its own as a door, which indeed it has . . .
>
> Within the restaurant you will find all quiet, orderly and clean. In extent it is only a rather spacious room of uncertain shape (though there are, of course, possibilities upstairs), but it has not the air of being confined to that one room . . . It is bounded on the north side, as our schoolbooks say, by the wide front windows, which are pleasantly half-curtained with vermilion gauze; on the south side, where the room tapers towards its end, by a much smaller window, which is always heavily curtained and may or may not look upon the mysteries of the Mont Agel backyard; on the west by a wall decorated with mirrors, stags' antlers, and heads of furry beasts, and broken by a small door which leads into the hotel, the famous cellars, and

the usual offices; and on the east side by a handsome counter
which runs along half the length of the wall . . .

This restaurant is no place for a poor man, you understand;
unless, of course, he happens to be with a rich one, as must now
and then happen in even the most luckless life. The very tables
are arranged with a rich sparseness; for they are placed only
around the walls, each with its red-shaded lamp. The centre of
the room is thus left unchallenged to a large brass contrivance
from which flow ferns, palm leaves, and all manner of
secondary flowers; on one side is a rack for papers; on its other
side is a small table weighted with various and unseasonable
delicacies, artichokes and asparagus, oysters and strawberries,
plovers' eggs and grouse, caviare and cantaloup.[4]

Nina Hamnett's drawings again bear out the accuracy of this
description, but its very existence transcends questions of veri-
similitude. Even at the time, it seems, there was a feeling that the
Eiffel was somehow different.

There was no particular reason why it should have been; like so
many other places and features of Fitzrovia, the Restaurant de la
Tour Eiffel, as it was more properly known, was there well before
the Bohemians arrived, hot-foot from the Café Royal, and still
there long after they departed. Indeed, some semblance of it
lingers even today. Renamed the White Tower when it transferred
to Greek ownership in 1943, the shop at 1 Percy Street is still used
as a restaurant. But although it has maintained the old Eiffel
Tower's reputation as one of the best – and most expensive –
establishments in the area, the modern White Tower has none of
the eclectic, artistic ambience that used to permeate its predecessor
and ensured its popularity.

For, as Arlen hints, the Eiffel Tower was more than a restaurant.
Anthony Powell recalls that it was 'treated almost like a club by
those *abonné* there',[5] while Nancy Cunard went so far as to
celebrate both it and its proprietor, Rudolf Stulik, in verse. A
rather mystical ode entitled 'To the Eiffel Tower Restaurant' first
appeared in 1923, tactfully near the back of a collection of her
poetry. After fifty lines it concludes:

> *I think the Tower shall go up to heaven*
> *One night in a flame of fire, about eleven.*
> *I always saw our carnal-spiritual home*
> *Blazing upon the sky symbolically . . .*

If ever we go to heaven in a troop
The Tower must be our ladder,
Vertically
Climbing the ether with its swaying group.
God will delight to greet his embassy
Wherein is found no lack
Of wits and glamour, strong wines, new foods, fine looks,
*   strange-sounding languages of diverse men –*
Stulik shall lead the pack
Until its great disintegration, when
God sets us deftly in a new Zodiac.[6]

Others might have phrased it better, but Nancy Cunard was not alone in her hymn to what she also called 'the Tower's beacon, the Tower's cheer'. In the early 1920s the restaurant really was the 'carnal-spiritual home' of a great many people.

Upstairs, and reached by a separate door, was that hotel which Arlen mentioned, an offshoot of the restaurant, which catered for respectable guests – Nina Hamnett met the Irish-Polish pianist Lady Dean Paul (Poldowski) there – as well as the more furtive carnal needs of some of the downstairs clientele. More important at the time, however, was the way in which, for a few years at least, the downstairs restaurant satisfied the 'spiritual' needs of its customers. For, like the Gargoyle, it was one of the first places in which Bohemia was at home and, in a neat reversal of the previous norm, society the guest.

Wyndham Lewis and the Vorticists had been early patrons and can even claim to have discovered the restaurant. Along with Ezra Pound, they had celebrated the launch of their influential magazine *Blast* at the Eiffel Tower in 1914. Later, Lewis had also had a hand in the decoration of one of its two upstairs dining-rooms, the so-called 'Vorticist room', which contrasted starkly with a plush, aspidistra-filled and 'far cosier' suite next door.

In those early days the Vorticists and Futurists had the place very much to themselves. But word soon spread. Long before 1920 they had been joined by representatives of the artistic mainstream. Augustus John, Nina Hamnett, Mark Gertler, Harold Gilman, Spencer Gore and many of the 'young Turks' who had been associated with the nearby Omega Workshops arrived shortly after the end of the First World War.

At about the same time the Eiffel Tower was discovered by the first adventurous members of society. Following in the wake of Nancy Cunard, these were the real-life counterparts of Arlen's Virginia Tarlyon, 'young women of patrician and careless intelligence', young men with private means and no early morning appointments, and a leavening of increasingly jaded Bright Young Things, all of whom were more than ready to forego the familiar West End beat in their ceaseless search for somewhere more interesting.

For a time it worked out well; and the classless, comfortable atmosphere of the Eiffel seemed to presage the shape of things to come. Bohemia retained the upper hand, but the tables were full every evening. Indeed, the early 1920s were the Eiffel Tower's high point. Freed from a reliance on somebody else's taste, in Percy Street at least (and on the pages of the Eiffel's visitors' book, known as the *Livre d'Or*) writers and artists were finally enjoying equality, if not complete independence. A new dispensation seemed to have been brought about among the tropical foliage and hunting trophies, a new world born in the restaurant's dim red light.

One night the place would be dominated by a tableful of squabbling European nobility; another by a gaggle of British politicians, intent on impressing their charms on a no less garrulous group of chorus-girls. There was Sickert; here a Sitwell or two. There was Herbert Asquith; here, surely, the magnificently effete novelist Ronald Firbank, struggling 'almost manfully with his asparagus'.[7] More often, though, it was the massive presence of Augustus John which presided over the feast as the Eiffel Tower's black-coated waiters floated among the tables, bringing a 'Sole Dieppeoise', perhaps, for Sickert, portions of 'Gâteau St Honoré' (a sickly, elaborate custard tart which nevertheless became one of the *specialités de la maison*) for the chorus-girls, bottle after bottle of the house hock, and then bills which even in the 1920s could come close to rivalling those at the Savoy.

It was, as its older clients recognised, all vaguely reminiscent of the golden-age Café Royal, albeit on a vastly reduced scale. There were differences, however. Chief among them was the fact that, whereas the Café had evolved over thirty years, the Eiffel Tower was the virtually instant creation of one man – its proprietor, Rudolf Stulik.

As fabled as his restaurant, Stulik has attracted at least as many stories. Augustus John recalled his once announcing that he was the product of a liaison 'in which the charms of a famous ballerina had overcome the scruples of an exalted but anonymous personage'.[8] Like so much of Stulik's talk, that was probably baloney, but it does go some way towards explaining his extraordinary success. For, as Michael Arlen observed of 'M. Stutz', the proprietor of his Mont Agel but an unmistakable portrait of Stulik: 'As every civilisation must produce a M. Stutz, so every M. Stutz must produce a civilisation.'[9]

The real-life Stulik had done exactly that. By the end of the First World War he had engineered at the Eiffel Tower just the sort of liaison between power and art which he claimed had given him birth. And then, having achieved it, he assiduously – and, as time went on, over-assiduously – nurtured it right up until the outbreak of the Second World War.

Born in Vienna of Jewish parents, portly, and with a moustache which gave him a certain resemblance to Lord Kitchener or the Emperor Franz Joseph, Stulik acquired the Eiffel Tower in 1910. Claiming that he was 'only a little *restaurateur*',[10] in reality he was an incurable romantic and the indisputable *genius loci* of the Restaurant de la Tour Eiffel in much the same way that Mme. Strindberg had been the only begetter of the Cabaret Club. Tristram Hillier, then an impecunious young student at the Slade, later recalled that in the mid-twenties:

> Stulik maintained a ratio of charges based upon what he estimated to be the wealth of his clients. For the fashionable, who liked to gather at night in what they imagined to be a Bohemian atmosphere, his prices were astronomical, but for the likes of myself, once accepted as a friend of the house, there was always a good *plat du jour* of some kind at a modest price, and generally people of interest to talk to or famous ones to watch with respectful awe.[11]

With the 'accepted' but still successful John, however, Stulik was not always so obliging. On one occasion he demanded that the artist clear an accumulated debt of some £300. Later, in the 1930s, he made him pay not only for his own dinner but an outstanding bill for Dylan Thomas's dinner, bed and breakfast. Ruthven Todd saw how he managed this:

'I know you treat me outrageously, Stulik,' [John] said, 'and you know I don't complain much. But forty-three pounds for lunch for two is a bit steep.' Stulik beamed sweetly. 'Is not for lunch only,' he explained. 'Little Welshman with curly hair.' He made a gesture above his own pate. 'He come here. He stay two weeks and eat. He says you pay.'

Sometimes arrogant and even peremptory – as in his occasional refusal in the 1920s to serve the newly popular whisky and sodas – Stulik was nevertheless adored. Some of his patrons, like Cecil Gray, remembered only his effusiveness. The composer was once sitting alone at the only table capable of accommodating 'five or six boisterous and wealthy would-be patrons'. He offered to move, but Stulik would have none of it:

'You are not only my customer, but my guest; not only my guest, but my friend! You will please to stay where you are; you will not move – I do not allow you to move! They can go somewhere else! I do not want them here! MR GRAY, I AM A VIENNESE!'[12]

Other diners enjoyed his outspokenness, especially when it was time to close. For, despite rumours that he 'never went to bed, never',[13] Stulik had a well-practised routine for emptying the restaurant when he felt ready to retire upstairs. 'Ladies and gentlemen, we close!' he would call in what Anthony Powell remembered as his 'Comic Opera broken English', following up a few minutes later with: 'Husbands and wives, we close! . . . Brothers and sisters, we close!'

And then, as his waiters took their cue, pulled down the yellow blinds, put up the shutters and extinguished half the lights, came the final warning: 'Lovers and sweethearts, WE CLOSE!'[14]

Coats, hats and opera-cloaks would be reclaimed, bills settled, and trysts made as the last of the casual diners were ejected onto the pavement of Percy Street. But for Stulik's trusted, accepted friends, of course, the evening went on regardless. On at least one occasion Nina Hamnett was helped out of the dark and shuttered restaurant through the hotel door and led all the way back to her room in Howland Street by two of the Eiffel Tower waiters after a private, post-prandial party. And she was not the only one, nor even the last to leave . . .

Great fun while they lasted, such 'Bohemian' binges neverthe-less seem to have had their morning-after. For, in reality, they were not particularly Bohemian at all, and appear to have amounted to little more than Stulik's cashing-in on the fame brought to his restaurant by its more flamboyant habitués. Anyone could be part of them; anyone Stulik knew, however vaguely – even Nancy Cunard. In 'To the Eiffel Tower Restaurant' she recalls

> Those old nights of drinking,
> Furtive adventures, solitary thinking
> At the corner table, sheltered from the faces . . .

Typically, her insistence on occupying the corner table was only one of the demands Nancy made on Rudolf Stulik's hospitality. She was, of course, the real-life original of Virginia Tarlyon in Michael Arlen's *Piracy*; and there is good reason to believe that she inconvenienced the Eiffel every bit as arrogantly as Virginia did the Mont Agel. Well before 1918, Arlen writes, Virginia had given herself permission to

> enter the Mont Agel at any hour of the night by the hotel entrance, having rung the bell; and she would sit in the deserted and shuttered restaurant, in the light of a candle stuck in its own grease on a saucer – it was war-time then, you understand. M. Stutz would leave her alone, guessing that it was for solitude she had come hither, this lady of high fashion in all her finery . . . she would write letters, sitting there, and every now and then she would sip her Vichy Water. Half a glass of Vichy Water would last Virginia a long time; but cigarettes would fade before her contemplation, a box of ten cigarettes would fade away . . . Her letters from the Mont Agel, addressed in that pencilled scrawl, would suddenly drop on studios in all parts of London, sometimes on very poor studios indeed, asking them what they were doing and if they were working well these days, and if they would care to come to luncheon with her one day, and naming a day for that luncheon, either at the Mont Agel, the Café Royal, or Belgrave Square. And sometimes, if it was a very poor little artist she was writing to, there would be a cheque tucked away in the letter.[15]

If it had only been 'solitary thinking'! If it had only been

Nancy! . . . But it wasn't; as early as 1922 more and more people were coming to the Eiffel only so that they could later claim to have seen Augustus John,

> to have sat and watched the bearded and significant figure of [Stulik's] most considerable patron – an epic figure, that! – and to have wondered whether that silent detachment betokened a great artist or a great vagabond.[66]

By the middle of the decade things were even worse, with the Bohemians once again finding themselves overwhelmed by fashionable society. Originally so daring, its occasional visits to the Eiffel in particular and Bohemia in general had become an arrogant and persistent gate-crashing. Nancy Cunard was by no means alone; she had brought her friends and they had brought theirs. Now, not only was it difficult to get a table at the Eiffel, the whole atmosphere of the place was changing. The boisterous *bonhomie* of the past had been replaced by a monied boorishness that was at once conceited and patronising, for John and his ilk were looking for far more than cheque-books and invitations to luncheon in Belgrave Square from their companions. (Indeed, the mere possession of the former was a positive liability: when John was asked to pay that bill for £300 he delved in his pockets and produced the cash.)

The whole situation was becoming untenable. It wasn't as if the Eiffel was the Gargoyle Club where the Bohemians were happy enough to temporarily swallow their pride, don evening dress, get only discreetly drunk and go through their paces. The Eiffel had been *their* restaurant, but now its days were numbered.

There was no big break; John, Nina Hamnett and the rest continued to use it, but on a Micawber-like basis, until somewhere better turned up. The extent to which it had lost its appeal by the end of the twenties, however, is well caught in the second of Nina Hamnett's two volumes of autobiography. *Is She a Lady?* tells the story of her life from 1927 in the same short, child-like paragraphs which had characterised its predecessor, *Laughing Torso*. But in comparison with the warmth and affection which mark that book's account of nights at the Eiffel, in *Is She a Lady?* the references are cold and factual. There is no suggestion of loyalty to it. By 1927, it seems, the Eiffel had become just another place to eat:

I dined at the Eiffel with Harriet Cohen and a musician friend of hers and after dinner Sir Henry Wood appeared. He asked us to drink some champagne with him. Harriet explained that I had just done a book with Sir Osbert Sitwell and he asked me to send him a copy.[17]

At the Eiffel Tower one evening, I met Ruth Baldwin, whom I had known some time before. She shared a house with Jo Carstairs, the motor boat racing girl.[18]

Soon the references cease altogether, for long before 1930 to all intents and purposes, John and his circle had moved on. It was a shambling, none too sober advance, but a vital one, for with it Bohemia irrevocably became Fitzrovia.

Augustus John was hardly sedentary. He was certainly not rooted to any particular studio in London, nor even to London itself for most of his life. But he was left standing in the years after the First World War by the constant travelling of Nina Hamnett. Her autobiographies describe a dizzying succession of Channel crossings, pleasure-trips and working holidays in Brittany, Paris and, not infrequently, the far south of France.

Born in 1890 – like John, at Tenby in South Wales – she was one of the first women to have been a full-time art student. Restless and rootless in London, she had gravitated like a moth to the bright lights of the Domino Room at the Café Royal and later to the Cave of the Golden Calf. Uninhibited and unabashed at being one of the very few females in a predominantly male world, she became an established member of the Bohemian set even before her first work was exhibited in 1913. (As proof of her good faith, the previous year she had persuaded Allan Odle to relieve her of what she had come to consider her boring, respectable virginity.) Even before she became, in later life, an almost caricatured Fitzrovian, perennially cadging drinks in return for scurrilous gossip in all the pubs of Rathbone Place, she was in many ways the archetypal Bohemian. It was not just her raffish lifestyle – for ever changing rooms and lodgings, never managing to keep track of the money she earned – she seemed to have a kind of pedigree.

Her frequent trips to France had left her, by the early 1920s, as familiar with the rather more stylish Bohemian circles of Paris as she was with the regulars at the Café Royal and the Eiffel Tower in London. She had paid her first visit to the French capital in 1912 (when she met up with Jacob Epstein, then working on his monument to Oscar Wilde in the Père Lachaise cemetery) and was back in the city two years later. But this time it was as more than a tourist. She rented a room in Montparnasse and threw herself into the wartime life of that quarter, quickly becoming a member of an artistic circle which included the likes of Modigliani, Derain, Maurice Vlaminck and Brancusi, and discovering the delights of Parisian café life at the Rotonde.

Part bar, part Bohemian labour exchange and social club, even more than the nearby Dôme, the Rotonde maintained the tradition of easy Bohemianism which had been established at the Café Momus and further refined at the Closerie des Lilas. It was a tradition which came more naturally to the French than to the English but, with its *bals* and impromptu parties, it was all very much to Nina's taste: her very English presence capped the former, while her nude dancing more than once stopped the latter. The war compelled her to return to London, but almost as soon as it was over she was back in Paris, determined to catch up on all she had missed.

There had not been a great deal. Although the Rotonde had closed (and left several new venues such as the Restaurant Baty and the Café Parnasse fighting for the Bohemians' trade) uncharacteristically Nina arrived at exactly the right time to play a full part in the upsurge of Parisian artistic life which happened at the beginning of the twenties. She was there in time for the opening of the Gaya bar in 1921, a sophisticated Right Bank nightspot where Negro jazz was played and Nina first met the composers Darius Milhaud and Francis Poulenc as well as Jean Cocteau and his protégé Raymond Radiguet. She was still there a few months later when the Gaya was transformed into a larger and more famous bar, the Boeuf sur le Toit, whose name commemorated the popular Cocteau-Milhaud ballet.

'*Une sort de Gibson-girl de faubourg*',[19] she was back in 1923 to sample the syncopated delights of two new 'American bars', the Dingo and the Jockey. Got up in a second-hand cocktail dress and cheap, Woolworth 'pearls', she was also a well-known figure in many of the plush, expensive night-clubs which were opening in Paris at least as fast as they were in London.

It all had its effect. Back in England, Nina looked around for something equally interesting. But her memories of the giddy Parisian social round made London seem dull. Even the Cave and the Eiffel Tower, where the ubiquitous Lady Dean Paul soon introduced her to Raoul Dufy, paled in comparison. So, as she was later to write, in the company of Augustus John and the perpetually self-effacing writer T. W. ('Tommy') Earp, she 'searched through London' for something different. There were definite shades of W. B. Yeats and Arthur Symons about this quest; certainly Nina at least really seemed to believe that an echo of the liveliness of the Rotonde (if not the brilliance of the Boeuf) was there to be found if one looked long enough.

But there were differences too. Thirty years younger and fundamentally less serious than any of the Rhymers, the trio set its sights rather lower; all they were after was 'a public house with a large saloon bar attached to which was an amiable proprietor'.[20]

The Fitzroy Tavern and Papa Kleinfeld, its 'guv'nor', fitted the bill exactly. A large pub on the corner of Windmill Street and Charlotte Street, it had opened in 1897. It had sawdust on the floor, First World War recruiting posters on the walls, a mechanical piano and a loud and lively clientele, even before Nina, John and Tommy Earp strode in one evening in 1926. Like many later landlords, Kleinfeld was an inveterate charity fundraiser and the ceiling of his saloon was festooned with small packets of money attached to darts which were habitually lobbed there by his customers. There was also a Christmas club whose members paid in their spare coppers each Monday evening.

It was all very different from Paris; but, for varying reasons, the down-to-earth, beery atmosphere of the Fitzroy exactly suited each of the trio. Nina Hamnett found it very conducive to work, for 'not only did one meet people but one did a lot of business there also'.[21] While Augustus John, and to an even greater extent Tommy Earp, revelled in it for less laudable but ultimately more characteristic reasons. One evening at the Eiffel Tower Cecil Gray had suggested to them that people drank to escape from themselves – and unwittingly managed to evoke entirely typical statements from both the artist and the writer:

Augustus demurred, saying: 'On the contrary, I drink in order to become more myself'; to which Thomas responded, quietly and gently: 'I drink because I like it,' which seems a very much better reason than either of the former alternatives, and probably very much nearer the truth in all three cases.[22]

There was one further reason for the otherwise inexplicable adoption of the Fitzroy Tavern: it was the ultimate bolt-hole. There, surely, the fugitive Bohemians thought, they could at last be themselves, untroubled by the likes of Nancy Cunard. For, as a telling anecdote of Nina Hamnett's demonstrates, although it did not quite work out like that, they were getting heartily sick of the 'tourists':

> One evening two people came to the Tavern – a smartly dressed woman accompanied by a rather dreary-looking man.
> They were introduced to me by a man I knew slightly and had come to see what they thought was 'Bohemia'. The first thing they said was: 'Are there any dope fiends here? We have been looking all over London for them.' I said, feeling and, I suppose, looking rather startled: 'Good gracious, no, the people in this quarter when they have a few pennies and want to feel excited only drink beer, or, if they can afford it, gin and whisky. I think that you had better go back to Mayfair if you want to find people who take drugs.'[23]

The couple beat an abashed retreat. They were not to be the last West End visitors to the pub (Nancy Cunard herself put a bobbed head around the door on more than one occasion) but by and large the Bohemians had it to themselves. It was somewhere in which they could let their hair down and entertain their 'friends'. The cabaret singer Elisabeth Welch remembers being taken there by the composers 'Willie' Walton and Constant Lambert one evening in 1933: 'I was very excited because of course I'd heard so much about it. It was also, I think, my first pub. We used to drop in every so often. Augustus John was always there, I remember – and always singing.'[24]

And well he might have been. After more than a quarter of a century the Bohemians had detached themselves entirely from society; and the pub had given them a new name. Bohemia had become Fitzrovia by throwing in its lot with the working classes for whom 'laughing, talking and regaling themselves with beer' were far more important than luncheons in Belgrave Square. Suddenly, connections were no longer important and under Papa

Kleinfeld's benevolent eye a new New World arose. By the early thirties it was firmly established, and already seedier and more seductive than anything which had gone before.

Word soon spread. Well before the beginning of 1934 it had reached the ears of a teenage Swansea poet. Concluding a long letter to a London friend he wrote:

> I hope to be coming up to stay with my sister in the next three or four weeks; no definite date is arranged yet, but I'll let you know as soon as it is; and, if nothing else, we can spend a few hours together in the Fitzroy Tavern.[25]

There was no valediction, just the name Dylan.

CHAPTER NINE

Enter Dylan Thomas

EVEN before his death in November 1953, just a fortnight after his thirty-ninth birthday, the solid reputation of Dylan Thomas the poet was irrevocably mixed with the more sensational notoriety of Dylan Thomas the Bohemian. But there was a sense of proportion: in his public and professional life at least, the one was properly predominant over the other. Editors published and paid for anything he cared to write. More than that, until the very end of his life they were also prepared to offer advances for work promised but never completed, nor even in some cases so much as started. His *Collected Poems*, first published in 1952, sold well on both sides of the Atlantic – far better, in fact, than volumes by the majority of his fellow-poets – and won Thomas the £250 Foyle's Poetry Prize. In Britain his sonorous, booming voice reached countless living-rooms whenever he broadcast for the BBC, for he was much, if increasingly reluctantly, used by the Corporation as a reader and actor on both the Home Service and the prestigious, newly established Third Programme.

For those who did not know – or those who chose to ignore – the other side, he was still the 'slightly dented cherub', the boy from Swansea whose poetry was 'pure fire compressed into holy forms'. Edith Sitwell stole that phrase from Walt Whitman, but she was far from alone in her eulogising. Remembering him as 'Gwilym' in his basically autobiographical *Autumn Sequel* (1954), Louis MacNeice described a Thomas who:

> . . . *stayed young and gay,*
> *A bulbous Taliessin, a spruce and small*

Bow-tied Silenus roistering his way
Through lands of fruit and fable, well aware
That even Dionysus has his day

And cannot take it with him. Debonair,
He leant against the bar till his cigarette
Became one stream of ash sustained in air

Through which he puffed his talk. The nights were wet
And incomparably alive . . .[1]

That is how it should have been. But there was another side to
Thomas. Somehow, in getting and, more pertinently, in spending,
he had laid waste his powers. Whatever MacNeice said, he was
neither truly young nor gay for very much of his life. In his later
years he could hardly have been described as spruce; he was
bloated rather than small, and not in the least debonair. Roistering
had become more than an endearing trait. Even before his death
less generous friends and acquaintances, fellow-poets and a wider
circle of drinking cronies had collected and polished a repertoire of
favourite stories featuring the Welsh Dionysus as abusive, violent,
none too clean – and seldom, if ever, sober.

'What will you have to drink, Mr Thomas?' 'Anything that goes
down my throat' – one anecdote from the many sums up them
all.[2] There are scores if not hundreds more: Thomas on all fours,
drunk and barking like a dog; Thomas stuck in a bar and failing to
turn up for a public reading; Thomas chasing girls around an
American college campus . . . Even now, a third of a century after
his death, the literary historian who is prepared to haunt the bars
and saloons of London and New York can still pick up scraps and
tatters of the legend. Elderly regulars, propped on stools in their
corners, will recite tired and threadbare tales of the times they
accompanied 'the poet Dylan Thomas' on gargantuan binges or
followed hard on his heels during desperate, dreadful all-night
debauches in search of beer, bourbon or, just occasionally,
women.

In the years since 1953 the circumstances surrounding his
seedy, sordid death in New York have added still further
pinchbeck glamour to the poet's beery, Bohemian image.
Succeeding biographers have pieced together the details of a
muddled, unsatisfactory story. Certainly Thomas had been on a

drinking bout in and around the Chelsea Hotel during which, he claimed, he had downed eighteen straight whiskies. Equally certainly, he was seen to have difficulty breathing on his return, in the early hours of 5 November. A doctor was summoned and unwisely administered morphine. But neither the precise sequence of events in the hours that followed, nor the reasoning behind the doctor's actions has ever been satisfactorily explained. All that is known for certain is that, later the same night, Thomas was admitted to hospital in a coma and, after four and a half days, during which he did not regain consciousness, he died on the morning of 9 November. There was a post-mortem (revealing, among other things, that his liver was fatty) and the medical authorities at the St Vincent Hospital decided that death was due to hydrostatic bronchopneumonia and 'acute and chronic ethylism'. Acute and chronic ethylism is a medical term meaning little more than alcoholism. 'As far as the pathologist was concerned,' says the poet's most recent biographer Paul Ferris, 'Thomas died of drink.'[3]

There are other, posthumously circulated, stories too. Stories relating to Thomas the supposed drug-addict, Thomas the incurable womaniser, even Thomas the repressed but rampant homosexual. All add something, however unlikely – and as the years go by it does become increasingly unlikely – to the legend. For, quite apart from the enduring popularity of poems such as 'The Force that Through the Green Fuse Drives the Flower', 'Fern Hill' and 'Do Not Go Gentle Into that Good Night', the familiarity of *Under Milk Wood* and the continuing demand for those *Collected Poems*, since his death Dylan Thomas has acquired a character grander and far grubbier than anything he had in life. In spite of himself and despite the known facts, in the popular imagination at least, he has become the very image of what a certain type of writer in the middle years of this century should have been. His way of life was at least as much an influence on the late fifties' and early sixties' 'beatniks' and 'beat poets' as the corpus of some 200 poems he left behind him. It was not chance, after all, which led an American folk-singer called Robert Zimmerman to rechristen himself Bob Dylan.

In this country too, rumours and memories of the poet's feckless, inebriated and irresponsible lifestyle set standards by which the rest of the Fitzrovia of the forties and fifties would come to be judged. Thomas was a legend in his own lifetime – and that was exactly the way he wanted it.

Dylan Marlais Thomas was born in Swansea, South Wales on 27 October 1914, a couple of months after the outbreak of the First World War. And, as he later wrote to the poet and editor Geoffrey Grigson, he 'developed, intellectually at least, in the smug darkness of [that] provincial town'.[4] He should probably have remained there or somewhere similar; for, however much he might have claimed to despise them, Swansea and the small towns of Pembrokeshire and Camarthen were to exert a crucial influence on him for the rest of his life. They are behind, and their physical presence is an inextricable part of the texture of his best and most characteristic work – *Under Milk Wood* and poems from such different points in his career as 'The Hunchback in the Park' and 'Fern Hill'. Their values and attitudes are at the centre of his early prose work *Portrait of the Artist as a Young Dog* in the same way as those of Dublin dominate its model, James Joyce's *Portrait of the Artist as a Young Man*.

But Thomas was not content to remain in Wales. He was eighteen when he wrote to Grigson in 1933. He had already had poetry published in London and was coming to feel cut off and out of things in Swansea. Like many other young men both before and since, he believed he was being stifled by that town's 'smug darkness'. Quite simply he yearned for the bright lights. He was impatient with the small-minded gentility he saw around him (and was to lampoon to such comic effect in *Under Milk Wood* fifteen years later) and his desperation is reflected in many of the letters he wrote at this time. 'It's impossible for me to tell you how much I want to get out of it all,' he confided to Pamela Hansford Johnson in October 1933, 'out of narrowness and dirtiness, out of the eternal ugliness of the Welsh people, and all that belongs to them, out of the pettinesses of a mother I don't care for and the giggling batch of relatives.'[5]

Getting out of it all meant going to London. There was nowhere else. London was where the lights burnt brightest and – probably of greater importance at this early stage of his life – London was where the poetry magazines were. Paul Ferris suggests that Thomas made his first visit to the capital in August 1933. It was essentially a business trip; the eighteen-year-old poet was looking for contacts among the editors of those magazines and is believed to have called on two of the most eminent, A. R. Orage at the *New English Weekly* and Sir Richard Rees who ran the *Adelphi*. He stayed with his elder sister Nancy and her husband Haydn Taylor on their houseboat which was moored on the Thames near Chertsey in Surrey and clearly found metropolitan life very much to his liking.

His antipathy to Swansea and his impatience with the cosy, middle-class comforts offered by his parents' home at 5 Cwmdonkin Drive made it inevitable that he would. But there are other reasons too why London was so important to Thomas. Even in 1933 he had decided that he was going to be a writer; in a letter he sent to the editor of the *Swansea and West Wales Guardian* the following year he even referred to himself, semi-seriously, as 'Mr Dylan Thomas, the literary critic and poet'. More significantly, Thomas had already decided that he was going to live the life of a writer. In another of the letters he wrote that year to Pamela Hansford Johnson (who was then his confidante and only later emerged as a writer herself) he confessed that he had already been trying to do this in Swansea:

> . . . I read on until twelve or thereabouts, when perhaps I have read [a] quarter of a novel, a couple of poems, a short story, an article on the keeping of bees in Upper Silesia, and a review by somebody I have never heard of on a play I never want to see. Then down the hill into the Uplands – a lowland collection of crossroads and shops, for one (or perhaps two) pints of beer in the Uplands Hotel. Then home for lunch. After lunch, I retire again to the fire where perhaps I shall read all the afternoon – and read a great deal of everything, or continue on a poem or a story I have left unfinished, or to start another or to start drafting another, or to add a note to a letter to you, or to type something already completed, or merely to write – to write anything, just to let the words and ideas, the half remembered half forgotten images, tumble on the sheets of paper. Or perhaps I go out, & spend the afternoon in walking alone over the very desolate Gower cliffs, communing with the cold and the quietness. I call this taking my devils for an airing. This takes me to tea-time. After tea I read or write again, as haphazardly as before, until six-o-clock. I then go to Mumbles (remember the woman of Mumbles Head), a rather nice village, despite its

name, right on the edge of the sea. First I call at the Marine, then the Antelope, and then the Mermaid . . .[6]

Rather self-consciously though this reads – Thomas was, after all, barely nineteen when it was written – in many respects it depicts an existence identical to the louche, 'Bohemian' lifestyle which Thomas adopted in later years. He always rose late. His letters show that hour after hour of his time was given over to reading and then to writing, writing anything in an attempt to ward off the fear that his first collection of *18 Poems* (1934) would also be his last, scribbling feverishly to assuage the terror that he was a one-book poet and written-out by the age of twenty . . . and then sloping off to the pub evening after evening in an attempt to prove to the world and himself that he really, really wasn't. In all essentials the die had been cast at Cwmdonkin Drive.

The only problem was that it was not easy to live the *vie de bohème* in suburban Swansea; there were persistent suggestions from his father that Thomas should get a 'proper' job, and frustratingly few fellow-Bohemians to mark his progress. As he soon realised, writers – and least of all the *real* writers, among whom the unknown teenager already included himself – did not live in Wales. They lived in London, in garrets and flats in Earl's Court and Chelsea or romantic top-floor rooms in Fitzrovia.

The only solution was to move, and Thomas seems to have taken the decision to do so by the end of 1933. His mind was certainly made up by the beginning of 1934. 'I believe I am going to live in London soon,' he wrote to his friend Glyn Jones in March of that year:

> but as, so far at least, no-one has offered me suitable employ-ment, living is rather an ambiguous word. I shall probably manage to exist, and possibly to starve. Until quite recently there has been no need for me to do anything but sit, read and write (I have written a great deal, by the way), but now it is essential that I go out into the bleak and inhospitable world with my erotic manuscripts thrown over my shoulder in a sack. If you know any kind people who want a clean young man with a fairly extensive knowledge of morbid literature, a ready pen and no responsibilities, do let me know. Oh, would the days of literary Patronage were back again![7]

Thomas was over-optimistic in his belief that he would be

moving 'soon'. It was not until November 1934 that he finally cut loose from Cwmdonkin Drive and set off for London. Sharing the expense and the adventure was another friend, the meticulous Swansea-born artist Alfred Janes. Bringing with them little more than 'typewriters, easels, bedclothes, brassières for lady models, & plum-cakes for Nelson's lions – a cherry or two for Eros, a copy of the London Mercury for Nurse Cavell',[8] the two arrived on 10 November and rented what the poet described as 'a large room with a bathroom and sort of inferior wash up adjoining'[9] at 5 Redcliffe Street, SW10.

Then as now, Redcliffe Street was a world away from the cosmopolitan busyness of Fitzrovia, a quiet road midway between Earl's Court and Chelsea whose only previous claim to literary fame is currently marked by a blue plaque a few doors away from No. 5. But few, if any, of its present population of clerks, students and short-stay tenants pay any more attention to the inscription which announces that 'Austin Dobson, 1840–1921, Poet and Essayist' once lived there than they do to the anonymous (and unmarked) front door of No. 5.

For Thomas too, life at Redcliffe Street fell some way short of the ideal. He was unused to the privations and cramped squalor of bedsit-Bohemianism and initially found it

> difficult to concentrate in a room as muddled and messy as ours is nearly all the time; for yards around me I can see nothing but poems, poems, poems, butter, eggs and mashed potatoes mashed among my stories and Janes's canvases. One day we will have to wash up, and then, perhaps, I can really begin to work.[10]

Doubtless, memories of the frankly rather pampered life he had enjoyed at Cwmdonkin Drive contributed to this disillusionment. Preoccupied with his intricately detailed still-lifes, Janes after all had neither the time nor the inclination to tidy up after the young poet and make the endless cups of tea and cocoa which Florence Thomas had provided for her son at all hours of the day or night. Not even the presence of Mervyn Levy, another Swansea artist-friend, in the same house could redeem the situation. 'I think I shall change my digs quite soon,' Thomas was rather dejectedly admitting to his Swansea confidant A. E. ('Bert') Trick little more than a month after his arrival.

But at least Redcliffe Street was a start. He had one foot in London and from then on, although he would never be a Londoner, it always remained his base. Night after night whenever he could afford it – and sometimes when he couldn't – Thomas escaped the cluttered claustrophobia and headed off to Chelsea, to the Anglesey and the Markham Arms in the King's Road, or took the Piccadilly Line underground from Earl's Court to Leicester Square and somehow found his way up through Soho to that same Fitzroy Tavern he had dreamt of back in Swansea.

The particular London into which Dylan Thomas pitched himself in the winter of 1934–5 had little or nothing in common with the stylishly hectic Bohemia of the previous decade. The world of the Gargoyle, the Eiffel Tower and the Café Royal (and, indeed, of the Café de Paris and the Eiffel's other chic and decidedly un-Bohemian successors) was as closed to him as it was to the majority of ordinary, native Londoners. Quite simply, he was still virtually unknown and did not have the private means to establish himself within that affluent *beau monde*, even assuming that he wanted to. (In his unfinished, quasi-autobiographical novel *Adventures in the Skin Trade* Thomas describes how his pseudonymous hero Samuel Bennet attempts to make 'a fine beginning' in London with only £8 10s. in his pocket, although even that paltry sum was 'nearly three pounds more than he had ever seen'.[11])

Thomas's first collection of *18 Poems* sidled off a small press run by David Archer at the Parton Bookshop in December 1934 and acquired for its author a garland of basically favourable reviews in the following few months. But although that was sufficient to launch him as a poet, it was hardly enough to promote him to the elite. It would be some time before this young writer began receiving invitations to luncheons in Belgrave Square, or their equivalent.

In the meantime, he whiled away his days in a more common-place world, in a city closer to the grey and shabby metropolis which forms the background to Patrick Hamilton's trilogy *Twenty Thousand Streets Under the Sky* (1935) and his later 'story of darkest Earl's Court', *Hangover Square*, than to the fantasy Belgravia depicted in the novels of Michael Arlen. Like George Harvey Bone's in *Hangover Square*, Thomas's was a London in which trams and underground trains rather than taxis shuttled him between Kardomah cafés, Lyons' Corner Houses and the numerous cinemas whose performance details filled column after column in the back of the old *News Chronicle*: 'There was "Astoria", Ger.5528. *Racket Busters* (A), 1.35, 4.20, 7.10, 10. *Rich Man, Poor Girl* (U), 12, 2.45, 5.30, 8.20. News, etc. . . . There was "Gaumont", Haymarket. Doors 10.45. Frank Capra's *You Can't Take It With You* (U), 11.20, 1.45, 4.10, 6.40, 9.10. *Don. Duck* (U) . . . There was "New Gallery" *Suez* (U) with Tyrone Power, Loretta Young, Anabella, 12.45, 2.30, 4.45, 7, 9.20. Disney's Col. *Farmyard Symphony* (U) . . .'[12]

Public houses rather than restaurants quite naturally became his meeting-places. He managed to keep the appointment with his friend Trevor Hughes and spent those long-promised few hours drinking with him at the Fitzroy Tavern. Many, many more such hours were to follow, both in and out of Hughes's company, at the Fitzroy and in a wide variety of other establishments. As well as the Anglesey and the Markham Arms, there was also the Plough, a dark, intimate and, in the popular mind, rather 'highbrow' tavern almost opposite the British Museum, whose role as a literary watering-hole the Fitzroy would later eclipse, and an infinite number of other pubs in Kensington, Paddington and the City which were merely convenient, or where the company was conducive and the beer cheap. All proved just as comfortable and every bit as seductive as the Marine, the Antelope and the Mermaid back in Mumbles.

Though he would later come to realise that his spells in London were ultimately destructive – periods of what he called 'capital punishment' – during his first few months there Thomas was in his element. Not unnaturally, in its pubs and out he lived a life far less pure and disciplined than Bert Trick, a fundamentalist Communist, and still less than his parents would have wished. There were certainly one-night stands with women, and equally certainly evenings when too many pints forbade such debauchery. Then, soon after closing time, he might be found shinning up Chelsea lamp-posts or boisterously gate-crashing parties with a group of recently acquired 'friends', quite understandably making the most of an unsupervised life away from home. But, fittingly picaresque though all this seems in retrospect – and it was, after all, the foundation of the legend – it represents only half the story.

It would be an over-simplification to depict the young Thomas as a mere provincial, a boy floundering out of his depth in pints of Bass and the man's world of the great capital. But it is clear that in these early years, and to an extent throughout the rest of his life, he did regard himself as an outsider, someone who was both temperamentally and intellectually at odds with metropolitan sophistication.

Possibly it was no more than a legacy of the middle-class decency with which he had been brought up by his schoolmaster father, but there was undoubtedly a stubborn streak of puritanism – or maybe it was nothing more than prim, suburban correctness – in his make-up. And this was at least as important a part of his character as the more publicised aspects of his behaviour. Even during the Second World War, when he was a scriptwriter at Strand Films in Soho and some degree of artistic flamboyance might have been acceptable, Thomas's dress and attitudes remained surprisingly conservative and proper. The short-story writer Julian Maclaren-Ross, with whom he shared an office, records that he turned up for work on his first day wearing 'a very respectable dark blue suit and a white shirt with a bow tie and celluloid collar, too tight round the neck and giving the effect of someone strapped in the stocks. In these clothes he might have been a young provincial tradesman or perhaps a farmer up in London for the day on business.'[13] Nor did he take kindly to Maclaren-Ross's suggestion that they keep a bottle of whisky in the office.

That inherent contradiction, the vital tension between what he was and what he knew he should be, was always there. His friend and first biographer, Constantine FitzGibbon, notes that (in a phrase from *Under Milk Wood*) Thomas's first two years in London were 'sardined with women' – but then he goes on to quote a most un-legend-like remark made by the poet in February 1936: 'Oh God, I'm so tired of sleeping with women I don't even like.'[14]

Like Arthur Ransome a quarter of a century earlier, Thomas seems to have arrived in London with a precise, indelible and sometimes priggish notion of his place in the scheme of things. Nor is this the only similarity between the two young immigrants for, although there is nothing to suggest that Thomas ever read *Bohemia in London*, on the surface at least, in his youthful 'dented cherub' phase he appears to be almost a reincarnation of its author. Like Ransome, he was within months of his twentieth birthday at the time of his arrival. Like Ransome again, he had not been to university; Thomas's education had stopped when he left school at the age of sixteen (having failed to obtain a school-leaving certificate), but he too was widely, if randomly, read.

Both writers were filled with a second-hand knowledge of Bohemia and determined to become a part of it all. They even ended up in virtually the same place and among very much the same type of people. Shortly after his arrival in Redcliffe Street, Thomas reported to Bert Trick that:

> This is the quarter of the pseudo-artists, of the beards, the naughty expressions of an entirely outmoded period of artistic importance, and of the most boring Bohemian parties I have ever thought possible. Slightly drunk, slightly dirty, slightly wicked, slightly crazed, we repeat our platitudes on Gauguin and Van Gogh as though they were the most original things in the world. There are, of course, scores of better people that I do meet, but these little maggots are my companions for most of the time.[15]

Not only is this strikingly reminiscent of Ransome's description of that 'Chelsea evening' when he first drank opal hush,[16] Redcliffe Street itself is rather less than half a mile from Ransome's original base in Lamont Road or Limerston Street, although this latter coincidence is not particularly significant. In the fifty years before the outbreak of the Second World War the whole of the Earl's Court–Chelsea nexus at the lower end of the King's Road was the traditional base for every type of writer, artist and 'pseudo-artist'.

There, however, the resemblance between Ransome and Thomas ends, for there were profound differences in the attitudes of the two writers to the unfamiliar world they encountered in the capital, differences which provide both an index of how far things had moved in little more than a quarter of a century and an important indication of the way in which Thomas saw himself during this period of his life. Most crucial was the fact that, whereas Ransome was content to remain among the opal-hush-drinking artists, albeit as a tweedy, diffident outsider, Thomas most certainly was not. He had not come to London merely to live the life of a Bohemian; fired by that Swansea puritanism, he had come with a mission. He had come to be a poet.

147

As he saw it, the empty posturing and conscious, deliberate and elaborately striven-for decadence of the pseudo-artists among whom he lived were ends in themselves. It was all just 'slightly wicked' play-acting (and maybe that word 'slightly', four times repeated in his letter to Trick, was what annoyed him most). More seriously, it was 'a menace to art'.[17] Ransome might have enjoyed 'going to that strange room to listen to the songs and tales, and to see the odd parties of poets and painters, actors and actresses and nondescript irregulars who were there almost as regularly as I.'[18] Thomas did not. To him it was all a sham which both angered and revolted him.

There was an almost bardic seriousness underlying his belief in himself as a poet, a seriousness which later led to his spending weeks and sometimes months refining and revising a single lyric. Right from the start, in his own eyes at least, he was that 'Mr Dylan Thomas, the literary critic and poet'. In contrast to the pseudo-artists who ultimately produced nothing, he was a real artist and therefore, and unlike them, licensed to be different.

Ever since his last months in Swansea he had been attempting to perfect this difference, struggling to live the life of a wholly new type of *poète maudit* or, in FitzGibbon's words, playing the role of 'the Rimbaud of Cwmdonkin Drive'. The ground-rules had been sketched out in his letters to Pamela Hansford Johnson; now he was living it for real.

Seen in this context, his drunkenness and not infrequent abusiveness make a kind of sense; they were no more than his equivalent of Oscar Wilde's Aesthetic posturing or Augustus John's equally boozy Bohemianism: trademarks which would get him noticed. Thus at one level he lost no time in boasting to Maclaren-Ross that he used to rub up his nose with his fist in front of a mirror every morning 'until it shone satisfactorily',[19] while on quite another he was assiduously cultivating an image of un-intellectuality if not of downright anti-intellectuality.

That was something he kept up until the end of his life. Even in the immediate post-war years, when his fame was at its height, he seemed genuinely alarmed by the critical attention paid to his every response and retreated into a defensive flippancy during interviews. As late as the early 1950s, when he was asked in New York to explain the meaning of his poem 'Ballad of the Long-legged Bait', he would say only that it was 'a description of a gigantic fuck'. At other times (and like many other creative writers) he point-blank refused to reveal anything at all about his methods of composition. Whatever the location, faced with clever-clever aesthetic chat, his instinctive reaction, followed on at least one occasion, was simply to unbutton and display his penis.

By the early 1950s it had all become routine; Thomas was trapped by the very image he had been at such pains to create. He was once asked why he drank so much, and could only reply: 'Because they expect it of me.'[20] But at the start, for the first ten years or so, it was brilliantly effective. Thomas more than succeeded in his attempt to *épater les bohèmes* and quickly proved himself to be not so much their equal but someone who could be wilder, freer and, when the occasion called for it, even more Bohemian.

Julian Maclaren-Ross wrote his *Memoirs of the Forties* two decades after most of the events he was describing had taken place, but his shock at Thomas's conversation on the evening of that very first day at Strand Films remained unabated. After work the apprentice scriptwriters had repaired to the Café Royal, ostensibly to talk over ideas for a film about the Home Guard. Maclaren-Ross, wearing a white corduroy jacket and carrying the silver-topped malacca cane which later became his trademark, ordered a Scotch. Characteristically, Thomas started on bitter – and then on Maclaren-Ross himself: 'Fucking dandy. Flourishing that stick. Why don't you try to look more sordid. Sordidness, boy, that's the thing.'[21]

Hit with increasing stridency, this note of 'sordidness' would resound through Fitzrovia for the next twenty years. But at the start none of those who first adopted it was consciously aping Thomas (in contrast to the 'beatniks' of the decade following his death who sadly and slavishly were). Many, in fact, were already independently evolving their own, rather similar, images. And, leaving aside questions about the range of his and their talents, the fact that it has come to be associated primarily with Dylan Thomas is largely an accident of chronology. For, in a way which echoed Augustus John's appearance on the scene a third of a century earlier, Thomas arrived in London at precisely the right moment. John, Nina Hamnett and their circle had instigated the break with society – with precisely the type of 'slightly wicked' pseudo-artist whom Thomas instinctively disliked – and adopted the Fitzroy Tavern just as the young Dylan was emerging as an adult and beginning to see himself as a character on a wider stage than that of the Swansea amateur dramatic society on which he had so enthusiastically strutted during his late teens.

One question remains, however. Why did Thomas in particular, and, more generally, the whole school of writers and artists who flocked to the Fitzroy and in later years the nearby Wheatsheaf, take such care to cultivate this image of cultural slobbishness? In part, the downwardly mobile progress of John and that older generation of Bohemians has already provided an answer; but for the writers at least there is also a broader background against which this change should be seen.

Viewed from South Wales, or indeed from anywhere other than the hothouses of literary London, the cultural landscape of the early 1930s must have seemed volcanic. After decades of polite, undemanding Georgian verse, the literary world was still trying to come to grips with W. H. Auden and that group of young writers (chiefly comprising Stephen Spender, Cecil Day-Lewis and Louis MacNeice) then quasi-affectionately known as 'MacSpaunday' or the 'Pylon Poets', after one of Spender's lyrics.[22]

Auden's first published collection, *Poems*, had appeared in 1930 when he was twenty-three. It marked a brilliant début. Critics and readers alike praised what F. R. Leavis (whose seminal study *New Bearings in English Poetry* appeared in 1932) called its – and by extension its author's – 'highly individual sensibility'. Despite one or two hiccups, such public paeans were to continue for the next thirty years. (As late as 1979 Auden's literary executor Edward Mendelson was still glibly describing him as 'the first poet writing in English who felt at home in the twentieth century'.)[23] But in private, opinions seem to have been rather more divided.

Parodies of Auden's (and even T. S. Eliot's) style by the seventeen-year-old Gavin Ewart had begun appearing in *New Verse* as early as 1933 and were to culminate a few years later in his justly celebrated 'Audenesque for an Initiation'. Three years older than Ewart (but still seven younger than Auden) in the early thirties Dylan Thomas too was unabashed by Auden's celebrity, and cast a somewhat colder, more humourless eye on the golden boy of the literary establishment. 'As a Socialist myself, though a very unconventional one,' he wrote in the spring of 1934, taking up Auden's much noticed 'commitment',

> I like to read good propaganda, but the most recent poems of Auden and Day-Lewis seem to me to be neither good poetry nor good propaganda. A good propagandist needs little intellectual appeal; and the emotional appeal in Auden wouldn't raise a corresponding emotion in a tick.

And that was not all. It would be nearly a year before a *Listener* review, which proclaimed his own *18 Poems* to be 'one of the most remarkable volumes of poetry that have appeared during the last few years',[24] and several other favourable notices raised him from obscurity, but Thomas saw no reason to remain in awe of his elders. Modern poets, he went on, singling out Auden in particular, 'have taken their public too much for granted, and have cut out all words that seem to themselves unnecessary, leaving their poems at the end written in an imaginative shorthand.'[25]

Although they are only part of a private letter to another, older, confidant (this time it is Thomas's schoolmaster friend Glyn Jones), in retrospect it is tempting to see these observations as a declaration of war. Beneath the forgivable arrogance of youth, a new type of poet is, surely, jockeying for position. He would himself never write 'good propaganda' – even his wartime filmscripts now seem to say more about Dylan Thomas than they do about life on the home front – nor would he every really concern himself about whether his readers understood him, but that early criticism of Auden amounts to the first sketch of a new aesthetic. With its implicit attack on the cliquishness of the establishment writers who were producing for a private coterie and did seem to be taking the wider public 'too much for granted', it is virtually a call for a broader-based and more democratic literature: a poetry for the people, by the people.

Nor was Thomas the only one expressing unease at the way things were going. As the thirties went on, this half-jealous, half-irritable reaction to the celebrity of the Auden group became one of the common factors linking the very separate talents of the Wheatsheaf writers. It is even apparent in the seemingly laudatory November 1937 'Auden Double Number' of the magazine *New*

Verse. An essay by its editor Geoffrey Grigson (born in 1905, but by his sheer, combative energy always on the side of the new) is ambiguously entitled 'Auden as a Monster'. In contrast, Thomas, whose views are included among 'Sixteen Comments on Auden', is almost fulsome, deprecating only what he called 'the boy bush-ranger' side of Auden.

Giving credit where credit was undoubtedly due, however, did not amount to a *rapprochement*. There would never be much of a consensus between those groups of writers whom Auden and Thomas have come to exemplify for, in life as much as art, they inhabited two entirely different worlds. Throughout his life, Thomas would touch, cadge and even con a variety of individuals out of cash; and his juvenile longing for a return to the days of 'literary Patronage' never left him. He would be seen on occasions at the Café Royal, and, as his fame grew, even at the Eiffel Tower; but he was the precursor of a new breed of Bohemian. He had promise, but no background, no devoted patron, and no private income. He was shabby, coarse and, both in person and in print, not infrequently incoherent.

Although in his later years, and particularly in the decade leading up to his death in 1973, much the same was true of Auden, it was all very different in the mid-thirties. Then, despite their own pose as left-wing 'rebels', it was Auden and his group of public school and predominantly Oxford-educated young writers who were tipped by the ageing mandarins of Bloomsbury as the coming men. More than that, they allowed themselves to be taken up by the literary establishment and, as Stephen Spender records, introduced to a

> civilised world of people who lived in country houses, pleasantly modernised, with walls covered with areas of pale green, egg-shell blue, or pale pink distempering, upon which were hung their paintings and drawings of the modern French school, and a Roger Fry, Vanessa Bell, or Duncan Grant. They had libraries and good food and wine. They discussed few topics outside literature, and they gossiped endlessly and entertainingly about their friends.[26]

For all that they remained a heterogenous collection. There was little other than a shared upper-middle-class background and, despite their left-wing political stance, a certain cultural conservatism bonding the Pylon Poets to each other, and still less which allied them to figures as different as Christopher Isherwood, the novelist and critic John Lehmann and the critic and editor Cyril Connolly. Yet their comparatively easy success on 'the right side of the tracks' (Auden's work was published by Faber and Faber, edited by none other than T. S. Eliot) made them natural allies in the face of the Bohemian invasion. To all of them, even the literary talent of Thomas and his friends (which they were quick to recognise and often to praise) could not quite make up for their personal 'sordidness'. If they were not quite the barbarians at the gate so feared by Leonard Woolf (whose novel of that name was published in 1939), the new generation which had, typically, occupied the pubs on the other side of Tottenham Court Road from the previously safe purlieus of Bloomsbury, still seemed as sophisticated as a rugger club.

Yet, looking back, it is clear that the Bohemians were the men of the hour. Even in the mid-thirties Bloomsbury and all it stood for was in retreat, if not terminal decline. Lytton Strachey had died in January 1932; Roger Fry less than three years later. The Woolfs had long since abandoned Gordon Square and were spending more and more time out of London at Monk's House, their Sussex country home. Clive and Vanessa Bell, the inheritors of the Omega spirit, were already well ensconced at Charleston. Despite Auden, the To Let signs had gone up, not just in quiet Bloosmbury squares, but over a much more valuable piece of real estate. Suddenly, it seemed, there was no longer any focus to London literary culture. Cyril Connolly noted that:

> at that time (the early thirties), poetry seemed to have exhausted itself; Eliot had gone religious, the Georgians moribund; Edith Sitwell appeared to be resting after giving us her *Collected Poems* of 1930 and Geoffrey Grigson had not quite started *New Verse*. *New Signatures, New Writing* – everything *new* but the *New Statesman*, was still in the womb.[27]

The Modernism which had exploded in 1910 with the first Post-Impressionist exhibition at the Grafton Gallery, and went on to inform every aspect of artistic and Bohemian life for a third of a century, was declining into middle age. On the one hand, its original daring had become decorum; the prim, self-satisfied, country-house decorum of late Bloomsbury. On the other it had

153

collapsed into the effete decadence which Thomas had encountered at those arty parties in SW10. In the centre, however, there was little more than 'ou-boum', the panic and emptiness which Mrs Moore had experienced at the Marabar Caves in *A Passage to India*, the novel by that tangential 'Bloomsberry' E. M. Forster which, coincidentally perhaps, achieved wide popularity only in the late 1930s, although it had first appeared in 1924.

Away in County Sligo, even W. B. Yeats had noticed the way things were going. His *Last Poems* show a return to the Irish mythology and folklore which had been so much a part of his first:

> Now I am in the public house and lean upon the wall,
> So come in rags or come in silk, in cloak or country
>   shawl,
> And come with learned lovers or with what men you may,
> For I can put the whole lot down, and all I have to say
> Is fol de rol de rolly O.[28]

Espousing all manner of disreputable causes, everything from Surrealism to support for the Spanish republicans, Dylan Thomas and his tribe did indeed come. Poets as different as Henry Treece, Alex Comfort, Nicholas Moore and Norman MacCaig flocked to the Wheatsheaf which had become *their* public house and quickly discovered that, if they shouted loudly enough, even the far-away Yeats could not put them down. With learned and not-so-learned lovers, they set about proving their Bohemianism by revelling in sordidness and being even more rebellious than their elders. The journalist turned poet Henry Reed (whose poem 'Naming of Parts' became one of the most anthologised of Second World War lyrics) neatly explained why. The Auden group had been rebels, he wrote,

> . . . it was therefore necessary that the newcomers should be rebels also, this time (it was almost a dialectic process) against the politically-conscious, over-intellectual writers of the early 'thirties.[29]

They were, though – these 'newcomers' – hardly more of a cohesive group than their predecessors. None of them managed to sustain their own fittingly combative label of 'Apocalypticism' for very long; none of their work showed the influence of any of

the others' except Thomas's (and all of it showed that). Like the
Auden group again, they held together only because they were
the men of the moment. But while that moment lasted they made
the most of it. For a few brief years the din was tremendous as the
presses roared and all manner of erratically appearing magazines,
broadsheets, periodicals and typographically-amateurish anthologies celebrated their contributors' new freedom from establishment orthodoxy.

They were heady, triumphant years for those who had
plumped for the Fitzroy and the spartan comforts of the other
pubs in and around Charlotte Street rather than the dry-sherry
intellectualism of Bloomsbury. Until everything changed with the
outbreak of war, it really did seem that 'another little drink
wouldn't do us any harm'. There was a distinct feeling of *Bohemia
triumphans* in the air, a euphoria which the poet John Heath-
Stubbs remembers all the more vividly for having only caught its
already-staling end.

And yet . . . in a wider context the Apocalyptics' victory was
rather less apocalyptic than it seemed. The centre was still
holding. Although the old Bloomsbury had, in Quentin Bell's
words 'slowly expired in still glowing fragments' by the mid-
thirties, its legacy lingered on. Normally so alert as a critic in both
the formal essay and the informal aside, Virginia Woolf for
instance does not seem to have ever deigned to mention Dylan
Thomas. The implication is clear enough: for all his posturing in
the Wheatsheaf and on the printed page he was ultimately
unimportant. Life would go on.

And it did. In the course of researching his biography of
Thomas, Paul Ferris unearthed a memorandum written by the
head of the Third Programme at the BBC (long the repository of
those still glowing fragments of post-Bloosmbury culture) as late
as December 1951. Its subject is the fees paid to the poet for his
occasional broadcasts. Thomas must never, it said, be put into the
'celebrity class' along with contributors such as T. S. Eliot, W. H.
Auden, C. Day-Lewis and E. M. Forster. No matter that the poet
Roy Fuller, the producer of many of his post-war broadcasts, found
Thomas 'the best all-round reader of verse that I ever produced
. . . almost Superman' when confronted with a lyric by Blake or
Gerard Manley Hopkins, to the Powers That Be he was not One of
Them. Nor would he ever be given a staff position. How could he

– hadn't he once (but only once) turned up drunk for a live reading, been discovered 'snoring in front of the mike with only twenty seconds left' and then gone on to slur his way through the poem he announced as an 'Ode on Saint Sheshilia's Day?'[30]

For all the bombast, then, Bohemia always remained a tribe within a tribe – as indeed it had to. Even after fifteen years the cultural commissars at the BBC might not have been impressed, but right from the start Thomas and its slurred and slushy rhetoric had been going down very well in the pubs around Rathbone Place – the pubs which, in the intervening years, were to become its natural home.

—— · CHAPTER TEN · ——

A District of the Mind

BY the mid-thirties the members of Boots Circulating Library and many thousands of other middle-brow readers could have been forgiven for thinking they knew all about literary pubs. Eric Linklater's novel *Poet's Pub*, which first appeared in 1929 and went through several impressions in the next few years, seemed to have said all there was to say about them.

Hence, everyone knew that they were quiet, oak-beamed country inns like the fictional Pelican at Downish, which even had its own Elizabethan Hall. True, the 'poets' who found themselves there tended to gather in its American bar sipping light and dark blue cocktails, inevitably called Oxfords and Cambridges, but they were poets, after all. You instinctively knew that there was another bar somewhere, a cosy snug staffed by buxom, apple-cheeked barmaids where the locals quaffed pints of ale in front of a roaring log fire.

Linklater's Pelican was that kind of place. To a far greater extent than even the Cheshire Cheese a quarter of a century previously, as late as 1929 it retained a gentle, Georgian ambience. Under the management of a frustrated poet called Saturday Keith, who had taken it over in a fit of pique after the *Times Literary Supplement* savaged his collection 'February Fill-dyke', it had apparently survived the profound social changes of the 1920s completely unscathed. Not that inconsequential events like the Wall Street Crash, the General Strike and the Great Depression would in any case have disturbed its well-heeled, county and distinctly un-Bohemian regular clientele. Old Colonel Waterhouse had arrived at the Pelican for a rest. Sigismund Telfer, the author of ' "Polyphobion", which was called the "New Poet's Bible" ', and

157

Lady Porlet 'who had never written anything (for she had rheumatic finger-joints) and never read anything (for she had no brains)', were there because they could not have survived anywhere else, except perhaps in the pages of one of Agatha Christie's contemporaneous murder mysteries.

In direct contrast, the real-life Wheatsheaf was an unpretentious boozer towards the top of Rathbone Place in central London. Although an ornamental engraved mirror now hanging behind the bar optimistically boasts that the place was once known as the WHEAT SHEAF [sic] HOTEL, it is extremely unlikely that it ever accommodated guests. One of the smaller pubs in the area, it simply would not have had the room. It was built during the early thirties by the brewing firm of William Younger, but in the then prevalent mock-Tudor style with armorial devices in its leaded windows and a wide street entrance to a rear courtyard which did give it some resemblance to an old coaching inn. The interior, however, was less remarkable. There was no Elizabethan hall and certainly no American bar, just a small public bar at the front and a long narrow saloon beyond.

Indeed, the Wheatsheaf resembled the Pelican far less than it did another fictional establishment. Had it really existed, the Midnight Bell, which gave its name to the opening volumes in Patrick Hamilton's trilogy *Twenty Thousand Streets Under the Sky* (coincidentally also first published in 1929), would have been its near neighbour and rival. Not only was it supposedly located just off the Tottenham Court Road, its clientele and even its décor were strikingly similar to those of the Wheatsheaf. In each pub the saloon bar was

> narrow and about thirty feet in length. On your right was the bar itself, in all its bottly glitter, and on your left was a row of tables set against a comfortable and continuous leather seat which went the whole length of the bar. At the far end the Saloon Bar opened out into the Saloon Lounge. This was a large, square room, filled with a dozen or so small, round, copper-covered tables. Around each table were three or four white wicker armchairs, and on each table there lay a large stone ashtray supplied by a Whisky firm. The walls were lined with a series of prints depicting moustached cavalrymen in a variety of brilliant uniforms; there was a fireplace with a well-provided fire; the floor was of chessboard oil-cloth, broken by an

occasional mat, and the whole atmosphere was spotless, tidy, bright, and a little chilly.[1]

That is Hamilton's depiction of the interior of the Bell, but it could easily have come from the definitive account of life at the Wheatsheaf and in the other, real-life pubs of Fitzrovia which lies at the heart of Julian Maclaren-Ross's fragmentary autobiography *Memoirs of the Forties*. The only material difference is that the walls of the Wheatsheaf's saloon were wood-panelled and lined with squares of various tartans, reflecting the fact that the pub was one of Younger's Scotch Houses. (They only finally disappeared when the pub was refurbished less than a decade ago.) Less obviously, its floor was actually covered with scarlet linoleum and its chairs upholstered in a more practical green cloth.

Like the Bell again, the Wheatsheaf was also little more than what in the 1930s was known as a dive. At the beginning of the decade at least, there would certainly have been no room for a poet, failed or otherwise, behind either of its bars. Indeed it was actually run by a no-nonsense triumvirate comprising of Redvers, who was always known as 'Red' and only wore a suit on Sundays; his unmarried sister Mona (who actually held the licence); and his wife Frances. Nor did poets or poetry figure at all prominently in conversations in either the public bar or the saloon at this period. Even the latter was filled with a crowd whose preoccupations were more prosaic. There were sharp-suited, brilliantined motor dealers with premises in the mews around Great Portland Street. There were tweed-suited 'antique dealers' from that end of the market, where even today they continue to believe that firing a shotgun at a piece of furniture is a cure for woodworm. Once in a while there were also heavily made-up girls and their men-friends who simply had nowhere to go.

Drinking at the same tables as these representatives of the down-at-heel, disreputable and sometimes downright criminal London *demi-monde* – some of whom were wont to disappear at irregular intervals with no warning and for months at a time – there was also a sprinkling of genuine drinkers who used the Wheatsheaf literally because it was their local. Chief amongst these, until her death in about 1950, was the elderly woman known as Mrs Stewart who was believed to live in one of the nearby Victorian tenement blocks.

Always neatly turned out in black silk, she let it be known that in the twenties she had been a member of the Montparnasse circle in Paris, even hinting to Nina Hamnett (who exhibited several drawings and water-colour portraits of her) that she had known both Hemingway and James Joyce. 'Down on her uppers', however, throughout the thirties and forties, Mrs Stewart was as much a part of the Wheatsheaf as the tartan on its walls. Every evening she would arrive shortly after opening time at six o'clock. Both Maclaren-Ross and Dan Davin (in a later and somewhat derivative account) describe how she would then buy the first of the bottles of Guinness she invariably drank and take it to her regular place at the corner of the bar. There, speaking to nobody and abruptly spurning any offers of help, 'like an ant with a straw' she would attempt to solve the crossword puzzles in two evening newspapers, timing her progress with an alarm clock brought for the purpose, oblivious of the changes which were going on around her.

And plenty were. For, despite (or in this case precisely because of) society's reluctance to visit such a place; despite its prostitutes, pimps and loud-voiced con-men; despite Mona's prompt and irrevocable time-calling and even Mrs Stewart herself – despite everything, well before the end of the 1930s the Wheatsheaf had become a real poet's pub and had replaced the Fitzroy Tavern as the headquarters of Bohemia.

With unconscious but none the less perfect symbolism, this realignment was marked by an event which took place in the saloon bar one evening in April 1936. On one of his occasional visits, Augustus John, the patron saint of the Fitzroy, arrived at the Wheatsheaf in the company of a sometime Palladium chorus-girl, Caitlin Macnamara. She had been his model and, briefly, his mistress; but things were changing in more ways than one.

John cannot have thought, when he insisted she meet a young poet of his acquaintance by the name of Dylan Thomas, that he was being anything other than the genial host. In retrospect, however, the introduction can be seen as a sort of fittingly pagan tribute from the Silenus of the old world to the cherubic Taliesin of the new generation. Certainly Thomas seems to have taken it as such for, as Caitlin herself recalled, he immediately claimed droit de seigneur and 'kind of fell all over me. Put his head on my knee and never stopped talking.'[2]

In later years Thomas liked to add that he and Caitlin were in bed together within hours. Whether that is true or not, they were undoubtedly married at the Penzance Registery Office a little over a year later, on 11 July 1937.

It is as difficult to ascertain any concrete reason for the virtual desertion of the Fitzroy as it is to give any precise date for the southerly migration to Rathbone Place which brought it about. Julian Maclaren-Ross ascribes it to nothing more than the fact that 'fashions, and rendezvous for writers and artists, change';[3] but Nina Hamnett is probably nearer the mark in seeing the annexation of the Wheatsheaf as the symptom of a wider development.

Always fiercely loyal to the Fitzroy (though, like John, a frequent visitor to many of its successors) she had later to acknowledge that, ironically enough, its virtual desertion at this time was at least indirectly brought about by her earlier decision to drink there. Remembering the late thirties in *Is She a Lady?*, she admits (not without a dogged trace of pride in the part she, John and Tommy Earp had played in it all) that:

> The neighbourhood of Charlotte and Fitzroy Streets was becoming daily more fashionable. The pubs were becoming so full in the evenings that it was difficult to get a drink at all.
> The news had circulated in the past few years that it was the only quarter of London where drink was cheap and the people amusing.[4]

It was not just the artists, attracted by the chance of encountering Nina or even Augustus John, and the new young hopefuls like Dylan Thomas who were causing the problem. The Fitzroy had long since been invaded by a vastly greater number of lesser mortals, all seeking asylum from the realities of what Auden was to call 'a low dishonest decade' in the collective fantasy that was to become Fitzrovia. There were 'grubby bands of supposed art students' who clogged up even the spacious bar at the tavern while they made 'atrocious' drawings. 'Sometimes rowdy medical students appeared'; and, as if that was not enough,

Daily the neighbourhood became more populated with Generals,

161

Colonels, Majors and Captains. How they got there and where they came from nobody knew. Some had come because the drinks were cheaper than in the West End and, in any case the company was the same: for every day they would find other old acquaintances whom they had either known during the war or before the war.

Now and then one of them caught the other out and he was universally denounced as 'bogus'.

One by one they would appear to mount or descend the social scale.

The better ones returned if they made some money to buy everybody drinks and others would be discovered in distant suburbs in worse pubs.[5]

Inevitably, too, there were the 'tourists', for this emerging new Bohemia and its haunts was proving as inexhaustibly fascinating as any of its predecessors to what it was still (just) possible to call society. In exactly the same way as Nancy Cunard, a new generation had taken to visiting the artists in their dives to round off an evening's entertainment. But, as Andrew Motion unwittingly makes clear in his biography of the composer Constant Lambert, there was little solidarity in these visits. Few if any of the evening-dressed tourists of the thirties would even have gone as far as Nancy in putting pen to paper; most in fact seem to have viewed the prospect of visiting the pubs in much the same way as their ancestors did an afternoon's outing to the Bedlam asylum. Motion quotes the novelist Anthony Powell's wife, Lady Violet, who visited a 'raffish-smart, bohemian, mysterious and extremely smoky' Soho jazz club called the Nest. He goes on: 'After one of her two visits there, Lady Violet said, "I had to have my dress cleaned because it smelt so appalling." '[6]

Powell himself was, at root, equally antipathetic. 'B. 1905; ed. Eton, Balliol Coll, Oxon', it was not unnatural that he should have been, nor that he should have bequeathed his own innate High Toryism to Nicholas Jenkins, the narrator of his twelve-novel sequence *A Dance to the Music of Time*. Though Powell does sneak himself into the pre-war world of the Eiffel Tower in the second part of his four-volume autobiography, volume ten of the *Music of Time* cycle and the last book of his autobiography both contain accounts of one episode which reveals just how far he was from the post-war Fitzrovia.

Late one evening Jenkins/Powell is persuaded by a literary

friend called Bagshaw/Bobby Roberts to forsake his more normal nocturnal round of cocktail parties and visit a pub in order to meet a young novelist called X. Trapnel/Julian Maclaren-Ross. Not in any real sense a Fitzrovian, Bagshaw/Roberts is nevertheless 'so wholeheartedly committed to the mystique of The Pub that no night of his life was complete without a final pint of beer in one of them.' In no such thrall to 'the angelus of closing time' – and even less of a Fitzrovian – Jenkins/Powell is quite obviously out of his element, pompous and prepared for the worst:

> The licensed premises [Bagshaw] chose for the production of Trapnel were in Great Portland Street, dingy, obscure, altogether lacking in outer 'character', possibly a haunt familiar for years for stealthy BBC negotiations . . .[7]

As if the attentions of these society interlopers were not enough, by the late thirties an entirely new breed of tourist had also arrived on the scene. Cruising the crowded pubs of Rathbone Place a few years later in search of that week's girlfriend, Julian Maclaren-Ross was to run into them at their worst:

> Through the fog [of tobacco smoke], at its thickest where the Public Bar was partitioned off, I could distinguish, leaning against the glass and wood, a group of young men swathed in scarves and smoking curved pipes, technically known to me as the Slithy Toves. To my dismay I caught sight of Vicky in their midst. A Tove with even more scarves on than the rest and wearing a polo sweater to boot swayed in front of her, talking nineteen to the dozen. She saw me at the same time and waved wildly, calling out: 'Julian! Come and meet Walter.'
> I looked round for my drink. It had disappeared, probably drunk by Bob. In a very bad temper I forced my way towards Vicky.
> She said: 'Julian, this is Walter. We were up at Cambridge together.'
> In an instant I was shaking hands with every Tove in sight. 'You can't all have been at Cambridge,' I said.
> 'No, I was at Oxford,' a Tove with an orange beard told me. 'I edited a magazine there. Are you an editor?'
> 'God forbid,' I said.
> 'Pity, because if you were, I've some poems here I'd like to show you. D'you know Tambi by any chance?'[8]

Generals, colonels, tourists, students, artists, Toves and writers of all descriptions and every level of competence: the Fitzrovians of the late 1930s had little or nothing in common. Unlike the Aesthetes, say, who behaved, dressed and even spoke in such a way that they were immediately recognisable as a group; unlike even the Edwardian habitués of the Café Royal, who at least had an allegiance to Nicols's premises in common, they were a uniquely disparate tribe. Though individual Fitzrovians were frequently featured in the press during the forties because of books published or pictures painted, it was as individuals. At the time there was no public conception of 'Fitzrovianism', no general caricature of a Fitzrovian, and certainly no rash of plays on the wartime stage satirising his fads and foibles.

Viewed from the inside too, Fitzrovia had none of the neat coherence with which it has been imbued in many later accounts and memoirs. Even during the war – when that Fitzrovianism was ostensibly at its purest, before a certain weary professionalism institutionalised the drunkenness and minimalised the work – it was nothing but a dream-kingdom, a district of the mind which meant cheap drink to some people, good company to others, and true artistic endeavour to only a handful. Sadly, if there ever really was a boozy, licentious principality of pubs and poems and high-falutin talk in the heart of London W1, it flourished for an even briefer period than that during which the Burgundian flag fluttered over London SW1 in the 1948 Ealing comedy *Passport to Pimlico*.

Indeed, it is quite possible that Mrs Stewart and her cronies in the saloon bar of the Wheatsheaf never even noticed it. For, despite the fulsome claims of later writers and biographers who have peopled the Wheatsheaf of the period with figures as varied as the composer and balletomane Constant Lambert, the novelist Malcolm Lowry and even the actor Charles Laughton,[9] seemingly with no more justification than the fact that they all drank and, therefore, ought to have been there, for most of its life Fitzrovia was no more colourful or exciting than any other district in the blacked-out London of the forties. The beer ran out there too, and sometimes even pubs as celebrated as the Wheatsheaf simply failed to open.

Thus it is wholly misleading to suggest that the Fitzrovian forties was a decade in which every night saw Dylan Thomas and

Julian Maclaren-Ross, a tight clique of Apocalyptic poets and other, similarly impecunious members of the new literati clustering amiably round the Wheatsheaf's bar. Equally, although Linklater's poets used to gather very clubbily in the American Bar of the 'Pelican' to discuss old books, it is as wrong to picture the Fitzrovian writers chatting idly to one another while waiting their turn to flick through a copy of that month's issue of *Horizon* as it is to imagine any of them being allowed to help Mrs Stewart with her crosswords.

If for no other reason, it is wrong because there were simply not enough writers to go round. In amongst the generals and colonels – bogus or otherwise – and the students, Toves and tourists, there were never more than about fifty of them. And since it was wartime, most of those were only in London infrequently and for short periods. On the hand-written frontispiece of his *Memoirs of the Forties* Maclaren-Ross in fact lists forty-one. But a sizeable number of them were at best only visitors.[10] No other account of the period, for instance, mentions the presence of Beverly Nichols or, still more improbably, Pablo Picasso, both of whose names Maclaren-Ross included.

Nor, it has to be said, does even his. Maclaren-Ross died before completing much more than a third of the projected book, and thus deprived posterity not only of his reminiscences of Nichols and Picasso but also of any coherent portrait of another of the characters on his list and ostensibly the most unlikely Fitzrovian of them all: 'His Majesty King Juan 1st of Redonda'. But, happily, this particular lacuna can be filled in by judicious reference to other sources.

It appears that when the English laid formal claim to the Leeward Islands, a collection of rocky outcrops some five hundred miles north-west of Trinidad in the West Indies – which they had first settled in the 1630s – Redonda, one of the very smallest, was somehow forgotten. Getting on for two centuries later, this omission was seized upon by the novelist M. P. Shiel who duly laid claim to the tiny territory and had himself crowned King Phillipe I of Redonda by an obliging bishop.

Matters did not end there, however, for Shiel bequeathed his 'kingdom' to the poet John Gawsworth, who thus became the Juan I of Maclaren-Ross's acquaintance and something of a joke in the pubs of Fitzrovia. He published 'state papers' and indulged in the rapidly tiresome habit of creating Redonan dukes and other nobles on the spot and whenever the mood took him. The novelist Laurence Durrell was ennobled one evening, so too was the poet John Heath-Stubbs (though he now admits to having mislaid his letters patent). Roy Campbell was appointed Master of Redondan Horse, and John Waller became a Redondan duke before he inherited his own, more tangible, English baronetcy.

As a joke it soon wore thin, although Gawsworth was not easily deterred. John Heath-Stubbs remembers that, 'decayed by drink', he finally raised virtually everyone he knew to the peerage. And then, shortly before defecting from the ranks of the Fitzrovian irregulars – and after unsuccessfully attempting to sell his title – he nominated a Tottenham Court Road publican as his successor to the throne of Redonda. Theoretically, therefore, the title continues to this day, vested in the name of that long-vanished 'guv'nor', now believed to be living in retirement in the north of England.

Julian would have honed and polished the whole story, cherishing but not necessarily embroidering the details of his own (inevitable, but now unprovable) elevation. It would have been one of the high points of the full *Memoirs of the Forties* which he planned to write.

And the tale of Redonda is not the least of the stories he should have told, the stories which might have linked more of his forty-one names more definitely to the Wheatsheaf or any other of the Fitzrovian pubs. That, ultimately, he did not, however, means that one is regretfully forced to discard his list and rely instead on other evidence for a realistic Who's Who of the heyday of Fitzrovia. And fortunately such evidence exists, for a very credible list of the Wheatsheaf's regular Bohemian clientele is contained in sketch of an evening at the pub which Alan Ross included in his obituary of the painter Robert Colquhoun.[11]

Maclaren-Ross noted that this 'described of course an evening on which absolutely everyone was there'[12] – going on to add that 'such an evening *could* and indeed sometimes did take place' – but Ross's 'everyone' still amounts to just thirteen names. In the course of the one-and-a-half-page essay he mentions Colquhoun and his fellow-artist Robert MacBryde, Maclaren-Ross, W. S. Graham, Fred Urquhart, John Minton, Keith Vaughan, Nina Hamnett, Tambimuttu, the Ceylonese writer Subramaniam, George Barker, Dylan (just 'Dylan') and even – this was the Forties, the

Blitz had drawn people together – John Lehmann, 'eyes narrowing over his cigarette holder [who] would assess the relative pleasures of company against the nuisance value of unwanted or rejected contributors to *New Writing*'. In retrospect that seems a more likely turn-out; but, bearing in mind Maclaren-Ross's important qualification, it is equally easy to imagine nights when Fitzrovia was entirely bereft of any literary presence.

Nor should we continue with the notion of an easy-going, harmonious confraternity of writers cosily clustered at one end of the bar. Such is the received impression, but as Dan Davin remembers,

> when Dylan came into the Wheatsheaf, he always turned right at the door; Julian, who never seemed to arrive in the Wheatsheaf but always to be already there, kept his station and standing at the corner of the bar on the left. And, when bitter ran out at the Wheatsheaf (the pubs were rationed and thirst exceeded supply) and it was necessary to cross to the Marquis, Julian, after a friendly salute to Dylan who might be with Augustus John and Nina Hamnett and sometimes his wife, Caitlin, would proceed to a distant table and his own court.[13]

Even in the early forties, the homely, wholesome Bohemia which Arthur Ransome had so signally failed to find, but which had nevertheless provided a spiritual home for W. B. Yeats, Augustus John and Nina Hamnett, was beginning to fall apart; the centre was not holding, precisely because there was no longer any real centre. (Nor would it be too long before everything collapsed into 'mere anarchy'.) As Davin suggests, even among the writers, evenings at the Wheatsheaf were seldom free from tension and a certain professional jealousy. Groups and sub-groups ceded and withdrew, while poets and editors ebbed in and out of favour. Indeed, one does not have to venture far into the labyrinthine complexities of the literary politics of the time to realise how divided the loyalties and allegiances of the Wheatsheaf's patrons really were.

In the chapter entitled 'Fitzrovia Nights' which lies at the heart of his unfinished *Memoirs of the Forties* – and must now be regarded as the basic vade mecum to wartime Fitzrovia – Julian Maclaren-Ross unsentimentally categorises all his fellow-literary drinkers as Regulars, Wits or Bums.[14] By all accounts he saw himself as a Regular, clinging to his place at the bar and doggedly remaining the centre of any conversation. Certainly all those beyond his immediate circle were summarily dismissed: the Wits, he notes rather acidly, could be 'distinguished by the fact that none was ever heard to say anything witty', while the Bums seem to have been little more than a sub-species of the genus Tove.

It takes no more than a peep round the door of the Wheatsheaf today to understand the major consequence of this rivalry. Even now, with its two bars knocked into one, the place remains too small ever to have accommodated mutually exclusive coteries of writers – to say nothing of its fair share of moth-balled generals, colonels, majors and hangers-on – with any degree of comfort. Small wonder then that those not of Maclaren-Ross's persuasion should have decided to foresake the Wheatsheaf's Scotch ale and wandered off to saloon bars new, effecting as they did so the second great transhumance which was to set Fitzrovia apart from anything which had gone before.

For not only was it more catholic in its membership and more casual than the Bohemia of Fitzroy Square, at its height it was also far more broadly based. The sheer number of people sucked into the post-John void made that inevitable, and accounts for the fact that, although the two dozen or so Fitzrovian Regulars could themselves seldom have drunk in most of them, their acolytes and hangers-on were able to make their presence felt in an extraordinary number of the pubs, clubs and cafés.

By the late thirties refugees from the Wheatsheaf had requisitioned half a dozen nearby pubs. By 1939 (when the outbreak of war halted and fossilised Fitzrovia's physical development) they had established regular visiting rights in as many again, while the first of what would be a large number of professional Fitzrovians were at the same time fostering friendly relationships with the proprietors of a few afternoon drinking-clubs. Thus in 1945 the descendants of Nina Hamnett, Augustus John and Tommy Earp, who had been content with no more than a place at the bar in the Fitzroy, had the freedom of an area which extended southwards from Goodge Street, across Oxford Street and on down through the greater part of Soho, almost as far as the stage doors of the Apollo, the Queen's, the Globe and the nearby, ever-open Windmill Theatre on the north side of Shaftesbury Avenue.

At the time, mastering it was an art which more than filled the odd seven-day or forty-eight-hour leaves of serving writers. Poets like Alan Ross and Roy Fuller, both of whom were in the Navy, and Gavin Ewart, Keith Douglas (d. 1944, Normandy) and Alun Lewis (d. 1944, Burma), among many others who found themselves in the Army, spent precious evenings peering around saloon bar doors on the lookout for a familiar face or two. Re-creating it today, however, is far easier; for a careful examination of the literature of the period and subsequent memoirs yields both names and locations for the key sites and many clues about why they were originally selected.

Not unnaturally disgruntled at the way in which they had been all but squeezed out of the Wheatsheaf, the refugees (whom it is convenient to continue calling the Wits and Bums) inevitably sought new shelter in pubs that were reassuringly close by. Curiously, there was no resurgence of interest in the Markham Arms or any of the other Chelsea pubs which had housed and watered the pseudo-artists of Redcliffe Street since the beginning of the century. For this reason, the true heart of Fitzrovia always remained midway between the Fitzroy Tavern and the Wheatsheaf, at about that point where Charlotte Street, Percy Street, Rathbone Street (originally Upper Rathbone Place) and Rathbone Place itself meet in what could almost be a corner of Montparnasse. Almost all the district's second-league pubs were in fact visible, or no more than a good bread-roll's throw, from the front windows of the old Eiffel Tower. (Broken in every sense of the word by his time there, Rudolf Stulik had sold up in 1938. The restaurant reopened five years later under new management and with a new name, which it still retains: the White Tower.) Indeed, the Marquis of Granby, on the corner of Percy and Rathbone streets, was almost opposite.

Hardly less celebrated than the Wheatsheaf itself, the Marquis was very definitely the next establishment on the mental list of pubs worth a visit which every newcomer carried in his head. Like virtually all the other pubs which the Wits and Bums discovered, it was very quickly visited by Maclaren-Ross and the Regulars and pronounced suitable by them too as a home from home when, for one reason or another, the Wheatsheaf was off-limits.

Even Maclaren-Ross would have had to struggle to make himself heard in the Marquis though; in comparison with the Wheatsheaf, it was a noisy, violent place, more so even than the

Fitzroy. Beginning with a sentence which graphically foreshadows what was to happen to Fitzrovia (and in its final years was to become even more of a way of life at the Fitzroy Tavern), Maclaren-Ross himself effectively sums up its ethos with a couple of anecdotes:

> Gigantic guardsmen went there in search of homosexuals to beat up and rob and, finding none, fought instead each other: one summer evening, in broad daylight, a man was savagely killed by several others in a brawl outside while a crowd gathered on the pavement to watch and was dispersed only by the arrival of a squad from Goodge Street Police Station nearby, by which time the killers had made their getaway in someone else's car. (Entering the Wheatsheaf shortly after this incident, I was surprised to find it empty except for a local tart known as Sister Ann, who told me equably: 'Oh, they've all gone to see the bloke being kicked to death outside the Marquess, [*sic*] dear,' and added that the sound of the thumps was somethink awful.)[15]

Just around the corner, in what is now Rathbone Street, was the Beer House (now rechristened the Newman Arms). Unremarkable in comparison with the Marquis, its one claim to fame was that, as its name suggests, it was among the very last pubs in England with a licence which forbade it to sell spirits. In some quarters, 'it was also known as "the Little Country Pub", with a degree of affection it didn't really deserve'[16] – but in none was it renowned for anything like the licentiousness suggested by the *trompe l'oeil* painting of a *décolletée* woman which now fills a bricked-up window on the top floor.

Slightly further away, at the very top of Rathbone Street, was the Duke of York, run by a proprietor, who announced himself by means of a large placard hanging behind the bar, which read:

> MAJOR 'ALF' KLEIN
> THE PRINCE OF GOOD FELLOWS

It was at its best on Sunday lunchtimes when customers were offered complimentary bowls of hot soup as well as the more normal free cheese. But for the rest of the week it remained predominantly a Bums' pub and was generally eschewed by Maclaren-Ross and the Regulars for precisely that reason.

Tucked down a side street, almost behind the Wheatsheaf, there was also the Bricklayers' Arms, usually referred to in the argot of the time as the 'Burglars' (or more pedantically the 'Burglars' Rest') after a night-time visit by thieves. Their principal target seems to have been the spirits optic, for it was discovered the following morning that they had had to spend a few hours on the premises sleeping off the after-effects of the raid. But in general the Burglars was, in Maclaren-Ross's words, 'a quiet house, useful for a business talk or to take a young woman whom one did not know well', and we may be quite sure that he was not the only Fitzrovian who went there for both reasons.

Quiet too was the Black Horse, back in Rathbone Place. Quiet as the grave, one might almost say; for not only had one of its previous managers drunk himself to death on the premises, the pub itself was distinctly funereal. It must have been one of the last in London to have retained both a strict Ladies bar ('where old dears in dusty black toasted departed husbands in port and lemon') and the schizophrenic attitude that, though it was there to serve drink, the very act of imbibing alcoholic liquor should be made as uncomfortable as possible. There was (and still is) an ornate, moulded ceiling, but Maclaren-Ross records that in the 1940s the pub was furnished with black leather settles, its various bars reached only via a bleak tiled passage.

Redeeming all this, however, was the Horse's location. At the very southern end of Rathbone Place, it was a handy jumping-off point for the late-night raiding parties which regularly left Fitzrovia proper and crossed Oxford Street, bound for the wilder purlieus of Soho. Highly unpopular with landlords on both sides of the divide, there was one very good reason for these otherwise inconvenient and unseemly dashes.

Prior to the local government reorganisation of the 1960s and 1970s, London was a patchwork of separate boroughs, all of which exercised considerable local autonomy, not least in the field of licensing. And this had serious effects on matters as crucial as closing times. The Wheatsheaf, like the Fitzroy Tavern, was the wrong side of a borough boundary which ran down Charlotte Street. On the very fringe of the Borough of Holborn, it had to close at ten-thirty, while a pub like the Marquis of Granby, literally on the other side of the road, and even the Beer House, came under the jurisdiction of the burghers of the Borough of Maryle-bone and, like the pubs and clubs of Soho (which marked the northernmost extent of the City of Westminster), could remain open, and serve alcohol, until eleven o'clock.

In the strict sense of the term Soho was not, of course, Fitzrovia, although at least until the late forties Fitzrovia was frequently thought of as an extension of Soho. Even today some of its survivors still talk fondly of the district as 'North Soho'.[17] Maclaren-Ross did not, and thus, although he was himself well known in many if not all the establishments on the southern side of Oxford Street, his essay on 'Fitzrovia Nights' remains true to its title and ignores them. Nevertheless, it is not difficult to discover their identities and something of their individual styles from other writings, notably his own collection of short stories, *The Nine Men of Soho* (1946).

The first port of call, chiefly because of its relative proximity to Oxford Street, was the Highlander (now the Nellie Dean) in Dean Street. 'We don't drink there until half-past ten,' Tambimuttu told Maclaren-Ross but, as the latter was soon to find out, even if Tambi didn't, other people did. The

> early evening clientele was composed mainly of people younger than myself: the boys in tweed jackets with leather inserts at the elbows, the girls in white blouses and slacks with shoulder-slung bags. These I afterwards found out were university-educated assistant cameramen, sound technicians, secretaries and continuity-girls from various documentary companies affiliated to the Ministry [of Information].[18]

Slithy Toves many of them might have been, there purely because of the Highlander's proximity to their Dean and Wardour Street offices; but – and for similar reasons – the pub was also much frequented by such hardened Fitzrovians as Arthur Calder-Marshall and Dylan Thomas during their periods of enforced wartime cooperation with the British film industry.

Nearer the Shaftesbury Avenue end of Dean Street, where it crosses Old Compton Street, were two further pubs. Both were too far away from the heart of Fitzrovia to be of much use to the licence-beating late-night immigrants. But on the other hand, each was only a few hundred yards from the Café Royal, whose back room continued to offer occasional hospitality throughout this period to those Fitzrovians who could afford its dinners. The Swiss Tavern (now newly reopened as Compton's) was a cavernous place at 53 Old Compton Street. A favourite of Dylan Thomas's – in a complex, punning verse letter he described himself and Tommy Earp as 'two spooned swiss pillars'[19] – the Swiss was also where Maclaren-Ross first ran into the ubiquitous Tambimuttu. And around the corner, at 49 Dean Street was a much smaller establishment, always referred to as the 'French'.

Then officially known as the York Minster, and now as the French House, the French remains the least changed of all the Fitzrovian watering-holes. In the thirties and forties it was managed by, and had been nicknamed in honour of, Victor Berlemont, the first Frenchman to hold a publican's licence in London. Today, unmistakable because of his luxuriant moustache, he still presides over the small bar, smiling benignly down from a photograph. But although the licence has passed to his son Gaston, the small pub continues to recall the years of Victor's incumbency.

On the staircase there still hangs a reproduction of the call 'A Tous les Français' – *La France a perdu une bataille! Mais la France n'a pas perdu la guerre!* – made by Charles de Gaulle from his Quartier-Générale at 4 Carlton Gardens, SW1. The bar walls are still covered with the signed portraits of a vanished generation of jockeys, cyclists, airmen, actresses, revue artistes and, most of all, boxers, handsome but sexless in the health and efficiency poses of the day. One Alexandre Poizat ('Champion de France, 1935–1938') inscribed his 'à Victore Berlemont, avec ma bonne amitié'. Another hailed Berlemont *père* as an 'ami des sportifs'. Elsewhere are displayed the felicitations of a youthful Lena Horne, a ten-by-eight of the music-hall act Moris and Vane – 'regards from The Boys' – and a photograph of Jack Dempsey across which, on 24 May 1926, the champ scrawled in uncertain capitals 'TO VICTOR BERLEMONT WITH BEST WISHES'.

Beneath them all, however, greeting his wine-drinking regulars and keeping a wary eye open for outsiders, these days Gaston – Berlemont *fils*, his moustache as proud and lush as his father's – genially talks down any reference to Fitzrovia. 'Dylan Thomas? He had a farewell party here before he left for America. So did Brendan Behan. Neither of them came back . . .'[20]

Set in the heart of Soho, both the Swiss and the French were ideal lunchtime meeting-places for those bent on an afternoon's drinking in the area's private drinking clubs. Officially, joints such as these were open to their members only, but membership was cheap and easy enough to obtain: anyone's for a few shillings and no questions asked. For that one got the dubious privilege of virtually round-the-clock drinking, throughout the afternoon and long after the more rigorously supervised pubs had closed in the evening. But, private or not, the majority of these clubs remained mere joints. Most had also to offer food or some form of entertainment, usually no more than a pin-ball machine or one-armed bandit, in deference to the terms of their licence; although even that did not stop their continually being visited, raided and occasionally closed down by justifiably suspicious policemen.

Accordingly, many flourished for no more than a matter of months, although one or two lasted long enough to become accepted as important parts of the Fitzrovian and later, more general Soho scene. Chief amongst these was the Caves de France. Although officially a club – Daniel Farson remembers that in the fifties 'a young wrestler with the head of a Greek god' was employed to bar access to non-members[21] – the Caves was for most of its life treated as just another pub.

But it was, of course, a pub in which last orders were never called at lunchtimes. Throughout the afternoons its owner, Mme. Philippe, an ex-soldier called Frank, and Secundo Carnera the barman, kept its 'members', glasses filled from a high bar which ran the length of the dark, narrow room. And, seated at tables and chairs ranged along the opposite wall, under the 'staggeringly bad' paintings of one Baron von Schine, those members kept up a level of wit and conversation which, Farson remembers fondly, 'would rank with that of the Café Royal or the Algonquin in their heyday'. Certainly, something of the Caves's atmosphere seems to have infected Julian Maclaren-Ross, for it was there that, with heavy hints of Robert Louis Stevenson, he was accustomed to adopt a new demonic persona:

'I am Mr Hyde today. You must call me Mr Hyde,' he said. Then he turned to the barman, Secundo Carnera, and called out haughtily, 'Have there been any messages for Mr Hyde?'

'No, Joolian, no. No messages for Meester Hyde so far,' replied Carnera, that most accommodating of men.

It appeared that he became Mr Hyde when he was feeling particularly vengeful or sinister.[22]

Amongst a host of lesser establishments there was the Jubilee, on the upper floors of a building next to the White Tower in Percy Street where the proprietors, in an apparently backward nod to the old Cabaret Club, had engaged Nina Hamnett to cover the walls with murals. There was the Horseshoe Club – Dylan Thomas's 'Wardour-street smithy'[23] – and another called the Byron in Greek Street. Slightly more reputable, there was also the Mandrake Club in Meard (or, as it was always pronounced, *merde*) Street.

The creation of a Russian emigrè called Boris Watson, along with the Caves it was one of the few clubs which seemed to get the Fitzrovian milieu right. Lurking, like so many others from the Cabaret onwards in a basement, its bar was always well stocked and presided over in the final days of Fitzrovia by a barmaid called Ruth, whom Daniel Farson remembers as 'Soho's version of the barmaid at the *Folies Bergère*'. But its continuing success probably had more to do with the character of its proprietor. According to Farson, Boris Watson was 'a large, unkempt man with swivelling, suspicious eyes', but he nevertheless had the knack of giving his customers what they wanted at any specific moment. In a later incarnation he appeared as the *maître d'* at the White Knight, a chess club in the Strand which flourished at the height of the 'beatnik' era, when of course chess clubs were second only to milk bars in popularity with a whole generation of goatee-bearded, duffle-coated Outsiders. Still later, as things got more affluent, Watson surfaced again, this time as the proprietor of a Hampstead restaurant.

Optimistically harking back to the gay society-Bohemianism of the twenties – and preserving something at least of the style of that decade with its rickety lift, mirrored though fast-fading opulence and, until they had to be sold, the two Matisse murals – there was also still the Gargoyle Club with its prominent site on the corner of Meard and Dean streets. Augustus John continued to use it, certainly until the mid-forties; so on a very occasional basis did many more ordinary Bohemians. But for the hungrier, thirstier and indeed poorer Fitzrovians its high membership fee meant that it was usually as far out of reach as it was seemingly out of touch.

More within their means were the cosmopolitan cafés and restaurants which abounded both around Charlotte Street and, in even greater numbers, in Soho. The Chinese and Indian restaurants which are now so much a part of both areas had, like the even more recent rash of fast-food take-aways, still to make their appearance. In Charlotte Street, at l'Étoile, at the café Madame Buhler ran by the side of the old Scala Theatre (an establishment much patronised by Julian Maclaren-Ross) and at the also vanished Schmidt's, the cuisine was European, the *spécialitées de la maison* reflecting the nationality of the individual proprietors. The same was true at Bertorelli's, which even today is still run by a descendant of the four Italian brothers who established it in 1912 and still trading from its original premises at Nos. 19–21, opposite the Fitzroy Tavern. In what is now called a 'Café Italien des Amis du Vin' and has been considerably expanded to include a wine bar, brasserie and restaurant, it was well known in the thirties and forties that a cheap and very basic plate of spaghetti was always available.

Further south, on the corner of Dean and Old Compton streets in Soho proper, was the Café Torino. Over its marbled-topped tables, exiled Spanish anarchists and defeated Republicans idly plotted the overthrow of General Franco in the years following the Spanish Civil War, becoming so much a part of life at Torino's that for a time the café was fondly known as the Madrid. But from eight-thirty in the morning it was also full of native British exiles and outsiders. Mr and Mrs Minella, its Italian proprietors, kept their prices so low, and were even known to offer credit, that Torino's was for many years one of Fitzrovia's favourite haunts.

Much coffee was also drunk at Madame Valerie's patisserie further along Old Compton Street, while Fava's restaurant in Frith Street served cheap(ish) meals, although in the early fifties Daniel Farson only discovered that the 'superb' steak he had eaten there was horse-meat when it was too late to matter.

All in all, it didn't amount to much. North and south of Oxford Street, Fitzrovia was a shabby, tawdry kingdom even then, not much for anyone to be proud of. Yet one man was, and the shabbier and more desperate it became, the more he clung to the irredeemably tarnished glamour of those Fitzrovian nights.

Like the hero of some lesser tale by Dumas or even Anthony Hope, Julian Maclaren-Ross's background was rather less than remarkable. He was born in 1912 at South Norwood, near Croydon in Surrey. He received an unexceptional education in England and France and is first heard of in 1936, married and living the prototypically thirties life of a salesman among the avenues and roadhouses of Sussex. He was then in lodgings in the seaside resort of Bognor, spending his days demonstrating vacuum-cleaners for Hoover and Electrolux, a period of his life he was to recall in his later novel *Of Love and Hunger* (1947). Before long, however, all that folded. He embarked on a new career as a landscape gardener, but with an equal lack of success.

Hitler's invasion of Poland came at precisely the right time, for Maclaren-Ross was conscripted in 1939 and abruptly removed from this world of small-time failure. (Even his marriage had been a short-lived affair which was finally terminated in the divorce court.) In that sense he had what people referred to as a good war. He started writing, or at any rate began to have sketches of Army life published ('A Bit of a Smash' by J. Maclaryn-Ross [sic] appeared in the June 1940 edition of *Horizon*), and was demobbed in 1943 with the beginnings of a reputation; the promise his widely praised collections of short stories *The Stuff to Give the Troops* and *Better than a Kick in the Pants* (which appeared in 1944 and 1945 respectively) appeared to fulfil.

Searching for editors during periods of leave in the years before his demobilisation he also discovered London, and in particular the Wheatsheaf. Indeed, it is hardly too simplistic to say that all the disparate elements of his life only finally came together at this period. Not only was Fitzrovia's undercurrent of shady wheeler-dealing reminiscent of so much of the thirties roadhouse talk of Bognor, moving through it all as a serving soldier and published writer for the first time he had a recognised role in the scheme of things. And, naturally arrogant and self-obsessed, as the years went by he found his talent uniquely well honed to the task of immortalising that milieu of which he discovered, or made, himself the uncrowned prince.

Even today, *The Nine Men of Soho* has an immediacy and

directness which can be ascribed to this new-found confidence. Far more than the majority of the reminiscences of those who were also there, with *Memoirs of the Forties* it remains the best account of the way things were in and around the Charlotte Street of the middle forties. Right from the start of the first story, Maclaren-Ross re-creates in almost journalistic detail the texture of day-to-day life at the time. With the potency of popular music, his fluent references to blackouts, beer shortages, clothing coupons and gin and limes for one-night-only girls summon up a *Dalton's Weekly* world where, in 1940, beer was 6*d*. a pint but a seven-room flat in Percy Street out of the question because of the exorbitant wartime rent of 6 guineas a week.

Yet at the time it was not so much his writings which seemed to sum everything up as his very personality. More so even than Thomas, he was the embodiment of his time, a man whom it would be impossible to imagine living at any other, in the recent past at least. Perhaps the closest resemblance is, as Dan Davin has suggested, to the poet Richard Savage, that spiritual companion of Arthur Ransome who was born in 1697. There are certainly similarities between the two, or at any rate between the public face of Maclaren-Ross and the portrait of Savage which his friend Dr Johnson gives in *The Lives of the English Poets*.

Like Savage, Maclaren-Ross 'did not lose the opportunity which success gave him of setting a high rate on his abilities, but paid due deference to the suffrages of mankind when they were given in his favour, he did not suffer his esteem of himself to depend on others, nor found anything sacred in the voice of the people when they were inclined to censure him'. Nor was that the only trait which the two writers had in common. Maclaren-Ross too was:

> always accustomed to an irregular manner of life, [and] he could not confine himself to any stated hours, or pay any regard to the rules of a family, but would prolong his conversation till midnight, without considering that business might require his friend's application in the morning; and, when he had persuaded himself to retire to bed, was not, without equal difficulty, called up to dinner; it was therefore impossible to pay him any distinction without the entire subversion of all economy . . .

From the more recent past, one more resemblance is worthy of note. In a felicitous phrase, the critic Ronald Bryden once dubbed

Joe Orton 'the Oscar Wilde of Welfare State Gentility'. It was a professional judgement (made after the West End opening of *Loot* in 1966) and largely based on the playwright's style. More loosely applied, however, the description fits Maclaren-Ross every bit as well. Not only did he seem to be consciously emulating Wilde in the insouciant way in which he carried that silver- (or was it gold?-)topped cane, he too evolved a style that was peculiarly his own. Like some literary spiv, he habitually wore dark glasses, a voluminous camel overcoat and a fresh carnation. He took taxis wherever he went, whatever the state of his perpetually precarious finances and, less endearingly, dominated any conversation of which he found himself a part.

His behaviour too was pure Wilde, even if the extravagances of Aestheticism had sometimes to be sacrificed to the make-do-and-mend exigencies of austerity. As Dan Davis records:

> His irregular habits were as regular as being short of money allowed. Midday in the pub till closing time, a late lunch at the Scala restaurant in Charlotte Street, roast beef with as much fat as possible and lashings of horse-radish sauce. A stroll to look at the bookshops in Charing Cross Road and to buy Royalty, his special jumbo-sized American cigarettes. Opening time again at the Wheatsheaf till closing time. A hurried dash to the Highlander which closed half an hour later. Back to the Scala for supper and coffee. At midnight the tube home from Goodge Street . . .[24]

There were even rumours, quite conceivably started by Maclaren-Ross himself, of an exotic background. One such, typical of many, had it that he was the son of 'a magnificent Indian lady (Bengali?); and the obvious source of his male beauty.'[25] But that is, at the very best, unlikely. Even his regular drinking companions make no mention of it; nor – unrepentantly heterosexual as most of them were – do they appear to have noticed his 'male beauty'. The few surviving photographs of him at this period do suggest good looks, but they are the regular, dark-haired, square-jawed good looks of a fighter pilot rather than the retouched, epicene beauty of the matinée idols of the day. However, age did not seem to wither them, nor were they staled by drink like so many of his contemporaries'. They remained with him until his death in 1964: a BBC television documentary made earlier that year (and directed by Anthony Powell's son Tristram), showed the fifty-two-year-old writer looking like nothing so much as an impoverished, suburban Richard Burton.

Despite it all, however, Maclaren-Ross was in the last analysis a tragic figure, for ever a man of the forties long after Fitzrovia and the world beyond had forgotten austerity, all but the most minor forms of rationing and even the Festival of Britain. In this respect it is perhaps appropriate that he is now best remembered as a function of that time. He was, by his own admission, 'a professional writer as opposed to a professional literary man'[26] – and about the last of the line. Gissing and Ransome, G. K. Chesterton and, at the beginning of the century, even Shaw had been proud to call themselves that; but, for a whole variety of reasons, by the end of the forties it was becoming impossible for anyone else to do so, and it has remained that way every since.

For Maclaren-Ross the fifties were in any case little short of a disaster, 'a decade which I could well have done without'. He remarried, had a son, tried to reform, and produced only a stream of generally inferior work, hack literary journalism and the first of the many memoirs and reminiscences which would intermittently preoccupy him for the remainder of his life. He died of a heart attack in 1964.

All of 220 years previously, in a passage towards the end of his *Life of Richard Savage*, Dr Johnson had already written his epitaph. In exactly the same way as Savage, the post-war Julian Maclaren-Ross

> proceeded throughout his life to tread the same steps on the same circle; always applauding his past conduct, or at least forgetting it, to amuse himself with phantoms of happiness which were dancing before him; and wittingly turned his eyes from the light of reason, when it would have discovered the illusion, and shown him, what he never wished to see, his real state.

Michael Arlen: In direct contrast to Gissing, Michael Arlen presents a self-created image of debonair suavity, modelling himself perhaps on Ivor Marlay, the hero of his novel *Piracy*, 'a man with no ties and plenty of money'.

(Above) *Fitzrovia Nights I: The French*: Apparently taken some time before the Second World War, this evocative photograph of the French suggests that, although the pubs are still there, precious little remains of the fabric which the Fitzrovians knew.

Fitzrovia Nights II: The Fitzroy Tavern: Although the Fitzroy Tavern had been largely deserted by the London Bohemian community before 1939, it continued to have its supporters. This photograph appeared in *Picture Post* in 1949, illustrating a feature on the favourite pubs of various celebrities. The Fitzroy was nominated by the journalist Ian Mackay, left. Note too the charity money, still pinned by darts to the ceiling.

Dylan Thomas: An unusually relaxed Dylan Thomas, photographed in 1946 and apparently making the most of a break from the 'capital punishment' of Fitzrovia. But such days were numbered. Within a few years this jaunty youthfulness would be overtaken by the bloated alcoholism of The Legend; within eight Thomas would be dead

Fitzrovia Goes to War: Osbert Lancaster's *Landscape with Figures – III* (originally the frontispiece to the January 1942 edition of *Horizon*) presents a witty and detailed sketch of the effects of war on a cosmopolitan corner of Fitzrovia. The Marquis is open, a couple of Toves are heading for the 'Café Suisse' – but where are the writers?

LANDSCAPE WITH FIGURES—III

OSBERT LANCASTER

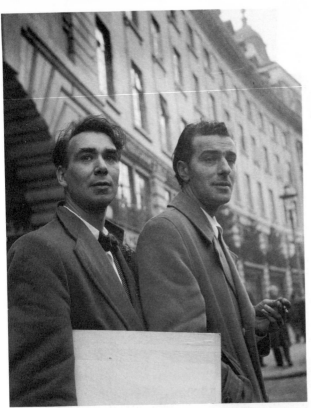

Robert Colquhoun and Robert MacBryde: Characteristically, it is Robert MacBryde (*left*) who carries the canvases as he and 'the great master' Robert Colquhoun emerge from the Café Royal into Regent Street one afternoon in 1951.

The 2i's Coffee-Bar: For Colin Wilson, Colin MacInnes and the other Angry Young Men who created a new Bohemianism in the mid-Fifties, 'coffee-spots, speak-easies and spielers' were the new meeting-places. Soon, visiting cafés like the 2i's became 'the chic-est thing to do amongst the juniors'. It was only old hands like Julian Maclaren-Ross who asked where everyone had gone.

CHAPTER ELEVEN

Whistling in the Blackout

HOWEVER much it may now seem otherwise – and however much he would have liked it to have been that way at the time – despite the favourable notices his stories attracted, Julian Maclaren-Ross's was not the only name with which conversations in the Wheatsheaf and the Burglars were larded in the early forties, when London was (in Robert Hewison's phrase) a city under siege. Others too were dropped, albeit less frequently and with rather less reverence: Henry Moore, John Piper, 'Johnny' Minton, George Barker, Charles Hamblett, Tambimuttu, Fred Urquhart, Roy Campbell, Ruthven Todd, John Waller, Charles Wrey Gardiner, Fred Marnau, Peter Brooke, Derek Stanford, Arthur Calder-Marshall . . .

With the exception of the first three, however, they were largely literary names, for well before 1940 it had become very clear in Bohemia at least that the artistic impetus of the first quarter of the century had long since faltered. Despite the efforts of the Chenil and other galleries, the thirties had seen nothing to compare with the excitement of the Post-Impressionist shows, Sickert's Saturday afternoons and the old Omega Workshops.

Even the International Surrealist Exhibition, which opened in June 1936, had ultimately proved little more than a flash in the pan. Nina Hamnett, of course, was there for the opening, at which Salvador Dali gave a speech from within a diving suit. So too was the painter Cecil Collins, who recalls that the French Surrealist André Breton and his wife were also among the guests. She had 'a piece of steak on her shoulder. The blood was running down to a notice on her back saying "EAT ME". Herbert Read [the art critic] looked round and said: "This is the dawn of a new age." And I remember thinking: No, not a dawn, a sunset . . .'[1]

While the Apocalyptics and virtually everyone else made sure they were seen at the New Burlington Gallery during the later run of the show, Collins's and not Read's became the more typical reaction. For, despite high hopes and an extraordinary range of exhibits, far from galvanising the avant-garde, the exhibition remained something of a cultural sideshow, a social rather than a serious artistic event; a spectacle to be laughed at rather than applauded. (It is, however, unlikely that Dylan Thomas joined in the laughter: his biographers disagree about details, but all of them mention that he might or might not have contracted gonorrhoea from a woman he might or might not have met at the show.)

In retrospect such a reaction appears inevitable. Surrealism was always too alien and, quite literally, too *foreign* an influence ever to have had much appeal to the careful Camden Town and London painters of the thirties. Even the post-Auden writers seem to have found its literary manifestations a mystifying or at any rate unsatisfying cul-de-sac. In 1935 Dylan Thomas had assured Richard Church that he was not 'influenced by such a pernicious experiment'.[2] ('Every line [of my writing] *is* meant to be understood; the reader *is* meant to understand every poem by thinking and feeling about it.') Although the pernicious experiment did excite a small but vocal clique of younger Modernist artists – chiefly comprising Paul Nash, Henry Moore, Edward Burra and Barbara Hepworth who, with others, had banded together as Unit One in the early years of the decade – by 1936 even their enthusiasm was waning.

Nash, Burra and Moore were the only members of the unit to have exhibited in the International Surrealist show. Constructivism, rather than Surrealism, was by then accepted as the new style; and even the *London Bulletin*, which had rather belatedly come out in favour of Surrealism in April 1938 (with issues which ironically resembled nothing so much as copies of the *Blast* of a quarter of a century previously), had summarily abandoned its wayward protégé by the autumn of 1940.

It was hardly a betrayal, more an acceptance of the inevitable. ('The war, when it came,' says Cecil Collins, 'beat the Surrealists at their own game.') And indeed, within half a decade the whole of the British Surrealist movement had been ripped apart by internecine strife, a punchy section wholly devoted to Surrealism in the first edition of the journal *New Road*, which appeared in July 1943, only serving to intensify the arguments. At that time even the once committed Nash and Moore would probably have agreed with Cyril Connolly who noted the following year that, in Britain at least, 'Surrealism, the last international movement in the arts, is now in its decadence . . .'[3] And by then it wasn't just Surrealism.

The competing claims of Constructivism, the Camden Town Group, the London Group, Unit One and many another group and -ism had long since blunted the cutting edge of British art. Roger Fry had died in 1934 and left a vacuum. No single entrepreneur had emerged, and there was no latter-day Ruskin to guide public taste. In the immediate pre-war years the visual arts were indeed as confused as they had been in the pre-John nineties. Had it not been for Hitler, they might well have continued in such a state. But the outbreak of war changed all that, albeit by wreaking even greater havoc. For, no respecter of schools or schisms, in the first instance it threatened to abolish them altogether, since among the all-embracing powers which the Defence of the Realm Act and other enabling legislation had given the State at the outbreak of hostilities, there was a blanket prohibition of any open-air painting that was not expressly sanctioned. Nor was this sanction lightly given: in 1940 the Central Institute for Art and Design reported that 73 per cent of British artists were out of work, an unemployment rate which came second only to that of the theatrical profession in which, the *Spectator* noted in February 1940, some 15,000 (or roughly 83 per cent) of the country's 18,000 actors were then resting whether they liked it or not.

Like the cinemas and theatres of London, however, painting survived, although only by wilfully suppressing its own wilder fringes, the better to aid the common struggle. The stage began doing its bit with shows like Terence Rattigan's RAF drama *Flare Path*; the cinema was producing Noel Coward's *In Which We Serve*, together with *Mrs Miniver* and many another patriotic weepie as well as Laurence Olivier's *Henry V*;[4] and the painters too came up with a suitably small-scale, almost literally back-yard celebration of 'what we are fighting for'.

In many ways the work shown in the early years of the war by members of the universally supported Artists' International

Association was backward-looking and unashamedly nostalgic. The association's exhibitions, such as the one entitled 'For Liberty' (which was given in an air-raid shelter beneath the blitzed John Lewis's department store in Oxford Street) and its smaller shows, usually held in such venues as the Charing Cross Underground Station, featured work which could have been painted at any time in the previous twenty-five years. As late as 1940 Walter Sickert (then a venerable octogenarian) was still being celebrated as the country's greatest living artist. And for several years after his death in January 1942 a very Sickertian social realism remained the order of the day.

Nor were the officially sanctioned war artists doing much better. Selected and paid – out of a special £10,000 Treasury grant – by Sir Kenneth (later Lord) Clark's War Artists Advisory Committee, they found themselves depicting typical English scenes as well as the quotidian realities of life under siege, and adopting a manner which, in the light of all that had gone before, at the time seemed conventional and even polite, so anxious was it not to offend.

The first WAAC show was staged as early as August 1940. Paintings by Paul Nash and Graham Sutherland were hung in one room of the otherwise empty National Gallery in Trafalgar Square. Well before the outbreak of war its permanent collection had been evacuated to a quarry in Wales, and the building had found a new popularity as the venue for Myra Hess's lunchtime piano recitals. But ultimately it was the Recording Britain project, funded by the Pilgrim Trust, which was to bear most fruit. Intended as a national topographical survey, to provide some record of the country's landscape and architectural heritage, it too staged interim shows: a Record of Britain exhibition, which filled a few more of the echoingly empty rooms at the National Gallery in July 1941; and a collection of work by Sutherland, Henry Moore and John Piper, which toured British provincial towns during 1941 and 1942.

Over and above this nostalgic, propagandist function, however, Recording Britain was also important in other ways. Before it was wound up in 1943, it had given employment to a few at least of the hundreds of unemployed artists – Nash, Sutherland, Moore, Piper and Stanley Spencer were just five of the best known – and been instrumental in redefining the terms of British painting.

But that was not generally recognised until after the war. In the

London of 1940 and 1941 the few critics who bravely hailed it and all the other wartime initiatives as the harbingers of a new culture were generally thought to be merely making the best of things. And understandably so, for it was indisputably true that the majority of the capital's brightest young talents had disappeared. Some had been conscripted into the forces, others had simply upped and gone – Ivon Hitchens to 'paint the war out' in Sussex, Barbara Hepworth and Paul Nash to do much the same thing in Cornwall and Oxford respectively. Augustus John and Nina Hamnett were, inevitably, still around; but behind the blacked-out windows of the Wheatsheaf and in the darkened streets of Soho, if it was not already apparent in 1939, as 1940 dawned and the Phoney War gave way to the Blitz, it became increasingly obvious that Fitzrovia was going to fight its war with a pen rather than an austerity sable brush.

The nature of that war, however, had still to be clarified. Even in 1940, nothing was quite as clear-cut as it had been in 1914. When they took their place at the centre of the stage in the first decade of the century, the Fitzroy Square artists had done so with all guns blazing. Even while the country at large was embroiled in the First World War, they were still signalling their arrival with shows and exhibitions and a fusillade of committed manifestos. Sickert and his followers had, in fact, advanced on London *en masse*, for all the world like the disciplined lines of men who had gone over the top at Ypres and the Somme. Along with the Bloomsberries, long before 1918 they had made it plain that they recognised their own worth and considered themselves a central part of 'what we were fighting for'. Indeed, as the smoke cleared, no one seriously doubted that they would be among the inhabitants of the 'land fit for heroes' over which David Lloyd George intended to preside.

In direct contrast, a quarter of a century later Julian Maclaren-Ross, Dylan Thomas and the Apocalyptics took the city by stealth. Even before the more acrid smoke of the Blitz had dissipated, it was clear that, despite their ambition, despite all the name-dropping, London's new Bohemians were seeking an altogether more modest role for themselves. In both contemporary accounts and later memoirs they resemble nothing so much as guerrilla fighters. Their deeds, their work, was noticed, but they themselves come over only as elusive figures in the blacked-out night.

Nowhere is this more apparent than in the frontispiece of the special January 1942 'Irish Number' of *Horizon*. A cartoon by Osbert Lancaster with the title 'Landscape with Figures – III', it has nothing whatever to do with the articles by Patrick Kavanagh and Séan O'Fáolain, among others, and even the reproductions of paintings by Jack Yeats which fill the bulk of magazine. Instead, it depicts a busy street corner.

There are, of course, no street names; all manner of signposts had long since disappeared from the face of Britain, giving a concrete reality to the grey anonymity which characterised national life for the duration and for many years after. Nevertheless, the cartoon celebrates a recognisable urban landscape. There is a pub clearly labelled the Marquis of Granby; and although architecturally it is fundamentally different from the real Marquis in Rathbone Street and there are other, topographical factors which prevent its being taken as a strictly literal depiction of life at the top of Rathbone Place, it is virtually certain that Lancaster intended 'Landscape with Figures – III' to be seen as a fantasy portrayal of wartime Fitzrovia.

Indeed it was, and as a sturdy, propagandist portrayal at that, for it depicts a community totally committed to the war effort. The foreground overflows with uniformed figures of all descriptions. There is a sailor, and a member of the Auxiliary Fire Service. A military policeman in a tin hat is being lectured by a soldier, while a French officer disappears into the Café Suisse.

More particularly, Lancaster's cartoon seems to be saying that if London could take it, as the official slogan rather bullishly claimed, then so could Fitzrovia. For although a placard advertising that evening's *Star* bears the stark message 'ITALIAN CRUISER SUNK – OFFICIAL' and a barrage balloon is tethered in the distance; although a bomb has ripped an ugly hole in a four-storey terrace, and a newly-hung sign points the way to the nearest public air-raid shelter, all the shops are open. The firm of Stromboli continues to offer *coiffeur des dames* and permanent waving; next door, despite rationing and restrictions, Il Re de Napoli, the oddly named Café Suisse, manages to keep a menu in its window, while a *Librarie* still boasts a range of *Journeaux français* and even *Deutsche Zeitungen*.

Most characteristically of all, perhaps, the Marquis is still in business, its public bar doors thrown wide, its landlord caught in the very act of pulling a pint. Elsewhere, a taxi plies for hire, and an estate agent's board continues to advertise the availability of a 'two-roomed maisonette, to let on short lease'.

It is business as usual too for the ordinary, non-combatant inhabitants of the district. Just outside the Marquis, a well-dressed, Mrs Stewart-like regular belches discreetly into her hanky. A little way off, the sailor has been accosted by a couple of tarts. Blowsy and bored, another stares down from a first-floor window. A beggar is playing the violin beneath a sign showing the way to the nearest air-raid shelter. A dog cocks its leg against a lamp-post. A cat chews a fish bone in the gutter. Spivs with cigars and extravagantly tailored double-breasted suits scuttle about rather furtively, and outside the café there are even a couple of unscarved but unmistakable Toves.

Amongst all the cosmopolitan busyness, however, one element of the Fitzrovian scene is conspicuous only by its absence. Nowhere in the drawing is there any reference to the writers for whom the area is now best remembered. Ostensibly this is odd, since not only was Osbert Lancaster at least touristically familiar with the predominantly literary Fitzrovian world as it had evolved by the end of the thirties, he was also working for a consciously literary magazine which regularly published writing by many of Fitzrovia's leading names. By the beginning of 1942 regular readers of *Horizon* would have been familiar with the work of both Julian Maclaren-Ross and Dylan Thomas.

Why, therefore, is there no cane-carrying dandy jostling his way through the uniformed crowds, and no thick-lipped, curly-haired poet-figure propping up the bar in the Marquis? For that matter, why is the sailor chatting up two very obvious prostitutes and not offering to escort a flagging Nina Hamnett at least as far as her door?

It is difficult to provide any conclusive answer. Tentatively, however, one might suggest that, just as a close reading of accounts of the Bohemianism of Rathbone Place has already shown that its permanent population of writers was perhaps smaller than has previously been imagined, Lancaster left them out because, even in 1942, they were not among the typical, indigenous inhabitants of the area.

On a superficial, sociological level this was undoubtedly true. However many 6*d.* pints Thomas, Maclaren-Ross and the other Fitzrovians drank at the Wheatsheaf or the Marquis of Granby, it is wholly fanciful to imagine their having any real effect upon the economic life of the district. Even during the war, that was dictated by the success of establishments like the Napoli café and Stromboli's hairdressing salon far more than it ever was by the takings at the Marquis. None of the mainstream publishers and magazines on which the writers depended for both work and recognition was actually based in Fitzrovia. Nina Hamnett did continue to occupy a succession of rooms in and around Percy Street, but she was about the only one of the Bohemians who could accurately have been described as a local. Julian Maclaren-Ross commuted home by tube every evening, while Dylan Thomas generally found his increasingly temporary London bases a taxi or bus-ride away in the bedsitter land of west London.

Ironically, however, the years between the appearance of that January 1942 issue of *Horizon* and the present have provided another, retrospective answer to the question. For now it is possible to see the invisibility of the Fitzrovians in Lancaster's drawing as a reflection of their more general invisibility at the time. Now, quite apart from its piquantly nostalgic flavour, Lancaster's cartoon has come to embody one of the fundamental barriers to any analysis of the Bohemianism of the period: the fact that, at the very time when it was ostensibly at its height, the literary community of Fitzrovia was already talking itself down.

More than anyone else, Julian Maclaren-Ross was to blame for this. For although each effusively catalogues every pub visited, every story told and seemingly every pint downed in the blacked-out, rationed Fitzrovia of the forties, neither *The Nine Men of Soho* nor his later *Memoirs of the Forties* has anything much to say about the work he or anyone else was doing at the time. Even had they been available (and they were, of course, not published until the mid-sixties), the *Memoirs* would have told the aspiring young writer of the period less about how to survive than, a third of a century earlier, *Bohemia in London* had told his predecessors about the business of being a Bohemian. In that book Arthur Ransome had at least included chapters on 'Old and New Fleet Street' and 'Some Newspapers and Magazines', even if they did consist of descriptions of Fleet Street pubs and 'the gay way with reviewing' rather than hard-nosed hints about lineage, double-spacing copy, and fees.

In contrast, Maclaren-Ross concentrates on off-duty moments: the action of many of the stories in *The Nine Men of Soho* characteristically occurs between the end of the working day and the moment when the pubs closed at ten-thirty or eleven. Instead of a more orthodox literary autobiography's chapter by chapter accounts of the genesis of its author's writings, the *Memoirs* too peddle the seductive notion that, even by the late thirties, the actual business of creative writing had become an irksome chore, sometimes tiresomely necessary but always secondary to the real business of boozing.

Not unnaturally this was later to prove immensely attractive. Like lazy journalists resorting to the cuttings, later writers merely squatted in Maclaren-Ross's territory and made his highly personal district of the mind into the sought-after and ultimately concrete Fitzrovia of popular myth. But in doing so, like lazy journalists again, they short-changed the story. Even the *Memoirs'* odd hints about reviews written or scripts commissioned were ruthlessly edited out, the better to foster Fitzrovia's posthumous image of drunken dilettanteism.

By restoring them to their proper place, however, and by adding in other details from both published and unpublished sources, a completely different picture emerges. For although the outbreak of war curtailed and threatened to extinguish the visual arts totally, it had quite the opposite effect on literature. Despite the impression we now get from Maclaren-Ross and all manner of more recent writers, well before Osbert Lancaster's 'Landscape' appeared, work, of a kind, had become a central preoccupation for the Bohemians of London.

In the middle of September 1939 Dylan Thomas complained that 'my little money-sources – (apart from anything else) – are diminishing or dying. Soon there will not be a single paper paying inadequately for serious stories and poems.'[5] He did have a point. He was writing less than a fortnight after Neville Chamberlain's declaration of war, and already the literary world had begun to batten down the hatches. His plight and that of many freelance writers like him was very serious. The papers and magazines which had previously been delighted to employ them now had other worries. Far from concerning themselves with the 'inadequate' rates they were offering, by the end of 1939 they all seemed to be preoccupied with their own chances of survival, for the war was to have a grievous effect on them too.

None was completely immune; indeed, so general was the suffering that the history of one can effectively stand for all. Before the war the influential, weekly *New Statesman and Nation* appeared in a generous two-column format. Its first issue in 1939 (7 January) had run to thirty-six pages. After the outbreak of war, although its cover price remained 6*d.*, its history was one of decline. It greeted 1940 with a New Year issue (6 January) of twenty-eight pages, and twelve months later (4 January 1941) it was down to twenty-four. Bowing to the by then urgent need to conserve paper, from 3 January 1942 it abandoned its two-column page and adopted a cramped but more economic three-column layout. Allied to a further contraction in its coverage – and a consequent reduction in the number of writers it commissioned – this meant that from that particular issue on the paper filled just sixteen pages.

Graphic though they are, Thomas's complaint and the very literal contraction of newspapers and magazines such as the *New Statesman* still tell only half the story. For in 1939 and 1940 the Fitzrovian *libraries* and station bookstalls in every part of the country stocked a substantially larger number of magazines and periodicals which were prepared to treat literature – and poetry in particular – seriously and in more depth than they do today. This had nothing at all to do with the interests or altruism of their managers; rather, it was a reflection of the fact that a significantly greater number of titles was available.

And, as Robert Hewison has demonstrated,[6] even in 1943 and 1944 the bookstalls continued to display what now seems a bewilderingly wide array of broadly literary magazines and periodicals. Leaving aside titles intended for servicemen based overseas, the latest issues of such generally read weeklies as the *New Statesman*, the *Listener* and the *Times Literary Supplement* lay next to copies of *Augury, Bolero, Bugle Blast*, the *Caseg Broadsheet*, the *Cherwell, Eight Oxford Poets, Horizon, John O'London's Weekly, Kingdom Come, Life and Letters Today*, the *New English Weekly, New Writing and Daylight*, the *News Chronicle, Now*, the *Oxford Press*

Anthology, Our Time, the *Partisan Review, Penguin New Writing, Periscope, Poems of This War*, the venerable *Poetry (Chicago)* which had once employed Ezra Pound, *Poetry Folio, Poetry (London), Poetry Quarterly, Poetry Review, Programme, Resurgam Younger Poets, Salvo for the USSR, Selected Writing*, the *Spectator, Some Poems in Wartime, Time and Tide* and *Tribune* on the shelves.

Some periodicals had indeed gone out of business in the early months of the war (Hewison identifies the *Cornhill Magazine, Fact*, the *London Mercury, New Stories, New Verse, Purpose, Seven, Twentieth-Century Verse* and, most poignantly, the *Writers' Own Magazine*), but it is fair to say that the new writer, and particularly the new poet, in the forties would have stood at least as much of a chance of seeing his work in print and responsibly reviewed as the young or even the promising young writer of today. Obviously there was not a wholly free market. Not everyone would have wanted, or even been eligible for, inclusion or review in all the three dozen titles Hewison lists. There was a vast gulf fixed between *Horizon, Penguin New Writing* or *Poetry (London)* and, say, the *Caseg Broadsheet* and *Salvo for the USSR*, while the book pages of even some of the most well-established papers indulged prejudices every bit as strong as those on display in the preceding editorial columns. Anthony Cronin recalls[7] that when he took over from John Betjeman as the literary editor of *Time and Tide* it was irreverently known as the 'Sapphic's Graphic' on account of the strongly feminist line insisted on by its founder editor, Lady Rhondda.

In general, however, the magazines were after anything they could get, anything which would satisfy a national craving for literature which began to make itself felt in 1941. The previous year Cyril Connolly had unhappily acknowledged as much in his prefatory note to the first edition of *Horizon*:

> A magazine should be the reflection of its time, and one that ceases to reflect this should come to an end. The moment we live in is archaic, conservative and irresponsible, for the war is separating culture from life and driving it back on itself, the impetus given by Left Wing politics is for the time exhausted, and however much we should like to have a paper that was revolutionary in opinions or original in technique, it is impossible to do so when there is a certain suspension of judgement and creative activity. *The aim of* Horizon *is to give to writers a place to*

191

express themselves, and to readers the best writing we can obtain. Our
standards are aesthetic, and our politics are in abeyance.[8]

If Connolly was characteristically pessimistic about this 'irres-
ponsibility' and the suspension of literary judgement, others took
a more sanguine view. Behind the cries of those such as Thomas,
who were understandably worried by the effect they believed the
war would have on their careers, there were still those in Soho, in
both its northern and southern *départements*, who carried on
regardless. David Archer's Parton Street bookshop and press,
which originally issued Thomas's *18 Poems*, had closed in 1936
(although a new shop was open in the early 1950s in larger
premises in Dean Street). But not even the war could extinguish its
detached, gentlemanly spirit in which, war or no war, culture was
always separated from life. Another of Archer's discoveries, the
poet George Baker, recalled that the old Parton Street shop had
been 'full of bright marvellous books – lovely colours – the whole
place looked charming – rather like spring flowers'; and something
of that brightness and colour continued to pervade the literary and
poetic scene long after Archer himself had gone into temporary
exile in Glasgow.

For Bohemia, this separation of culture from life was ultimately
to prove fatal. It might even have been behind the fact that, as the
newspapers of the time were not slow to mention, unlike the First
World War, Hitler's War did not seem to be producing any real
war poets. On another level it can be seen as nurturing a different
type of war poet – on the one hand servicemen for whom the
specifics of battle were an irrelevance, and on the other a whole
phalanx of home-front writers for whom the war was a distraction
rather than an inspiration.

There were even more of these than there were publications
ready and waiting to publish their work. Many servicemen
discovered that the war had spawned its own literary sub-culture.
Fame of a kind came to many through the pages of such
commercial anthologies as *Wartime Harvest* (1942), *Poems from the
Forces* (1941) *More Poems from the Forces* (1943) and *Air Force Poetry*
(1944) as well as collections gathered by the Army Education
Corps and later published in a series of volumes called *Poems from
the Desert* (1944), *Poems from Italy* (1945) and *Poems from India*
(1946).

But, *pace* Thomas, the 'sordid' home-front poets – though they might have found themselves ostensibly spending the duration as fire-watchers, air-raid wardens, documentary film-makers or officers in the Auxiliary Fire Service – were also having their say. Their particular brand of what, in the broadest possible sense, one might term non-combatant war poetry, was ironically perhaps the finest flowering of their loud and gaudy Bohemianism.

Through a combination of circumstances, it is convenient to take Ruthven Todd as their exemplar. Born in 1914, and thus an exact contemporary of Dylan Thomas (though he was to outlive him by fifteen years), his first slim volume, *Proems*, had been published by a small press in the summer of 1938. A more comprehensive collection, *Over the Mountain*, followed in March 1939 under the more prestigious George Harrap imprint. In effect another one-book poet, Todd was, therefore, in a similar position to Thomas at the outbreak of war later that year. But without Thomas's doubts and self-pity, he faced the uncertain future with an apparent equanimity.

Julian Maclaren-Ross records that he first encountered him in the Highlander, shortly after his own demobilisation, 'and for once I can even be certain of the date: the Thursday before August Bank Holiday, 1943'. He was introduced by Arthur Calder-Marshall and his wife Ara, and having misheard Todd's name, spent an uncomfortable few minutes watching 'a febrile young man' whom he believed to be 'the Reverend Todd' making short work of a pint of bitter ('unlike Calder-Marshall it took him two goes'). Soon, however, the misunderstanding was ironed out:

Before I could apologize for having misheard the introduction, Ruthven Todd who now held a whisky in his hand said: 'I didn't get your name either. Who the hell are you anyway?'

I gave my name, Todd's whisky went down the wrong way, and when I'd patted him on the back he spluttered: 'But I discovered you!'

'I thought Cyril Connolly discovered me.'

'On my recommendation,' Todd shouted, his voice still pitched to carry above a crowd though the pub had now emptied around us. 'I happened to be in the *Horizon* office when your stuff came to light, I sat down and read it through, then I went straight to Connolly and told him: "Whatever else you do you've got to publish this bloke." And he did.'[9]

Nor, it soon became apparent, was that easy familiarity with Cyril Connolly Todd's only literary credential. Characteristically accepting his suggestion that they 'push off' for food and more beer at his flat in Mecklenburgh Square, Maclaren-Ross found himself in the company of someone perfectly at home in the unique and peculiar London literary world of the mid-forties:

> Famous names erupted rapidly from him, he seemed on friendly terms with every conceivable literary figure and, although still in his late twenties, to be himself a figure more of the Thirties than of the Forties. Now he worked as a bookseller's assistant at Zwemmers in the Charing Cross Road but also acted as a consultant on antique furniture to a Feature film company which paid him a small retainer, and had a new novel coming out from Wrey Gardiner who owned the Grey Walls Press.[10]

Although Maclaren-Ross does not mention it, Todd was also still writing. Uniquely, we now know about virtually every piece of literary work he undertook during the Second World War (and indeed throughout the whole of his career) because of the patient detective work of his son Christopher.[11] Thus it is possible to counter-balance Thomas's rather jaundiced view of the period with the actual experience of another Bohemian, and one who was by no means among the most celebrated of his time.

The comparison is highly instructive. Not only did some of Ruthven Todd's early poetry continue to appear throughout the war in collections ranging from Anne Ridler's *Little Book of Modern Verse* (1941) to the Penguin *Anthology of War Poetry* (1942), new work by him was also published in a very wide range of magazines and periodicals and a host of more modest anthologies with names such as *Calendar*, *Poetry in Wartime* and *Sailing Tomorrow's Seas*. Nor was that all. Christopher Todd's researches have revealed that, despite the time he must have spent at Zwemmer's bookshop, and despite a period at least of excessively heavy drinking – a friend noted during the war that 'he has given up drinking his two and a half bottles of whisky a day'[12] – by any standard his father was an extraordinarily prolific author during the war years.

In the period between Britain's declaration of war and VE Day (3 September 1939–8 May 1945) he published no less than nine books, and wrote a dozen or more reviews and articles for a range of magazines including the *Listener*, the *Times Literary Supplement* and *Horizon*. It should be added that many of those books were limited editions (sometimes running to no more than twenty-five copies and containing even fewer pages) but in amongst them were three major titles. *The Laughing Mulatto*, a full-length biography of Alexandre Dumas, was published in 1940; Todd's edition of Alexander Gilchrist's 1863 *Life of William Blake* took its place as volume number 971 in J. M. Dent's Everyman Library two years later; and *The Lost Traveller*, the 'new novel' to which Maclaren-Ross referred, appeared under the Grey Walls Press imprint in January 1944.

Noticeably, however, all three seem to turn their backs on the war; and in this context Maclaren-Ross's impression that Ruthven Todd was 'a figure more of the Thirties than of the Forties' has an extra resonance. For much of what has come to be seen as most typical of the literary Bohemianism of the forties also displays this blindness to contemporary events and embodies a curiously anachronistic, Archeresque detachment. It was as if a certain section of it had unilaterally decided to counter the bellicosity of popular sentiment and prove wrong all those who, like the *Daily Express*, were loudly proclaiming that 'There is no such thing as culture in wartime' by resurrecting something very close to the Art for Art's Sake credo of the nineties.

Thus in 1939 what can almost be seen as the *Yellow Book* (or, more accurately, the first of a series of *Yellow Books*) of the forties was being planned in the otherwise impeccably correct town of Billericay in Essex. For after its editor, E. M. Channing-Benton's conscription in the autumn of that year, the magazine *Poetry Quarterly*, which he had founded as *Poetry Studies* in 1933 and in the equally implausible location of Dawlish in Devon, had been taken over by his deputy, Charles Wrey Gardiner.

In Channing-Renton's hands *Poetry Studies* had been a polite, somewhat dowdy and wholly provincial periodical. Its pre-war subscription list of just 200 was headed by the name of Lord Alfred Douglas, although for a short time at least it did also include Dylan Thomas's. It was little short of a vanity publication and plainly had no future in the age of Auden and *New Writing*. But even the change of name did not seem to have affected anything below the masthead, for the first two issues of *Poetry Quarterly* (which appeared in the spring and summer of 1939) were just as bad. Indeed, had it not been for Wrey Gardiner's arrival as editor that autumn, the whole enterprise would now be long forgotten.

Gardiner, however, had big plans. Within two years, operating first from an office-cum-bookshop in the front room of Grey Walls, his mother's large house in High Street, Billericay, and only later from an office at Vernon Place in central London, he transformed 'PQ' into one of the major outlets for the new generation of poets.[13]

Issue after issue, and volume after volume produced by the Grey Walls Press, which Gardiner established in the winter of 1940, contained material by those whom Gardiner, like David Archer, seemed to have a special gift for promoting to greatness. Hardly any, as Derek Stanford has pointed out, was over the age of thirty-five; while even fewer had any sort of reputation. That was about all they had in common. It was not until Gardiner decided that he needed an assistant and gave the job to the young poet Alex Comfort (then a medical student at a nearby hospital where, incidentally, a future GWP poet, Denise Levertoff was also training as a nurse) that PQ and, more particularly, the Grey Walls Press side of things swung in the direction of the Apocalyptics.

That it did, however, was to prove crucial. Many of the group proper were to make their first appearance in *Lyra*, an anthology edited by Comfort and Robert Graecen which appeared in 1942, but before the end of the war a sort of watered-down Apocalypticism had become the house style and the Grey Walls Press list had expanded to include full volumes by Comfort, Nicholas Moore, Fred Marnau and Ruthven Todd among others.

Fittingly too, its editorial stance was also consciously literary, as is revealed by a glance at the contents of another periodical which Gardiner launched during the war. *New Road*, financially backed in the first instance by Nicholas Moore and ultimately run by Fred Marnau, first appeared in 1943 and was to continue for a further four years. It was intended as nothing less than an annual index of 'new directions in European art and letters'; however, its early volumes (which have recently been reprinted) can now be seen as some of the most eloquent testaments to Fitzrovia's wartime doctrine of pure culture.

No matter that 'about Wrey swarmed the young wartime poets: servicemen and women, civilians, nurses and land girls, conscientious objectors, those in reserved occupations or classified as unfit.'[14] No matter that John (later Sir John) Waller was one of his poets and that half a decade earlier, in December 1939, he had refereed a swim across the River Isis by the undergraduate editors of Oxford University's two magazines *Kingdom Come* and *Cherwell* in an attempt to counter stories of the effeteness of the younger generation which were circulating even then. By 1944 *New Road* too had perfected that air of Olympian detachment from day-to-day reality.

That year's 279-page hardback issue included a substantial selection of poems by Alex Comfort and John Bayliss (its co-editors), Christopher Fry, Laurence Durrell, James Kirkup, Norman MacCraig, Nicholas Moore, Stephen Spender, Dylan Thomas, Ruthven Todd, Vernon Watkins and Charles Wrey Gardiner himself. There was also an introduction outlining the editors' principles. For although the book had begun with Derek Stanford's worried 'essay on modern art and society' and Alex Comfort's own musings on 'Art and Social Responsibility', when it came to the choice of poetry, the editors seemed perfectly happy to employ wholly different criteria:

> None of the poems which we have included were [*sic*] written with one eye on the rifle and the other on the public. The following selection represents a section of English literary work which we have felt to deserve reissue in a permanent binding.[15]

Perhaps by now we should not be surprised. For if the hitherto obscure wartime career of Ruthven Todd and the parallel but now largely forgotten development of both *Poetry Quarterly* and *New Road* were symptomatic of the time, and if Charles Wrey Gardiner is only now beginning to emerge as its *éminence grise*, the more widely known exploits of another of its 'characters' also boil down to little more than a plaintive, petulant whistling in the blackout.

Do you know Tambi by any chance? . . .

It was not entirely surprising that the Slithy Tove singled out 'Tambi' for special mention – and not, say, Cyril Connolly or even Charles Wrey Gardiner – when he discovered that Julian Maclaren-Ross was a writer. For 'Tambi', more formally J. Meary Tambimuttu, had personal qualities which transcended even his position as a director of the now defunct publishing firm of Nicholson and

Watson and the editor of their magazine *Poetry (London)*. Something of them at least comes over in Maclaren-Ross's own description of one of their first meetings.

Tambi merely approached him one evening at the Swiss and asked whether he had a book to sell:

> 'I'm not a bookseller,' I said.
>   Tambi said: 'No no, I mean a book you have written yourself. I am empowered by my principals to offer a one-hundred pounds advance.'
>   'Sorry,' I said.
>   Tambi said: 'One hundred and fifty.'
>   'Not possible,' I said.
>   He said: 'Two hundred. That is the top.'
>   I said: 'We're not in the bazaar.'
>   Tambi's prehensile pink tongue darted out like a chameleon's from between his purple puckered lips. 'I will have to consult Nick and Wat,' he said, 'before I can go higher.'
>   When I explained that I was already under contract to Cape, he said: 'A pity. My imprint would give an added lustre to your work.'[16]

Egregious is the word most often used to describe Tambimuttu, for the Sri Lankan-born Indian was like nothing that London had ever seen before. (Beside him even his fellow-countryman, the short-story writer Subramaniam paled into insignificance.) He was dirty, occasionally dishonest and frequently untrustworthy. Professionally he was unreliable and totally disorganised. He would borrow money on the flimsiest of pretexts and never return it. He would pick fights and then retreat into bruised bewilderment when his opponent retaliated, usually with a clenched fist but sometimes more imaginatively, as when the Indian writer Mulk Raj Anand emptied the contents of an ash-tray into his beer during another evening at the Swiss. He was rumoured to sleep in a Turkish bath during the winter because he could not stand the cold. He was, as he told everyone, a prince in his own country. He would be fêted whenever he chose to return; 'gold-dust would be smeared upon the meat . . .'

Yet somehow he never did, preferring to remain in London where, by 1939, he was universally known as Tambi. He liked to boast of his friendship with T. S. Eliot (adding, rather improbably, that the famously reticent Eliot was 'really a wild man, like me!').

He had cheek or *chutzpa* rather than real charm, and one talent which excused everything else: he was an inspired and universally respected editor.

He had established *Poetry (London)* in 1939, christening it, according to one story at least, out of admiration for the august and by then venerable *Poetry (Chicago)*. Whether that is true or not, the journal's subsequent success was largely due to his own extraordinary flair. It was widely believed at the time that he never actually read the submissions that reached him but relied instead upon instinct and the feel of the paper on which they were written. Certainly he was no intellectual. He had not been to university, he admitted to Julian Maclaren-Ross; but of course he 'could have a degree conferred, Honorary you know. From Oxford, I know many professors there.' Indeed, his own literary creations amounted to a slim and undistinguished volume of verse, entitled *Out of This War* and inevitably one of the first volumes issued by Poetry (London) Books, and a 'jazz musical comedy' which had apparently been performed at the Regal Theatre, Colombo some time prior to his arrival in London in 1937. All in all, his style of editorship has accurately been described as one 'in which eccentricity was always cheek by jowl with near chaos.'

Although 'Nick and Wat' provided him with an office in Manchester Square, he preferred to do most of his business in the Hog in the Pound public house in South Molton Street – a venue he seems to have made peculiarly his own – or on extended fraternal visits to the Wheatsheaf and the Swiss. Poems bulged from his pockets or were lost altogether. Wrey Gardiner used to tell the story of how he had been summoned to Tambi's flat to read a 'first-rate' new poem by Dylan Thomas. But when he arrived the precious manuscript had disappeared. Only after a frantic search was it discovered – floating in a chamber-pot beneath Tambi's bed . . .

The wonder was not that *Poetry (London)* appeared at all, for it often didn't. Originally advertised as a bi-monthly, just ten issues appeared between its launch in 1939 and the end of the war in 1945. The real wonder was the calibre of the writers and illustrators whom Tambi coaxed, cajoled or instinctively knew would contribute, despite the fact that deadlines came and went, payments were at best long delayed and, when an edition did finally see the light of day, more than one contributor found himself billed for what he had eaten and drunk at the launch party.

It is not an exaggeration to claim that every poet of any note in the early 1940s was sooner or later represented, for Tambi's tastes were catholic to say the least. If a poem of Walter de la Mare's took his fancy, it was included, cheek by jowl with work by Kathleen Raine, George Barker or David Gascoyne. Much the same rule applied to the illustrations he commissioned; indeed, looked at today *Poetry (London)* (which has also recently been reprinted) is as accurate an index of the coming names in the visual arts as it is of those in literature. Henry Moore, Graham Sutherland, Ceri Richards and Mervyn Peake are all represented.

Behind it all, however, there is still the same emptiness. Although the specific other-wordliness of *Poetry (London)* sprang largely from the character of Tambimuttu himself, something in its sheer eclecticism echoed the uncertainties of wartime Fitzrovia. Tambi himself, of course, came through it all unscathed. He continued to edit *Poetry (London)* until 1947 when he decamped to New York and tried to start all over again. But *Poetry (London) – New York* was even less successful than the old *Poetry (London)* he had left behind. Both closed within a couple of years. Unabashed, Tambi moved on to other ventures. In 1979 he launched a *Poetry (London)/Apple Magazine* after an unlikely merger with the Beatles. But that too was a failure. At the time of his death in June 1983, he was working with Mrs Indira Gandhi on plans for an Indian Arts Council in Great Britain.

Even more than Julian Maclaren-Ross perhaps, both Tambi and *Poetry (London)* were the products of their times, and their times were the late 1930s. For as his *Times* obituary put it: 'Poetry (London) always seemed an unlikely survivor of the austere economic climate of the Forties.'[17] Much the same could have been said of Tambi. He too never really moved on from the gentlemanly, casual and unknowingly doomed Bohemia in which he had first cut his teeth.

The tragedy was that he was not alone. For when the Prime Minister, Neville Chamberlain, addressed the nation on the morning of Sunday, 3 September 1939 from the Cabinet Room at 10 Downing Street, and announced Britain's declaration of war on Germany, he also pronounced what amounted to a death sentence on Bohemia. Few, if any, of its denizens took it as such at the time; to them it would have been unthinkable. But within no more than a matter of months the truth had begun to dawn. Inevitably, the war was going to have a cathartic effect on every aspect of British society. It was not something from which any group or individual was able to opt out. The Bohemians, however, tried their best to do just that, and sadly went on whistling long after their tune had been drowned by the noise of exoloding bombs.

CHAPTER TWELVE

Te Palinure Petens

STRUCTURALLY, Fitzrovia suffered less in the Blitz and the sporadic, but none the less destructive, bombing which followed than many other parts of London. Madame Buhler's café on the corner of the Scala Theatre in Charlotte Street was destroyed in 1942; but by that time all the paraphernalia of life on the home front, which is such an integral part of Osbert Lancaster's *Horizon* cartoon, had brought the day-to-day realities of wartime life to Rathbone Place in the same way that it had to every other part of the capital.

Shortages – 'Yes, we have no bananas!' – were as apparent in London W1 as they were everywhere else. Snoek, powdered egg and in all probability the wholesome but unappetising Woolton pie were as large a part of its diet as they were of any other section of the community's. More crucially perhaps, there were times when the pubs did not open until seven o'clock, or even later: inevitably it was Julian Maclaren-Ross who recorded that, because of a beer shortage, there was an especially fraught period during which the Burglars remained closed until eight.

If all this gave wartime in Fitzrovia something of the character of a perpetual Sunday afternoon, it should also have had the effect of establishing some form of solidarity between its inhabitants and more ordinary Londoners. By and large, however, it did not. Although the title at least of Dylan Thomas's poem 'A Refusal to Mourn, the Death by Fire, of a Child in London' suggests an angry defiance akin to Mrs Miniver's, as we have seen, the overwhelming majority of the work produced by his contemporaries virtually ignores the reality by which they were surrounded and by which they were ultimately to be destroyed.

Hardly more than two miles away, for instance, something like 500 people had been killed by a German air-raid, targeted on the East End and the nearby London Docks, during the night of 7 September 1940, a raid which was later seen as marking the beginning of the Blitz proper. And things were to become a lot worse before they showed any signs of getting better. Nine months after that opening salvo, on 10 May 1941, a single night raid killed another 1,436 Londoners and injured 1,792 more. Buildings, including the chamber of the House of Commons, were destroyed throughout an area which extended in an easterly direction from Chelsea as far as the Thames marshes. Although the rubble continued to smoulder for the next eleven days, even that failed to disturb the Bohemians' self-centred complacency.

Many, indeed, seemed to treat the Blitz as an inconvenient, external writer's block. They grudgingly relegated to the bottom drawer plans for the Great Novel (plans which in all probability they had been discussing in the Wheatsheaf since the mid-thirties) and instead began keeping diaries into which they poured their futile anger at the unfairness of it all. Thus, while even Stephen Spender was noting in the autumn of 1939 that, 'I feel so shattered that I cannot write at all', George Orwell was fulminating at 'the impossibility of writing books with this nightmare going on'.

At that time, the real nightmare was only just beginning, even though some hint of what was to come might have been discerned through the cracks which were even then beginning to open up in the fabric of society. The Blitz put considerable strains on what had previously been considered the innately British, and therefore somehow inexhaustible, qualities of fair play and the quiet acceptance of one's lot. It was conveniently overlooked in the popular mythology of the time, but as night raid followed night raid, social tensions began to run high. Revolution was never seriously contemplated; although at the height of the bombing the Communist Member of Parliament Philip Piratin did lead a group of homeless East Enders up the Strand in a rather half-hearted march on the Savoy.

Not for the first time, London was exhibiting something of its own version of the old Disraelian spectre of the Two Nations. Consensus was fast disappearing in the face of perceived inequality, and nowhere was that inequality more marked than in the basic matter of the provision of air-raid shelters.

For a year and more after the autumn of 1940 these became the nightly refuge for hundreds of thousands of civilians in London and England's other metropolitan centres. Hastily constructed brick and corrugated steel Andersons (named after the then Minister for Home Security, Sir John Anderson) offered a measure of semi-subterranean security in suburban back gardens. In the inner cities, steel tables with flap-down, wire-mesh sides, dubbed 'Morrisons' after Home Secretary Herbert Morrison, became the centrepiece of many a ground-floor kitchen, while brick-built communal shelters appeared on numerous street corners.

Although they were at first officially forbidden as places of public refuge, London's Underground stations rapidly upstaged all these and came to symbolise the capital's plucky, public defiance. It is estimated that between 100,000 and 200,000 Londoners regularly used them, crowding onto their platforms every evening, well before the last train had left, in search of a cramped, proletarian security. 'In the infernos of the Underground the poor wretches take up their positions for the night's sleep at 4 o'clock in the afternoon. The winter must surely bring epidemics of flu, even typhoid,' Cecil Beaton noted in his diary in October 1940.[1]

Miraculously, it didn't; but only because the authorities, who had no alternative but to accept the Underground's nocturnal occupation as a popular *fait accompli*, were forced to do all they could to ameliorate conditions. As and when they became available, bunk beds, chemical lavatories and even libraries were provided. In some shelters the London County Council offered regular evening classes. In others East Enders were treated to concert parties organised by both the Council for the Encouragement of Music and the Arts (CEMA, a direct ancestor of today's Arts Council) and the Entertainments National Service Association (ENSA).

Such delights, however, were little more than temporary diversions from the filth and degradation which were the more enduring realities of life in the tube shelters. The official photographs which Bill Brandt took of East End shelters in 1940 and Henry Moore's well-known drawings give some idea of the general conditions, but the scribbled notes beneath a preliminary drawing on one page of Moore's sketch-book are perhaps more illustrative of their fundamental squalor:

Te Palinure Petens

TILBURY SHELTER

Figures showing faces lit up – rest of bodies in silhouette.
Figures lying against platform with great bales of paper above also making beds.
Perambulators with bundles.
Dramatic, dismal lit, masses of reclining figures fading to perspective point – scribbles and scratches, chaotic foreground. Chains hanging from old crane.
Sick woman in bathchair. Bearded Jews blanketed sleeping in deck chairs.
Lascars Tunnel (bundles of old clothes that are people).
Bunks with women feeding children.
Dark wet settings (entrance to Tilbury).
Men with shawls to keep off draughts, women wearing handkerchiefs on heads.
Muck & rubbish and chaotic untidiness around.[2]

Not surprisingly perhaps, it all had an effect on those, generally more fortunately placed, Londoners who arrived at the tube stations in the mornings, bound for desks in banks, offices or ministries. Even today, after nearly half a century, they can still recall the scenes and even more vividly the *smell* which assailed them as they stepped out of their trains at Bank, Piccadilly Circus and Leicester Square.

But if life was nasty and brutish for those who had no option but to file down to the shelters every evening, conditions in the subterranean refuges available to those members of society who opted – or were, more rarely, constrained by their hush-hush or reserved occupations – to remain in central London, were very different.

Until it received a direct hit in March 1941, the Café de Paris, which had opened in the basement of the Rialto Cinema in December 1940, offered a pampered few the chance to forget all about the war and wallow in an otherwise vanished luxury. There was always a band playing in its elegant, *belle époque* salon – which had been modelled on designs for the ballroom of the *Titanic* with what now seems an overweening arrogance – and although it was virtually unobtainable everywhere else, for those who could afford it, there was always champagne too.

Ultimately safer, the Savoy, the Grosvenor House, the steel-framed Dorchester in Park Lane and many other luxury hotels also converted their basements into air-raid shelters at the beginning of hostilities, as they were legally obliged to. At the Dorchester they made over the Turkish Bath for the duration; and there, noted Cecil Beaton who was among those who 'beetled off' to Park Lane at the first sign of trouble, 'the noise outside is drowned with wine, music and company . . . Cabinet ministers and their self-consciously respectable wives; hatchet-jawed, iron-grey brigadiers; calf-like airmen off duty; tarts on duty; actresses (also), *déclassé* society people, cheap musicians and motor-car agents.'[3]

But, like lesser establishments and restaurants throughout the country, even the Dorchester had also to abide by a whole series of government regulations concerning prices and services. It found itself, for instance, prohibited from charging more than a maximum of 5s. (25p.) for restaurant meals, although it managed to maintain standards by adding an obligatory 7/6d. (37½p.) cover charge, and then a further half-crown (12½p.) to the bills of all those who ventured onto the dance floor. No one complained, for with the demise of the Café de Paris, the Dorchester rapidly became a home from home for London's wartime society.

Nancy Cunard's mother Maud, by then long since self-recreated as the demanding hostess Lady Emerald, had returned from America in the autumn of 1941 and installed herself there,

> in two rooms that are overfilled with outsize Buhl and ormolu furniture left over from her more spacious existence. Here she shows complete disregard for the deafening guns firing below her in the park, and pooh-poohs the danger of bombs.[4]

Maybe her 'complete disregard' was just that, no more than an aristocratic hauteur, although Cecil Beaton goes on to add that, 'it was acutely embarrassing sometimes to hear her complaints about the inevitable frozen and ersatz foods to the waiter in charge of her dinner party.'

Maybe it was no more than the fact that all the superfluous furniture blocked her view. But whatever the reason, it is clear from both this and other accounts that Emerald Cunard retained a blindness to the privations of more ordinary, native Londoners which would have been clearly visible from the windows of her suite. No socialist himself, even John Lehmann was later to recall that:

[Emerald's] great house in Grosvenor Square, setting of the parties of her heyday, had become a melancholy, deserted casualty of the blitz. In her Dorchester suite she began again to entertain, sometimes to tea and cocktail parties, but mainly to dinner parties, keeping up the spirit and tone of an already vanished epoch with astonishing courage, attack and verve, although in her late sixties and giving the impression of great physical fragility.

She was of slight build, with exquisite fingers and legs, advantages which were set off by the always impeccable elegance of her dress and the ropes of pearls and the diamonds which even at that time of almost ostentatious austerity she showed no sign of foreswearing.[5]

Nor was she by any means alone in this blindness. They might not have had the style of Emerald or even her rival hostess Margot Asquith (who was also sitting out the Blitz in a hotel and was once heard to remark: 'Now I am without a maid I have to ask the liftmen at the Savoy to get me out of my dress'), but the erstwhile Bohemians back in Fitzrovia seemed once again to be doing their best to emulate 'their lonely betters'. The phrase comes from a later poem by W. H. Auden ('Let them leave language to their lonely betters . . .'), but the image is entirely right.

For brief moments we glimpse them, as if through swirling clouds of smoke and brick dust: Nina Hamnett, Julian Maclaren-Ross and the others, going about their war. *Boom!* Just for an instant, there's Nina, drunk, in bed in the arms of a sailor – since the mid-thirties she had openly indulged a passion for boxers and the rougher kind of naval rating – cackling at her own good luck: 'We'll have to give coupons for them next winter!'[6]

Boom! – *ou-boum* – and once again the clouds part, revealing a different room, and Julian Maclaren-Ross. The year – 1944: 'the light was switched on in my bedroom and [the writer, Peter] Brooke stood over me stark naked, shouting: "Wakey, wakey, rise and shine. It's past four in the afternoon and I could eat a horse. I could eat fried cat."

'I said, perhaps a little crossly: "Better ring up the Ritz and find out if they've any," and Brooke forwith seized the phone: "That the Ritz? Put me on to the restaurant please. Restaurant? This is Colonel Sebastian Moran speaking. Have you any fried cat on the menu for tonight? What, no fried cat? Damn it sir what's England coming to I'd like to know. *No fried cat* indeed." '[7]

Caught somewhere between the two worlds of wartime London, in a bombed and rubble-strewn reality which should have been the new territory of Fitzrovia, one man at least tried to face up to the future.

Damn it, sir, what's England coming to, I'd like to know . . .

Squat, even ugly, he scarcely glanced at the way in which once bright terraces now resembled rows of broken teeth, hardly realised that buildings and churches which had once been familiar landmarks on his way to work no longer existed, so preoccupied was he by issues of a wider significance:

> As I waddle along in thick black overcoat and dark suit with a leather brief-case under my arm, I smile to think how this costume officially disguises the wild and storm-tossed figure of Palinurus; who knows that a poet is masquerading here as a whey-faced bureaucrat?[8]

Leaving aside the possibility of non-combatant guilt, there was no overriding reason why a poet like Cyril Connolly, the founder-editor of *Horizon*, should have had to indulge in such masquerading. Real poets like Dylan Thomas did not; and anyway the streets of wartime London were dark, and its citizens overburdened with problems of more fundamental importance. But such jejune play-acting was not only central to Connolly's very existence, on a broader, more basic level it also dramatised the predicament facing the whole literary community.

Throughout the war, questions about the function of a writer at such a time and the very nature of what they – 'We' – were fighting for were endlessly debated in the columns of the *New Statesman* and the *Times Literary Supplement*. But it was Connolly, writing as Palinurus, who was to cut through the ponderous sophistry of the periodicals and move the discussion onto an altogether higher plane.

He was never in any sense a real Fitzrovian, and still less a Bohemian; Eton educated, he was, rather, an example of precisely that type of professional literary man which Julian Maclaren-Ross was not. As such he was pivotally influential in the intellectual and cultural history of the forties as an arbiter of taste and a valued, if occasional, provider of work; but his importance to us today hinges on his self-appointed role as Palinurus, the conscience of the age.

He first assumed it in 1944 when he published *The Unquiet Grave*, a book which attracted considerable attention, and, indeed, something of a cult following in the weeks and months after its appearance. In large measure this was due to its pseudonymity. The title page merely proclaimed it to be 'A Word Cycle by Palinurus' (although the inclusion of passages like that quoted above meant that the real identity of its author was soon guessed, at least within the literary world). But the problems it raised did not end there. Trying to ascertain who-dunnit was critical sport second only to attempts at guessing the intentions of Whoever It Was in adopting that particular pseudonym. Palinurus was hardly a household name, but reference to encyclopedias of classical literature soon established him as a minor character in books V and VI of Virgil's *Aeneid*. Why, though, was the author of what seemed to be the diary of an Angst-filled year hiding his true identity behind that of the pilot of Aeneas's ship, a luckless individual who falls into the sea, escapes drowning when he is washed up on the shore of Italy, but is then murdered and his body left unburied by savage natives?

The theories were legion and their validity or otherwise in no way helped by the signed introduction which Connolly provided for a revised edition of the book which appeared in 1945. For in that he described *The Unquiet Grave*, ostensibly an account of the aftermath of a failed love-affair – 'a signal of distress from one human being to another' – as 'a war book'. There, not for the only time, he was being disingenuous. He had written a war book, although not in the same way as, say, the Poet Laureate John Masefield had when he wrote his Dunkirk epic 'The Nine Days' Wonder.' *The Unquiet Grave* does not celebrate 'little ships' and Spitfires, nor does it ever concern itself with blackouts, rationing, the Blitz and all the other privations suffered by those on the Home Front. It is a war book only in the sense that it is the story of a man at war with himself.

It is not bombs that Palinurus/Connolly is dodging, but the world in which he finds himself, a world he can describe only as 'a kind of Black Hole of Calcutta, where we are all milling about in darkness and slime'.[9] Innately predisposed to morbid pessimism, he flounders about in it for a year, convinced, after the break-up of the affair, of his own worthlessness. Only a matter of days before his fortieth birthday, he notes that he had dreamed that:

gin, whisky, sloth, fear, guilt, tobacco, had been appointed my inquilines; alcohol sloshed about within, while tendrils of melon and vine spread out from ear to nostril. My mind was a worn gramophone record, my true self was such a shadow as to seem non-existent and all this had taken place in the last three years.[10]

Over the same period many others had, of course, found shrapnel and bullets appointed their own, even less welcome 'inquilines'; and this decadent self-indulgence is a weakness of *The Unquiet Grave*. None the less it does not prohibit or even lessen the validity of Connolly's private unease, for the soi-disant pilot of the ship of literature felt himself to be negotiating waters as dangerous as any faced by the Atlantic convoys.

Even in 1942 and 1943 he was still privately debating the ideas which had fired his previous volume, *Enemies of Promise* (1938). In the opening pages of that he had admitted to 'one ambition – to write a book that will hold good for ten years afterwards'.[11] But then he had idly contemplated the notion from a position of what lesser mortals could have been forgiven for seeing as privileged ease. By 1943 that pose, if not the enquiry, had been overtaken by events. The Palinurus of *The Unquiet Grave* is still exercised by the idea of writing a masterpiece – 'He would like to have written *Les Fleurs du Mal* or the *Saison en Enfer* without being Rimbaud or Baudelaire, that is without undergoing their mental suffering and without being diseased and poor'[12] – but he is no longer at all sure of how to go about doing it. (Indeed, it has subsequently become a critical commonplace to point out that the nearest Connolly himself ever got to writing that masterpiece was *The Unquiet Grave*, a ludicrously ill-timed 'luxury liner run aground in the fog of war'[13] about his inability to do so.)

It was not that he had changed in the intervening five years. Rather, it was the world which had altered; we had all become engulfed by that 'darkness and slime'. Palinurus, indeed, had slipped from his perch into the ocean, and was there being tugged and buffeted by the currents and an undertow over which he had no control. This is the central theme of the book, and essentially the concept which underlay all the journalistic pontifications on the writer's role. Ironically too, it is the point at which creativity deserts Connolly. Spacing it from the surrounding text and setting it in upper case, he relies on a fragment of Virgil to make his point[14]:

TE PALINURE PETENS, TIBI SOMNIA TRISTIA
PORTANS INSONTI

['Looking for you, Palinurus, bringing you sad visions which you have not deserved.']

Palinurus was not the only one being hunted. Nor was Cyril Connolly the only one to see sad visions as he sat behind his desk at the *Horizon* office in Lansdowne Crescent, WC1. For even if the Bohemians affected to ignore them, well before 1944 they were beginning to crowd in upon some of the greatest names on the London literary scene.

The anxious calm of what later became known as the Phoney War or *Sitzkrieg* had been disrupted by the banging of the literary establishment's biggest drums. More than one took what was an essentially self-interested line, suggesting that we might just as well forget about Hitler since a national neglect of literature would itself bring about the end of Civilisation As We – or in this case, They – Knew It. The publisher Stanley Unwin even persuaded J. B. Priestley, A. P. Herbert and Sir Hugh Walpole to join a Committee for the Defence of Books.

Within little more than a year, however, the mood had changed dramatically. Whether it was because of the enforced idleness which filled so many hours for those on active service and so many blacked-out evenings for those at home, or whether it was a symptom of a deeper spiritual hunger, an unprecedented enthusiasm for reading and a concomitant demand for literature began to be noticed in the middle years of the war.

Tragically, however, they came at precisely the time when publishers were least able to meet them, for the industry was then at a lower ebb than at any period this century. On just one night (29 December 1940) fire bombs dropped by wave after wave of German Heinkels and Dorniers had fallen on the London premises of Longman, Collins, Eyre and Spottiswoode, Hutchinson and many smaller firms, destroying some 5 million books. The vast majority were, of course, the publishers' back-stocks and not war-books at all, but it made no difference. Paper rationing meant that it was impossible to reprint even new titles. In September 1939 it had been announced that firms would be allowed to buy only 60 per cent of the amount of paper they had used in the year ending 31 August 1939. By the end of 1941 that figure had been cut to just 37½ per cent. Consequently, the number of titles which appeared dropped as every year went by: in 1939 there had been 14,094; by 1945 there were fewer than half the number, and many of those were only cheaply reprinted classics . . .

Despite the difficulties, though, well before the end of the Blitz the publishing industry was back in business, doing its bit as best it could. The drum-banging died down, manuscripts were rescued from the shelves and the presses started to roll again. For publishers, booksellers and librarians at least, the scare was over; but for many writers it was only just beginning.

Holed up in the 'Ivory Shelter' into which he had crawled at the outbreak of hostilities, the cosmopolitan Cyril Connolly had noted in the final months of 1939 that, 'as human beings artists are less free now than they have ever been; it is difficult for them to make money and impossible for them to leave the country.' For many of those artists even that was pitching things a little high; they were less concerned with notions of freedom and foreign exile than with the very basic business of getting work done at all. And by and large, of course, these were the hacks and jobbing freelances of Bohemia who had published slim volumes and just about managed to scrape precarious, pen-to-mouth but none the less enjoyable livings in and around Fitzrovia throughout the middle and late thirties.

Up-turns in business for publishers and a national demand for books, which meant that virtually anything sold out within a few days of publication, were doing very little for writers. The publishers at what one might call the Dorchester end of the literary world might have resumed their lunches, but it is hardly an exaggeration to say that, up in Fitzrovia, many of their erstwhile authors and contributors were, metaphorically at least, huddled in the shelters and wondering where the next meal was coming from. George Orwell was by no means alone when he complained that 'the war had practically put an end to my livelihood while at the same time the government refused to give me any kind of job'.

As we have already seen, Dylan Thomas was faring equally badly, and in that same letter to John Davenport of 14 September 1939 he began what was to be a lengthy casting around for alternative sources of income:

Do you know of anything for me? I can speak & act too. Does the film-world want an intelligent young man of literary ability, 'self-conscious, pu~ ;h-drunk', who must (for his own sake) keep out of the bloody war, who's willing to do any work – provided of course that it pays enough for a living? I'm not expecting plums from the war – after all they must go to the kind of chaps who refused to give me anything out of the Royal Literary Fund – but I do want something.

The tone of his letter is, if anything, even more telling than its contents. Through his anger at the Royal Literary Fund's rejection of his application for a grant in 1938 (even though both T. S. Eliot and Edith Sitwell had pleaded his case) Thomas is explicitly grouping himself with the outsiders. He was never one of the establishment 'chaps'; far from 'plums', all he was after was a means of survival. In October 1938 he had estimated that 'thirty bloody pounds would settle everything'. The problem was that, even in 1939, there was no means of obtaining it other than by the frantic lobbying at which he would later become more and more adept.

Palinurus's sad visions were presenting themselves at every turn. The general hubbub and dislocation of war was making it impossible for virtually anyone to get down to serious work. Paper shortages, printing difficulties and the considerable problems faced by the editors of even the most prestigious magazines were all leading to a scarcity of commissioning fees, advances and other monies. And, above all, the Government – 'the Authorities' – were doing little or nothing to help.

Faced by the dizzying and very varied array of talent which then (as now) comprised the freelance market, there was nothing they could have done, short, perhaps, of establishing some literary equivalent of the War Artists Advisory Committee. But if the war effort had little or no need for serious literary practitioners, it had an almost insatiable appetite for a more pedestrian brand of hack. Accordingly, as the months went by and magazines and period- icals became even less able to pay adequate fees, large numbers of writers swallowed their pride and joined the legions of lawyers, journalists and advertising copywriters already working for various departments of the BBC and the Ministry of Information.

Those pointed in the direction of the BBC probably had a better time of it. From the very moment of their arrival many complained about the Byzantine complexity and petty bureaucracy of Corporation life. To feisty individualists like Geoffrey Grigson and George Orwell it was all very different from their previous existence. But there were moments at least when even they found themselves undertaking work that was fulfilling, even if it could hardly have been described as of high national importance.

Nevertheless, blithely assigned to the rapidly expanding Drama and Features Department as most of them were, many found that the posting ultimately meant a journey by blacked-out train to Evesham in Worcestershire where the department had been temporarily evacuated, and a provincial exile generally as footling, and in many ways even more disheartening, than their previous life in London. Gilbert Harding was not the only one who moaned that he had been marooned in a what was in effect a small-town metropolis. Very rapidly, he reported, Evesham had been 'inundated with young persons of either or doubtful sex carrying Siamese cats and teddy bears'.

Back in London things were hardly less difficult, although one wartime recruit at least was having a good war. The poet Louis MacNeice found working for the BBC very much to his liking and was to go on to enjoy a triumphant post-war career as a drama producer at Broadcasting House. But in 1941 and 1942, before the days of his adaptations of Apuleius and other writers, and his evocative (and at the time almost extravagant) recreations of the lives of Byron, Marlowe and Chekhov, he too served his time on the propaganda front. Among his first programmes were several talks for the series *The Stones Cry Out*, primarily aimed at reassuring American audiences about how well London was withstanding the Blitz. Collecting material for these by clambering among the smoking ruins of the city with his producer, MacNeice visited St Paul's Cathedral, Dr Johnson's house in Gough Square and even the bombed-out Royal College of Surgeons, in the flooded ruins of which he was momentarily disconcerted to find a perfectly preserved fetus, floating among the debris 'like a small soapstone Buddha'.

But, as an extraordinary quantity of contemporary writing makes clear, even the mundane task of transforming experiences like that into edifying and broadcastable material was real work when seen in the context of the ineffective paper-pushing which filled the days of those writers seconded to the Ministry of

Information. There, in partitioned-off offices in the once grand rooms and even the corridors of what had been London University's Senate House building in Malet Street, Bloomsbury – in what its inmates called 'the Big House' – no one seemed to have any idea about how the particular talents of a generation of writers should best be used. Certainly – and incredibly in the light of the roll-call of those who eventually worked there – there was no recognition of the fact that, in the words of an anonymous contributor to the *New Statesman and Nation* in 1940:

> Among the free-lances – painters, authors, poets who keep the pot boiling by writing reviews of books or art criticism, unattached journalists, playwrights, actors, singers, teachers of music, interior decorators and the like – are to be found many of the most intelligent, well-educated and valuable members of the community.

Graham Greene, Julian Maclaren-Ross, Arthur Calder-Marshall and eventually Dylan Thomas were among those co-opted into the ministry and its various offshoots responsible for the production of propaganda of every kind. But, as J. B. Priestley realised, their talents were almost wantonly squandered: 'There were plenty of writers, innocently anxious to serve their country, working there in Malet Street. Not one of them was given a position of any importance and authority: lawyers, advertising and newspaper men came first.'

Even more damningly, Graham Greene drew on his first-hand experience of life in the Big House for a sketch which appeared in John Lehmann's *Penguin New Writing* as early as September 1941. Ironically entitled 'Men at Work', it charts one day in the life of Richard Skate, an employee of the Ministry of Propaganda. Like every other, the day is almost wholly taken up by the drafting of pointless agendas and attendance at equally pointless meetings:

> Long before he reached the room where the Book Committee sat he heard a familiar voice saying, 'What we want is a really colossal campaign . . .' It was King, of course, putting his shoulder to the war-effort: these outbreaks occurred periodically like desire. King had been an advertising man, and the need to sell something would regularly overcome him. Memories of Ovaltine and Halitosis and the Mustard Club sought an outlet all the time, until suddenly, overwhelmingly, he would begin to

sell the war. The Treasury and the Stationery Office always saw to it that his great schemes came to nothing: only once, because somebody was on holiday, a King campaign had really got under way. It was when the meat ration went down to a shilling; the hoardings all over London carried a curt King message: 'DON'T GROUSE ABOUT MUTTON. WHAT'S WRONG WITH YOUR GREENS?' A ribald Labour member asked a question in Parliament, the posters were withdrawn at a cost of twenty thousand pounds, the Permanent-Secretary resigned, the Prime Minister stood by the Minister, who stood by his staff ('I consider we are one of the fighting services'), and King, after being asked to resign, was instead put in charge of the Books Division of the Ministry at a higher salary. Here it was felt that he could do no harm.[15]

With its references to the Ministry of Propaganda, to entry-passes, lifts, corridors and an ambience in which even teaspoons had to be locked away when not in use, Greene's story reads almost like an early draft of George Orwell's *Nineteen Eight-Four*. It too is a chilling account of life in a bureaucratic system; but the most revealing aspect of Greene's satire is its almost routine acceptance of the Artist as Bureaucrat. Unlike Orwell's Winston Smith (an expendable clerk who just rewrote back copies of *The Times* to bring the past up to date, a task which amounted to 'merely the substitution of one piece of nonsense for another') Greene's hero, Richard Skate is a struggling, well-meaning creative writer. He fancies himself as a playwright, although before the war he earned most of his living by teaching, but even he has been reduced to the level of a salaried advertising copywriter.

Ultimately, this was the saddest of the visions which, unbidden and to some extent at least undeserved, pursued the real-life Skates of Fitzrovia in the final years of the war. Long before 1944 they had joined Palinurus in the water and, floundering there, they could have done a lot worse than turn back to that anonymous *New Statesman* article of April 1940 for an indication of the reception they would get when they eventually washed up on a post-war shore.

For, with uncanny accuracy, it had already predicted what lay ahead. It was entitled 'The Liquidation of the Free-Lances (By One of Their Number)' and it concluded with these words:

Taking a long view, the section of the new poor in which I am especially interested – the free-lances – seems to me doomed. No young writer or artist, after this war is over, will dare to be without a safe job. We shall become, more than ever, a nation of employees, bossed by captains of industry. Authors, subject to good behaviour, will be paid a weekly wage by publishers and drafted to their appropriate departments – fiction, science, belles-lettres. Artists will have to pass examinations before admission, as salaried workers, to the studios of Advertising Agencies, Piccadilly Portraits (limited), or Complete House Furnishers. ('We can do you a landscape in best quality oils, for five guineas.') There are few enough independent journalists today: in five years there may be none. Fear of starvation, rather than Fascism, will effectively destroy the free expression of ideas and the 'honour and dignity of the free mind'. When the free-lance is finally liquidated, our art and literature will all be produced by little men in striped trousers, Anthony Eden hats and rolled umbrellas, who are punctual at their offices and incapable of dangerous thoughts.[16]

— · CHAPTER THIRTEEN · —

Sohoitis

IRIS Murdoch's first novel, *Under the Net*, was published in 1954. Set in a timeless post-war present which could be anywhere in the previous five years, it concludes with its hero and narrator James, 'Jake', Donoghue making his way back to Soho. A writer and translator by trade, in the previous 250 pages he has nevertheless been implicated in the physical destruction of a film studio, engineered the midnight escape of a patient from a hospital ward, liberated a latter-day Lassie and been led on a wild-goose chase around Paris. So it is not, perhaps, surprising that when he gets back to his old stamping-ground, the whole place seems dull:

> It was the rush hour. I threaded my way through the crowd with the dog at my heels, and turned down Rathbone Place. Soho was hot and dusty, sulky idle and senseless with the afternoon. People stood about waiting for opening time. In an upper room someone was playing a piano. Someone else picked up the tune and whistled it, going away into the distance. I walked along Charlotte Street. The scene trembled and shimmered before me perhaps with the heat or perhaps with fear. Like one pursued I quickened my step.[1]

For all its knowing references to Rathbone Place and Charlotte Street, this whole episode presents north Soho – for Jake does not venture south of Oxford Street – as a curiously characterless place. It emerges as a faceless, timeless, decent district of small, old-fashioned shops which appears to have little or nothing in common with the humming, vibrant Fitzrovia that Julian Maclaren-Ross and Dylan Thomas had celebrated less than a decade previously. Fear had never been one of *its* ingredients; nor had even the most casual of visitors felt impelled to quicken their step as they walked its streets. So what had happened?

In a word, the war had happened. There had been nearly six years of fighting. In London alone, hundreds of thousands of tons of high-explosive bombs had wrought more chaos than anything since the Great Fire in 1666. Still further damage – to morale as much as to property – had been caused by the jet-propelled *Vergeltungswaffen* 'reprisal weapons', nicknamed V–1s and V–2s, which began raining down in the summer of 1944. Cumulatively, all this had irrevocably changed the face of the capital.

Physically, the scars were all too apparent. Although, as we have seen, Fitzrovia's wounds were minimal, many other parts of the metropolis, notably the City and the working-class areas surrounding the docks, had been reduced to little more than rubble. For those who lived or worked there, nothing would ever be the same again. Everywhere, the ruined, ravaged landscape was vivid and individual. Iris Murdoch catches its unique character exactly in her account of Jake's desperate City pub-crawl, much earlier in the novel:

> From the darkness and shade of St Paul's Churchyard we came into Cheapside as into a bright arena, and saw framed in the gap of a ruin the pale neat rectangles of St Nicholas Cole Abbey, standing alone away to the south of us on the other side of Cannon Street. In between the willow herb waved over what remained of streets. In this desolation the coloured shells of houses still raised up filled and blank squares of wall and window. The declining sun struck on glowing bricks and flashing tiles and warmed the stone of an occasional fallen pillar.[2]

There were other, less tangible, changes too. The reassuring spirit of the London of the 1930s had been one of the major casualties of the Blitz. The clubby, essentially cohesive, gentlemanly city of eighteenth-century terraces and Edwardian exuberance, Victorian red brick and Dickensian back alleys against which the post-Wildean London Bohemianism had flourished, had been bombed out of existence. Even in 1941 when Noël Coward wrote his song 'London Pride' in celebration of 'our own dear town', there was precious little of it left. And though its verses were overtly up-beat and propagandist ('London Pride is a flower that's free'), one couplet at least did strike a more honest, note:

> *Nothing ever can quite replace*
> *the grace of London town.*

In due course the property boom of the 1950s and 1960s would try to do exactly that, endowing what remained with the 'thrusting', 'dynamic' but ultimately heartless grace of its day. But in the interregnum there was an uneasy period of shabbiness which continued well beyond the end of the 1940s. It was not something to which even native Londoners quickly became accustomed. Queues and shortages were one thing – and manifestations of that shabbiness which were also to remain a fact of life well into what was optimistically hailed as a New Elizabethan era – but behind them lay a deeper malaise. Looking out over the post-war ruins, one real-life Jake Donoghue in particular felt it more acutely than many of his peers:

> He tried to squeeze out some childhood memory that should tell him whether London had always been quite like this. Were there always these vistas of rotting nineteenth-century houses, their sides shored up with baulks of timber, their windows patched with cardboard and their roofs with corrugated iron, their crazy garden walls sagging in all directions? And the bombed sites where the plaster dust swirled in the air and the willow-herb straggled over the heaps of rubble; and the places where the bombs had cleared a larger patch and there had sprung up sordid colonies of wooden dwellings like chicken-houses? But it was no use, he could not remember: nothing remained of his childhood except a series of bright-lit tableaux, occurring against no background and mostly unintelligible.[3]

It is too simplistic to say that George Orwell was Winston Smith, the hero of his last novel *Nineteen Eighty-Four*, and the 'he' of this paragraph. But, though it was never a secret, it is only in recent years that critics have drawn specific attention to the manner in which the dehumanised London, which forms the backdrop to *Nineteen Eighty-Four*, is hardly more than a poetic extrapolation of the London of 1947 and 1948, the years of the novel's composition.

In real life there was, of course, nothing quite as gross as 'the

Party's' plastering of every vertical surface with portraits of Big Brother. (The photographs of a belligerent Winston Churchill which were still tacked onto the walls of public bars and East End sitting-rooms had an altogether different iconographic significance.) But by 1947 many a bomb-site had sprouted 'colonies of wooden dwellings', in reality the factory-produced prefabs which were bolted together by the thousand to alleviate the pressing housing shortage. Up until the very end of the decade there were also hortatory slogans, hardly different from those of the 'Waste Not, Want Not' variety which had been such a feature of wartime life. 'EXTRA EFFORT NOW MEANS BETTER LIVING SOONER', promised one, and you did not need to be an Orwell to realise that that boiled down to virtually the same as the second slogan of the Party. The new Prime Minister, Clement Atlee, who had come to power in July 1945, was no Big Brother; but his plans for economic revival also necessitated a national recognition that 'Freedom is Slavery', for another 'duration' at least.

Helicopters did not hover outside the windows of flats in what was still (just) the capital of the British Empire in the way that they did in the London that was 'the chief city of Airstrip One'. But at a deeper level it is still possible to hear in *Nineteen Eighty-Four*'s description of 'the enormous pyramidal structure of glittering white concrete' that was the Ministry of Truth an echo of London University's stark, white concrete tower from which the wartime Ministry of Information had exercised such totalitarian control. More tentatively, there is also the suggestion that, somehow, despite the winding-down of the ministry, that degree of control never seemed to lessen, even after VE Day.

Subtle, to a large degree unofficial and even self-perpetuating, it nevertheless affected every aspect of life; and the arts were by no means immune. Perhaps this should not surprise us. Long before the war they had fallen under the unofficial control of a mandarin elite whose lofty concerns for their general health and future transcended any immediate connection with individual artists or artefacts. Now, it was only natural that in the wider climate of authoritarianism these same individuals should further consolidate their position. What is surprising, however, is the extent to which they were willing to change their ground in order to do so.

Thus, in the second edition of his own periodical *New Writing and Daylight*, which was published in September 1946, John

Lehmann was arguing exactly the opposite case to that which he had advanced only five years previously. Then he had admitted to a fear that 'the war was going to make all serious literary activity impossible'.[4] Now he was opining that, 'the war awoke something in human beings, a revolt, often only half conscious, against the material values and dogmas of our civilization, a deep craving to live in some other way than under the iron compulsion of time's progress, which art and literature were called upon to satisfy' . . . and which, of course, he and the others of that elite had been instrumental in supplying.

That is by no means the end of his extended, and very typical, argument; for, forgetting all about the fears expressed by the likes of Cyril Connolly, J. B. Priestley and the anonymous *New Statesman* free-lancer that the establishment and expansion of bodies such as CEMA and the BBC amounted to an increasing degree of state control of the arts, Lehmann goes on to welcome such a move:

> Cultural diffusion and cultural competition have come to stay, though they both involve a state intervention and a national self-consciousness in artistic matters which is less characteristic of our country than any other in Europe . . . [But] this development of agencies to sustain the artist, to give him a place of dignity and respect in the community, and to bring him within the reach and understanding of millions from whom he was absolutely divided in an earlier epoch in our industrial civilization, all this is the fulfilment of the dreams of thinkers and idealists for generations.[5]

More and more it appeared that 'little men in striped trousers, Anthony Eden hats and rolled umbrellas' really were going to be the artists of the day. They would be the ones 'sustained' and given 'a place of dignity and respect in the community'. And, such was the magnanimity of Lehmann and his ilk, they would have it whether they wanted it or not. No longer would there be any need for shilly-shallying outside dives like the Wheatsheaf. Fulfilling 'the dreams of thinkers and idealists for generations', Lehmann at least was inviting them all to eat in the BBC canteen.

His words looked fine on paper. Indeed, they still read like a sort of literary protocol to the Beveridge Report, holding out the hope of a nationalised gas-and-water aesthetic well suited to the prevailing ethos of Atleeism. In any other period they might well have remained mere words. They would have been applauded in principle but quickly dismissed, in one of the more graphic phrases of the time, as a lot of 'hot air', just one man sounding off in a small magazine. The late 1940s, however, were exceptional times. In the same way that Beveridge's equally unlikely plans bore fruit, quite against the run of probability, something very close to Lehmann's dreams came true. In the weary euphoria that marked the establishment of a National Insurance scheme and a National Health Service, no one really noticed that their casual, parallel implementation was also proving the truth of another of the slogans of the decade. For, as people also said in the 1940s, Careless Talk Costs Lives.

Intervention, centralisation and general accessibility were concepts wholly foreign to, and ultimately fatal for, Bohemia. The immediate reactions of George Orwell and his like to Lehmann's and many other, similar proposals for an unprecedented (albeit long dreamt-of) degree of artistic centralisation have gone unrecorded, although it is not entirely coincidental that in *Nineteen Eighty-Four*, in the face of 'state intervention', Winston Smith's only free writing took the form of subversive diary entries.

They cannot, however, have been wholly favourable; indeed Brendan Behan's reaction a few years later to Cyril Connolly's *Sunday Times* obituary of Orwell himself conveys something of the writers' unchanging scepticism at the doings of the cultural elite. ' "Listen to this, Brendan," I said', Anthony Cronin has recalled. And he goes on:

> I read him the closing passage of Cyril Connolly's famous obituary: 'But the gardens of the west are closed, and there is no place now for the writer to wander . . .' A look of intense fury came over Brendan's face. 'Arrah sweet and holy Jasus, would you mind telling me what fucking gardens of the west did you and I ever wander in?' he asked.[6]

Lehmann was offering municipal parks rather than gardens, in the west or anywhere else. But for that he can nevertheless have received few thanks in the Wheatsheaf. For, viewed from the outside, his and even the official plans for the establishment of an Arts Council (to carry on in perpetuity the work begun by CEMA) must have looked like a retaliatory strike by society on all that Bohemia had so painfully garnered to itself in the previous half century.

Now that everything was focused on, and paid for by the nation, there seemed to be no need for a plethora of small magazines, independent shows and the even now modest rewards of private patronage. Despite the promise of those BBC dinners, Bohemia had entered a terminal phase before anyone even thought of taking it to one of the new public wards. For, by 1947 it had become clear that the successful artists of the peace were going to be quite unlike even those unfettered individuals who had made a go of things during the war. They were going to be those who could best come to terms with bureaucracy; those who first learnt to work, on short-term contracts at least, with organisations like the Arts Council and the BBC.

It was here, however, that the new reality hit hardest, for these newcomers were not just time-serving parvenus, the demobbed servicemen and young Toves of the Maclaren-Ross myth. We have already seen that Louis MacNeice found conditions at Broadcasting House wholly conducive to real work. He was by no means alone; also among the first to notice the way in which things were going were several other figures who were already coming to be seen as members of Bohemia's elder or, at any rate, pre-war generation.

It has been quietly excised from the legend, but even Dylan Thomas showed every sign of changing his ways in the immediate post-war years. He joined the National Liberal Club, for instance, and was entertaining friends in its spacious premises in Whitehall Place, London by 1947. Even more gallingly for those who persist notions of him as merely an indigent drunk, a rootless visitor to every Fitzrovian drinking den, he was also proposed, and accepted, as a member of the Savage in 1949.

He was a survivor, as his letter to John Davenport of September 1939 had shown, and he adapted better than most of his contemporaries to the changing times. Thus it comes as no surprise to find him working for the BBC in 1947; and wholly appropriate that his most substantial piece of work that year was a twenty-five-minute radio feature called 'Return Journey.' A semi-dramatised account of an imaginary return to Swansea, it is interesting today for two reasons. In its format it is a very early precursor of *Under Milk Wood* of 1953, while in its message it neatly encapsulates the Bohemian reality of 1947.

Thomas himself played the Narrator and described a picaresque odyssey through the shops, pubs and hotels of the town in search of a well-known character from the past:

> He's five foot six-and-a-half. Thick blubber-lips, snub nose, curly mouse-brown hair and one front tooth broken after playing a game called Cats and Dogs in the Mermaid, Mumbles. Speaks rather fancy. Truculent, plausible, bit of a show-er off – plus-fours and no breakfast, you know. Used to have poems printed in the *Herald of Wales*. There was one about an open-air performance of *Electra* in Mrs Bertie Perkins's garden in Sketty. Lived up the Uplands. A bombastic, adolescent, provincial Bohemian with a thick-knotted artist's tie made out of his sister's scarf – she never knew where it had gone – and a cricket shirt dyed bottle-green. A gabbing, ambitious, mock-tough, pretentious young man, and moley too.

Nowhere, however, in the still-smug darkness of that provincial town could he find anyone who so much as remembered that anachronistic, adolescent ghost. 'What d'you want to find him for? I wouldn't touch him with a barge-pole,' said a preoccupied hotel barmaid. No . . .

The harder he searched, the more fruitless Thomas the Narrator's quest became. In exactly the same way that the war had erased all signs of once familiar stores like Stead and Simpson, Curry's Bicycles, Boots's Cash Chemists and Tucker's fish shop in the High Street, it had also obliterated all traces of the young Bohemian.

That, however, was in Swansea. Back in London things were different. If Dylan Thomas himself was for long periods conspicuous only by his absence, there was no shortage of candidates anxious to assume his place at the bar of the Wheatsheaf. Just as it had turned its back on the war, so Fitzrovia reacted to the changed circumstances of the peace with what can at best be described as blithe indifference and at worst as blind ignorance. Shoring its few remaining fragments of dignity against the ruins of the present, it ordered another round of pints, huddled closer in upon itself and pretended that everything was just as it always had been.

It was not as if there had been no warnings. 'Only beware of Fitzrovia', Tambimuttu had told Julian Maclaren-Ross as early as 1943. And he went on:

> 'It's a dangerous place, you must be careful.'
> 'Fights with knives?'
> 'No, a worse danger. You might get Sohoitis you know.'
> 'No I don't. What is it?'
> 'If you get Sohoitis', Tambi said very seriously, 'you will stay there always day and night and get no work done ever. You have been warned.'[7]

Now, however – as Tambi himself slipped away to New York – neither Julian Maclaren-Ross nor any of the other pre-war Fitzrovians chose to remember his words. Consequently, like a particularly virulent strain of pneumonia, what amounted to an epidemic of Sohoitis was already finishing off the war-weakened body of Bohemianism. Inertia had set in, and The Image (or at any rate an image, the rigor mortis-like rictus of irresponsible, drunken pleasure) had finally taken over. For not only had the idea of the boozy, feckless Bohemian by now become firmly established in the public consciousness – the pseudo-John figure of Gulley Jimson had first made its appearance in 1944 with the publication of Joyce Cary's novel *The Horse's Mouth* – the caricature had also become a role-model for Bohemia itself. By 1947 saloon bars of Soho and Fitzrovia, still well-filled with the tottering relics of the days of their pre-war eminence, were being further crowded by the arrival of a host of younger writers and artists, all intent on carving themselves a slice of the action by living down to the once-fanciful but now increasingly-accurate beeriness of their elders.

Demobbed servicemen whose previous experience of what they were now again calling 'Soho' amounted only to what they had been able to accomplish on a forty-eight-hour pass; younger men who had not seen active service at all; returning 'conshis' and newly-arrived 'non-Blitzers', they comprised the first – and last – generation of post-Fitzrovian Bohemians. Some, like Brendan Behan, appeared with impeccable credentials, liked what they saw but did not stay. As Anthony Cronin has shown, Behan and a coterie of other Irish writers including Patrick Kavanagh and Flann O'Brien (Myles Na Gopaleen) had their own, similar

Bohemia with its headquarters at the Catacombs in Dublin anyway. Others, who had followed something more nearly approaching Arthur Ransome's path, pitched up in the Wheat-sheaf with nothing to offer but the conviction of their own innate but untried Bohemianism. 'My naïvety was almost obscene,' Daniel Farson has recalled of his arrival in 1951, 'but as soon as I stepped into Soho I felt that I belonged.'

Most were, or at least believed themselves to be, artists of one kind or another (even Farson had come to London to take up a job as a *Picture Post* photographer) and indeed on one level their arrival in 1945 and 1946 and 1947 can be seen as a re-establishment of the status quo of the late thirties. This was not quite a return to business as usual, however; for, in a way that was perhaps more superficial than Orwell's, the work which those artists were exhibiting at this time also demonstrated something of the changes which had overtaken Britain.

It had been dubbed 'Neo-Romanticism', and not without reason since the exigencies of war had driven the painters back on to themselves and British artists of the past (notably those two Romantic visionaries, William Blake and Samuel Palmer) for inspiration. Grafted on to the obstinate stump of thirties Surrealism, this referential approach effectively defined the parameters for artists such as Cecil Collins and Keith Vaughan. Taken together with an upsurge of interest in a purer, almost documentary style which had been aroused by shows of work from the Recording Britain project (its first, back in 1941, had been followed by many more and by other, similar exhibitions; notably the 1945 showing of an influential series of paintings by John Piper, all of which were based on Renishaw, the Sitwells' family home) it provided the perfect palette for visions of an austerity arcadia.

Indeed the painting of the peace hardly differed from the 'offical' Central Institute for Art and Design-approved work of 1940. Only a very fine line separated Henry Moore's shelter sketches from the post-war figure drawings of Keith Vaughan, John Piper's wartime pictures of bomber stations from the later thorny and troubled canvases of Graham Sutherland and Ceri Richards. Nor was it entirely coincidental that many of the Neo-Romantic landscapes of the latter continued to be directly inspired by the earlier, 'Apocalyptic' verse of his fellow-countryman, Dylan Thomas.

227

It would be wrong, however, to see this arcadian and sometimes downright whimsical Neo-Romanticism as primarily the art of Fitzrovia. It was to a far greater extent 'Establishment art'; in the early years of the war the work of those who have been called the 'senior' Neo-Romantics had already been taken up and given an enthusiastic imprimatur by such cultural bastions as the ballet. As early as 1941 Graham Sutherland was designing sets for Frederick Ashton's production of *The Wanderer* at Sadler's Wells. Two years later, John Piper had been responsible for the set and costumes of *The Quest* (a new work set to the music of William Walton), while the whole collaboration reached its apotheosis in 1948 with Michael Powell's film *The Red Shoes* which not only starred Léonide Massine and Robert Helpmann but celebrated Neo-Romanticism in virtually every shot.

But Sadler's Wells was, as always, at the wrong end of town; and Piper and Sutherland and all the other mainstream Neo-Romantics were, at best, only casual and occasional visitors to Fitzrovia. And with the end of the war in 1945 and the opening-up of the prospect of foreign trips and something approaching a *rapprochement* with the wider world of Europe, few were prepared to stop off for more than the necessary night or two in London on their way to warmer climes. As early as 1946 John Craxton and Lucian Freud had discovered Greece, and Leslie Hurry was in Avignon where, the following year, he was to be joined for a time by Francis Bacon and Graham Sutherland.

In exactly the same way as it did in literature, however, Fitzrovia maintained a distant, parodic connection with current movements in art. The rest of London might have been celebrating the achievements of Sutherland at 'The Wells' and John Piper at Covent Garden, but at the Wheatsheaf they were drinking to what was even then called an 'urban romanticism' of their own. Unfortunately, however (though wholly typically), no one paused to notice that many of the drinks had been bought by one of those who should have been receiving them.

Ever since 1940, the painter John Minton had been recording an altogether different Britain from that of the lonely country houses and shattered Regency terraces which appealed to Piper, Nash and Sutherland. At the height of the Blitz he had discovered the East End of London, an area to which he was to return again and again throughout the forties. The drawings and paintings he made there, at Poplar and Wapping and Rotherhithe, are muscular and full of angry corners in a way that contrasts sharply with the more decorous, intricate and fancifully detailed drawings (such as *Recollections of Wales*, 1944) which he was simultaneously producing. But then such contrasts were an essential part of Minton's life.

When he died, almost exactly one decade later, in January 1957, the press gave him a spectacular send-off. 'Mystery of the "gifted" artist', shouted one paper, before gleefully revealing that he had taken a massive overdose of pills. 'Yesterday there died a purple, melancholy genius', proclaimed another, but it was the *Reynold's News* obituarist who best caught the nature of his subject. 'London's artists are mourning the loss of Johnnie, their brightest star,' he began – and did not flinch from going on to describe Minton as a 'sad-happy alcoholic'.[8]

It was an apposite phrase, for by the mid-fifties 'Johnnie' was exactly that. But in his case at least, the alcoholism was almost incidental. One has only to compare the brooding intensity of John Deakin's masterly photo-portrait (see Plate 23), taken around 1954 (or, come to that, the melancholy vulnerability visible in earlier portraits of him by both Lucian Freud and Michael Ayrton) with Minton's own expansive self-portraits to understand something of the problems which the sad-happy dichotomy caused him. The heir to a fortune from his family's fine china and porcelain business, he has been laconically characterised by Michael Wishart:

> Johnny was very obviously manic. In frantic pursuit of love or even companionship, he dissipated himself to the hilt, while spending a useful inheritance on useless pursuits, such as nights of black dejection or blacker oblivion. The waste of self and money amused his followers.[9]

He was, of course, homosexual – but he had arrived on the scene at a time when just about everyone else was too, or so it must have seemed to the sturdily heterosexual Maclaren-Ross and all the other pre-war Fitzrovians. And tragically, for he was a fine and sensitive draughtsman, it is this aspect of his character – his extra-mural pre-occupation with what David Mellor has identified as 'Youth, the young (male) as (art) object',[10] and what can be more prosaically described as his obsession with sailors – together

229

with his 'alcoholism' and association with all the more traditionally anti-social aspects of Bohemian behaviour for which he is now best remembered.

Equally tragically, he was by no means alone. Minton's career, in fact, only exemplified a general trend. All the key members of the post-war generation are now better remembered for their spectacularly graphic private lives than they are for their work. In comparison with their manic bingeing and flagrant lawlessness, even the image projected by Julian Maclaren-Ross paled into a polite and decorous insignificance.

It was as though a collective decision had been reached: as though there had been an extraordinary general meeting of the whole of Fitzrovia at which it had been unanimously decided that austerity was too boring and that they would have no part in it. It might perhaps have been better if there had. That way, there would at least have been some formal basis for the retrospective eulogising of contemporary memorialists. Here is George Melly, uncharacteristically cast in the role of Nero, and fiddling as late as 1987:

> The fifties were a time of austerity, of punitive conventions, of a grey uniformity which would astound even the most enthusiastic defenders of the current puritan back-lash. Soho was perhaps the only area in London where the rules didn't apply. It was a Bohemian no-go area, tolerance its password, where bad behaviour was cherished – at any rate in retrospect. Only bores were made unwelcome.[11]

At any rate in retrospect . . . Too fly to fall for such a convenient theory, Melly (who was there, and later to write *Revolt Into Style*, the most persuasive of many explanations of the Sixties) uses that single qualification to contextualise what would otherwise be standard gush. For the great meeting never took place, and Sohoitis rather than consensus remains the best diagnosis of what was happening. Work continued to be at a discount.

Thus, when we hear of Francis Bacon – who had been exhibiting since 1935 but was rocketed to a notorious sort of fame by the exhibition of his *Three Studies for Figures at the Base of a Crucifixion* at the Lefrevre Gallery in 1945 – it is as a member of the Colony Room and not as an artist. When John Deakin is remembered it is as a 'character' (' "*Uno* gin, *per favore*,' said Deakin') and not as a distinguished and technically accomplished *Vogue* photographer. And whenever the survivors of this punishing circus talk of the old times today and reminisce about 'The Roberts' – as they unfailingly do – as often as not they completely forget to mention that both of them were painters too.

As much as or even more than John Minton, Robert Colquhoun and Robert MacBryde have come to stand for the whole period. The many lurid stories of their private life have upstaged those of everyone else, and assured them of a posthumous fame as the ultimate embodiments of the 'urban romanticism' of the late forties which, like so much else, began as earnest endeavour but came to a premature end in the gutter. Yet this is certainly not the way in which, at the start, they themselves saw things happening. Although the former is now considered worth little more than a shortish chapter in the more comprehensive art histories of the period – and MacBryde is usually denied even that – both arrived in London determined to prove themselves as serious artists.

They were Scotsmen – Colquhoun was born at Kilmarnock in 1914, MacBryde at nearby Maybole a year earlier – and had first met at the Glasgow School of Art in 1932. From that year on, according to a mutual friend, 'they were one person' and separated only by military service. (Until he was invalided out in 1941, Colquhoun was an ambulance driver for the Royal Army Medical Corps; MacBryde was tubercular and therefore exempt from war work.) They came to London – where for three years they shared a Notting Hill studio with John Minton – and enjoyed fame of a kind. But even then MacBryde was consciously neglecting his own work, doing the shopping, arranging exhibitions and generally immersing himself, as he put it, in the business of being 'the servant of the great master'.

And in those early days a master was what Colquhoun showed every sign of becoming. By 1947 no lesser figure than Wyndham Lewis had noted that, with his 'Existentialist' paintings of beggars and other urban characters, he was 'generally recognised as one of the best – perhaps the best – of the young artists. That opinion I cordially endorse.'[12]

But 1947 was also the year in which it all began to go wrong for 'The Roberts'. 1947 was the year in which they contracted Sohoitis. They began to drink heavily, they were evicted from their studio – it had been rented to them for working in by day, not for 'drunken orgies' by night – and from that moment on they became almost permanent features on the Fitzrovian landscape. Their fellow-artist John Craxton has recalled that it was they who first 'took me into Soho – I would never have dared to go in on my own – to places like the French Pub and the Swiss. I preferred jitter-bugging to drinking, but the others liked beer. Colquhoun used to get very drunk.'[13]

'I met them only rarely but on every occasion they [were] extremely drunk and behaved unpleasantly to all within earshot',[14] the critic John Rothenstein (William's son) has remembered. And quite how unpleasantly they could behave is borne out by his description of their first meeting with the poet George Barker: 'They became friends immediately (even though MacBryde crushed a small wineglass in his right hand which cut Barker's as they shook hands).'[15]

Surprisingly, the friendship with Barker was to endure for the rest of the Roberts' lives.

But, even in the late forties, the likes of Minton and the Roberts, George Barker, Dan Farson and the journalist and novelist Colin MacInnes were attracted to Fitzrovia by more than the beer. The influx of the post-war newcomers had fundamentally altered the nature of the area and the whole character of London Bohemian-ism. Both had become brasher, more dissipated – and more *sordid* than even Dylan Thomas could ever have wished. Drinking had been replaced by alcoholism, high spirits by a short-tempered liverishness and, above all, the easy aimiability of the early Eiffel Tower and Fitzroy Tavern days had been supplanted by both professional jealousy and the *arrivistes'* unwarranted assumption that anything went.

There are any number of examples of this, and they all show just how far freedom had become drunken truculence, and how easily Bohemianism could – and did – become sheer boorishness.

Daniel Farson recalls one evening when he arrived at the Caves de France. 'Get me a whisky will yer?' Robert Colquhoun was saying, banging the bar to attract attention. Trying to order his own drink, Farson was button-holed by Robert MacBryde. 'Why don't you fuck off?' he said.

Anthony Cronin describes an occasion on which he and his wife invited the Roberts to spend a night at their suburban house in Wembley. Even without drink – there had been a bottle of whisky, but MacBryde dropped it on the platform of Wembley underground station – it was to be a night during which Cronin, at least, realised just how far the Bohemianism of what was then the fifties was at odds with the values of suburbia. In his autobiography *Dead as Doornails* he recounts how, after a quarrel, a naked Colquhoun snatched up a carving-knife and chased the equally-naked MacBryde around the front garden, to the shocked amazement of the neighbours, of the Cronins' lady lodger, a reader for Boots's library, and above all of her elderly mother: 'Oh my gawd. Niked. Niked as the day of judgement. And 'e's got a knoife,' she cried . . .[16]

But perhaps most telling of all was the pervading ambience at the Colony Room. Originally just another of the members-only drinking clubs, the Colony opened in 1948. Inevitably, however, and with surprising alacrity, it subsequently became – and has remained – an integral part of the new Soho (so much so that regulars will tell you that it did not open in 1948 but on 15 December that year).

Fabled as the haunt of Francis Bacon and the likes of Deakin and, on occasions, Colin MacInnes, it was the creation of Muriel Belcher, and reflected her particular character. For although the Colony's barstools were originally covered in leopard-skin and the bar itself was clad in bamboo and festooned with greenery (in contemporary photographs it suggests a village-hall set for *South Pacific*), Muriel was even more special, maintain many of the regulars of those early days. A onetime nightclub owner, they go on, she had a genius for mixing people. There were artists like themselves, but also 'drab little numbers' like the heiress Olga Deterling, 'fucking bores', and middle-aged homosexual men whom Muriel always called 'Miss' in exactly the same arch, 'camp' way in which she still occasionally referred to that 'Miss Hitler'.

'Members only!' she'd bark at any newcomer who poked a nose around the door and whose face she disliked. With her friends, however, it was a different story. She mothered the new age, they say, for there was always a welcome – albeit one couched in her own, inimitable terms: *Hello cunty!!*

But, however hard they tried to live an unbuttoned *vie de bohème* amidst the Austerity, the willow-herb and the hardship of the late forties – and they did try *very* hard – the new wave of artists and photographers was left standing by Nina Hamnett. For, displaying her undoubted talent for keeping a pigeon-step or so ahead of the times, once again she was amply justifying her unofficial title as the Queen of Bohemia. But this time there was a difference.

Under a different dispensation, she had been the intimate of John, of Sickert and, in Paris, of Cocteau, Modigliani and Gaudier-Brzeska. Now it was all gone. She continued to work, in fits and starts, but – as even she recognised – by the late forties she had become little more than a museum-piece. Ruthven Todd recalled that when they were initially introduced (by Dylan Thomas) her very first words betrayed exactly that. Alluding to the sculpture for which she had sat to Gaudier-Brzeska nearly thirty years previously, the poor befuddled Nina said: 'You know me, m'dear . . . I'm in the V & A with me left tit knocked off!'[17]

Not that she wasn't still good company – of a sort. Making the rounds of the saloon bar at the Burglars or the Fitzroy, she would indiscriminately approach old friends or complete strangers. *Mine's a double gin, de-ah!* she would say in unexpectedly old-fashioned, cut-glass tones, *I'll have a double gin!* . . . and then attempt to reward their enforced hospitality with stories. Sometimes they were of that vanished Paris, tales of evenings at the Dôme or the Rotonde; sometimes they were of John and Sickert – more often, it seems, they were more basic descriptions of the times she had had with her boxers and sailors.

They were 'lovely stories', according to one young American admirer, 'filled with words like shit . . . fuck etc. Good Anglo-Saxon talk.'[18] And when even they failed she could always sing. John Heath-Stubbs can still recall some of the equally 'lovely' ballads and limericks with which Nina would regail any company:

> *A maid again I'll never be,*
> *Till apples grow on the orange tree.*
> *He told me that he loved me so,*
> *So he upped my skirts and he had a go.*
> *A maid again I'll never be,*
> *Till apples grow on the orange tree . . .*[19]

By and large, however, by the late 1940s Nina had become something of an embarrassment to friends and strangers alike, for she managed to transcend even the rather tattered Bohemianism of the time. Hardly able to afford to eat, in the immediate post-war years she was living in conditions of almost unbelievable squalor in two top-floor rooms at 31 Howland Street. Her many 'visitors' there have left vivid descriptions of the bugs, or the 'little deposits of rat turds' on Nina's bed and of the wholly inadequate sanitation. There was only a small wash-basin on the landing which her landlady was to accuse Nina of 'misusing' when she attempted to evict her in order to sell the house in the spring of 1947. ('What do you mean, a woman urinating in the sink? It is not possible' – the magistrate's comment at the ensuing court hearing provoked loud laughter in Fitzrovia where they knew by then that Nina was even less like other women than she had ever been.)

The secondhand Worth dresses and Woolworth pearls had long gone. Her biographer Denise Hooker notes that, even in public, by now Nina often 'looked like a scarecrow'. A few years earlier she had persuaded Ruthven Todd to print up a pile of postcards with which she bombarded friends and relations. 'WHAT DO YOU DO WITH YOUR OLD CLOTHES?' they asked. 'Do you give them to the SALVATION ARMY or the poor? If so, DO NOT, REMEMBER NINA.'[20] They did – some of them at least – but contemporary photographs still show a Nina inadequately filling shabby, hand-me-down jackets; the beret perched rakishly on her head ill-concealing her lank, greasy and receding hair.

'I took my grey dress to the cleaners and, my dear, it just shrivelled up because of the gin soaked into it over the years. All they gave me back was a handful of dust.' However much she played up to the image, in the artificial (but ironically equally hand-me-down) Bohemia of the late forties it did not quite work. It was too late.

When she died, in 1956, she was only sixty-six; but Daniel Farson (then just twenty-nine) remembers that 'I was so young that I thought of her as older than that.' He was not the only one. To the new generation of Fitzrovians that he represented, the half-forgotten names which she mentioned and her tales of nights at the Dôme and even the Fitzroy Tavern, were no more than stories of a long-vanished era. Their new world of 'Neo-Romanticism', de-mob suits, *Picture Post*, ever-expanding 'advertising agencies', a BBC hungry for young talent, and a beery, post-war optimism seemed to have nothing in common with the old crone who rattled a battered tobacco tin under their noses.

Got any mun, de-ah? . . .

They still recall her advances, still 'do' her voice – and still remember their outraged, self-righteous refusals. And only now are they admitting that they were mistaken. For only now do they see that in reality they owed it all to her, even their very presence.

At the time, however, it was different. Only the newly returned gentleman-publisher David Archer seems to have repaid the debt. 'No, Nina. Not again!' he had snapped one evening when she went through her whole routine and shook that old tin in front of him at the French – but then he went away and thought better of it. He returned, pressed a ten-shilling note into her hand and – typically – produced a bunch of flowers.

— · CHAPTER FOURTEEN · —

Deaths and Entrances

THE artist Keith Vaughan was not much of a Bohemian. Too quiet ever to have been more than a fellow-traveller bumping along in the noisy wake of John Minton and the Roberts, he nevertheless provided the ultimate epitaph for the boisterous, bawdy and short-lived post-war Fitzrovia. There was, he once told Noel Barber, 'a brief period in the late forties when artists and workers congregated at two or three Soho pubs, like The French House or The Wheatsheaf, but for some reason this habit broke up.'[1]

Through its perfect pathos Vaughan's wistful sentence carries within itself the answer to all its implicit longing. For Vaughan – who was after all included in Alan Ross's list of the Wheatsheaf's regulars – should have realised that things 'broke up' largely because of that very congregation of 'artists and workers'. There never was any necessary connection between the remnants of the Bohemia and the 'workers' – workers of any description, but least of all the sailors and homosexual 'rough trade' of whom Vaughan was inevitably thinking. (Among his most treasured possessions was an album of his own snapshots of naked young men, not all of which had been taken as *aides-mémoire* to his numerous drawings of similar subjects.)

The times were getting out of joint. In the last stages of Sohoitis, Bohemia was losing all connection with its parent-society. Thus, although it apparently struck late-night diners at the Gargoyle in the early fifties as no more than 'bad form' for John Minton to turn up with a party of sailors – so intent were they all on cherishing bad behaviour – the Metropolitan Police and various borough watch committees were beginning to take a dimmer view

237

of things. In particular, they began to look into the ritualised encounters of Vaughan and his like and those 'workers'. And, inexperienced as they were in the ways of Bohemia, what they found at the French, the Wheatsheaf and elsewhere seemed rather more than mere bad behaviour.

John Heath-Stubbs recalls that well before 1950 in both Fitzrovia and Soho proper 'homosexuality had become a sub-culture within a sub-culture. There were a number of recognised homosexual pubs. At various times I could name the Fitzroy, the Newman Arms and the Admiral Duncan. Right up near Riding House Street there was one which was always full of rent-boys. And of course there was the Golden Lion. The Swiss at times was a "queer pub", and the Highlander became one in the late fifties or early sixties.'[2]

Others who were there have also commented on this proliferation of what were then generally – and factually rather than pejoratively – known as 'queer pubs', although most too have pleaded a sort of Fitzrovian Fifth Amendment. In their reminiscences many invoke Soho's traditional tolerance of the individual and the different and hedge themselves around with statements about what fun these pubs were. Others present oblique apologies that, really, they were too busy to notice anything out of the ordinary going on. Nevertheless, it is clear that there was an explosion of homosexual activity in Fitzrovia in the late 1940s and early 1950s. And, just like the Bohemianism it was subverting, it too in these early years centred around the Fitzroy Tavern, which was by then under the management of Charlie Allchild, who had married Papa Kleinfeld's daughter and subsequently taken over the pub's licence.

The legalisation of homosexual acts between consenting adults would not come about for another two decades, but it is wrong to imagine that evenings at the Fitzroy, the Newman Arms or the Golden Lion were furtive, guilty affairs. For although things were very different from the way they are today, surprisingly the tone was in many ways more strident – or perhaps just more desperate – than that of the legalised, commercial 'gay scene' as it was to evolve in Soho and for that matter everywhere else during the 1970s.

Now, Soho's few gay pubs – there is none in Fitzrovia proper – pump out a uniform mixture of high energy – 'hi NRG' – disco music, 'spritzers' and gassy, over-priced lager. At the time of writing the current generation of rent-boys has deserted the Golden Lion for the raunchier bars of Earl's Court. The King's Arms in Poland Street has established a reputation as a discreet lunchtime meeting-place for the leather-and-denim 'clones' who work in the small publishers and commercial film companies at that end of the new Soho. Only the recently-opened Compton's, a phoenix which has risen in premises which once housed the Swiss, is out on the streets and hustling for trade. Large advertisements in London's gay and 'alternative' press coyly suggest that it is the place to 'meet your friends or make new ones'.

There were, of course, no advertisements in the forties or fifties, but word soon got round. John Minton, Keith Vaughan, the Roberts and any number of other homosexuals of the time had no difficulty in discovering that, for the price of a pint in Fitzrovia or elsewhere, one could not only meet one's friends (not always the point of the exercise) but 'make new ones' and gain entry to a forbidden world. And just how extensive that world was is demonstrated by a spate of letters and reminiscences of the fifties and early sixties which appeared in *Capital Gay*, a London gay newspaper, during 1987:

Ah yes, I remember it well.

Places like The Witch's Brew, Bobby's Bar, Robin's Nest, The Pink Panther and the notorious 'Place'. Bermondsey Baths, Jermyn Street, and The Imperial. All-night parties every weekend, jazz at The Coleherne Sunday lunchtimes . . .

The Martinique was a tacky all-night joint off Oxford Street. We sat around stoked up with Boots's amphetamine, pretending we were having a ball. There was a character called Ernest Page who told fortunes, and I also remember [Lady] Brenda Dean Paul, the famous heroin addict (Yes, it was that unusual then) wandering round like a ghost in blue tinted glasses . . . I saw my first drag act – Phil Starr, I think – at the Fifty club in Soho, and was astonished when told it was a man. Bobby's in Lisle Street was a real dive . . . The Kalabash behind the Paris Pullman was equally tacky, with illusions of grandeur. Leon the owner, covered the walls with photos of beautiful boys, and a very old lady took your coat, and was rumoured to have known Oscar Wilde.[3]

The whole 'scene' has also been well described in John Lehmann's extraordinary, quasi-autobiographical novel *In The Purely Pagan Sense*, which in its later pages graphically depicts the post-war, pre-Wolfenden London in which monied, middle-class homosexuals like Lehmann and Minton stalked the bars in search of 'rough trade' or the perpetually elusive sailors and guardsmen. (The staples of any homo-erotic story in the days of Wilde, even by 1950 these fabled guardsmen were in fact fast becoming fond memories, their greed and occasional violence at the Fitzroy, the Marquis and elsewhere having proved their downfall. As Maclaren-Ross observed, some of them at least enjoyed what would later become known as 'queer-bashing' and were even capable of turning on one another. Sailors, who were generally of a lower social class and anyway had shorter periods of leave, were more sought-after by those who disdained the company of non-combatant 'tricks'.)

Even in London, however, Lehmann ranged widely, right across the West End and up into Mayfair. The pubs he mentions are – inevitably – cloaked in pseudonyms; but, as we have seen, he was never a Fitzrovian mixer. *In the Purely Pagan Sense* therefore understates the concentration of activity in the area's pubs. Quite how much there was and indeed how noticeable it ever became remains difficult, if not impossible, to assess in the present, more tolerant climate. But it is beyond doubt that in the mid-fifties the Fitzroy Tavern was raided by the police and, with exquisite irony, Charlie Allchild was charged with running a disorderly house at the very premises in which thirty years previously London's always-disorderly Bohemia had come of age.

Disorderly, in fact, hardly seems the word for it. At the ensuing trial, the police evidence inevitably described the Fitzroy as nothing less than a 'den of vice'. It was occupied 'for the most part', their counsel went on, by

> quite obvious male homosexuals who dyed their hair and rouged their cheeks and behaved in an effeminate manner with effeminate voices. The other occupants were to a very large extent made up of servicemen – sailors, soldiers and marines. There can be very little doubt that this house was conducted in a most disorderly and disgusting fashion. These perverts were simply overrunning the place, behaving in a scandalous manner and attempting to seduce the members of the forces.[4]

Daniel Farson is surely right in describing this account as 'wilfully extravagant'; indeed, it seems to owe more to observations of the prissier, more self-consciously 'artistic' world of the fifties which was later to be re-created by Quentin Crisp in his book *The Naked Civil Servant*. But if Farson errs on the side of generosity in his tolerant *apologia* for the Fitzroy, he is guilty of disingenuousness to say the least in his reporting of the 'astonishment' of the brewery at Allchild's subsequent acquittal. To John Heath-Stubbs it came as no surprise at all. It was common knowledge, he says, that Charlie Allchild had 'bribed the police quite shamelessly until there was a change of Police Commissioner in 1955.'

Ultimately, however, neither that fact nor the verdict really mattered. For although Allchild left the Fitzroy soon after (and Farson and Heath-Stubbs agree that the pub has never been the same since his departure), although the rent-boys and sailors moved on, the damage had been done. Fitzrovia had been pushed one step closer to its final disintegration among the sex-shops and strip-clubs which would blossom in the Soho of the sixties.

At the time, however, there were other, more obvious signs that its number was up.

The Moka coffee-bar was established in Frith Street, Soho in 1953. Distinguished from the innumerable pre-war cafés and patisseries, many of which continued to thrive, by its roaring, spluttering *éspresso* machine, it was the first of scores of coffee-bars which were to open in London and in towns and cities throughout the country before the end of the decade. Soho, in particular, was soon overrun by them. The next few years saw the arrival of the up-market Partisan in Carlisle Street, and the House of Sam Widges, once a pub on the corner of Berwick and D'Arblay streets which had been painted scarlet and hastily re-opened as a 'coffee lounge'. In addition, there was Le Macabre in Meard Street where coffins were used as tables, Heaven and Hell (or, as its neon sign had it, 'Heaven & HELL') in Old Compton Street, and a small but vital establishment named the 2i's (in a punning reference to the two Irani brothers who owned the freehold) which opened right next door to the expansive, split-level Heaven and Hell in the spring of 1956.

Among them all, and there were many, many more, it was the

241

2i's which got things right – which was, in the argot of the time, 'hep' and even 'copacetic'. The words which appeared on its signboard at the end of the fifties were no idle boast: by then the 2i's really was 'world famous' and the 'home of the stars'. In the pre-Beatle era, when London and not Liverpool was still the centre of everything, it had become the Cavern Club of its day, *the* place to go, *the* place to discover new talent. Managed by two Australian ex-wrestlers Paul Lincoln and Ray Hunter, it had early on begun presenting music in the evenings. The 'skiffle' craze was at its height after the unexpected success of Lonnie Donnegan's recording of the Leadbelly classic 'Rock Island Line', which sold more than a quarter of a million copies and became an unexpected No 1 in May 1956, and to the enterprising Paul Lincoln at least live music seemed as good a way as any of keeping the coffee-bar full.

The Vipers, led by Wally Whyton, were the 2i's first band. An amorphous group of anything up to eight performers, at one stage their regular line-up included Jet Harris and Hank Marvin – although they were later to leave and join Cliff Richard in a group then known as the Drifters which achieved greater success when it changed its name to the Shadows. But the Vipers were by no means alone. Justifying the 2i's boast that it was the 'home of the stars' was the fact that Cliff Richard himself (then known as Harry Webb) and two more of Britain's 'rock and rollers' had started their careers there. The fashion of the day was for short, angry stage names (Billy Fury, Marty Wilde, Duffy Power) and so the pair, who arrived at the 2i's as Tommy Hicks and Terry Nelhams, left as Tommy Steele and Adam Faith respectively.

Paul Lincoln's daring had paid off. He had been among the first to see that the skiffle boom, which lasted until about the end of 1958, had galvanised a generation. But it was Lonnie Donnegan who later explained why. In an interview with the music journalist Tony Palmer he pointed out that, with its washboard-and-tea-chest-bass simplicity and rudimentary three-chord structure, skiffle was the ideal music of the time. Guitars were still hard to come by in the lingering aftermath of Austerity, but that no longer mattered. Skiffle's very backyard, amateurish spontaneity (Donnegan received a flat fee of £3/10s. and no royalties for 'Rock Island Line') was all part of its appeal.[5] Not many of Britain's suburban teenagers in the mid fifties could emulate the open, American rebelliousness so apparent in the voice of Elvis

Presley, but skiffle gave them both a more suitable sound and a home-grown cause to rally round.

And rally round they did. Wally Whyton (who remained Wally Whyton and went on to become a children's television presenter) remembers that the 2i's 'simply couldn't contain the droves of people who wanted to see where it was all happening – after all it was only thirty feet by ten feet – so Paul [Lincoln] opened a 2i's Club around the corner in Gerrard Street.'[6]

By 1958, when all this was happening, it was the only sensible thing to do. Soho and even Fitzrovia proper had been taken over by a new generation of Bums. Julian Maclaren-Ross would probably have recognised them as the successors of the Slithy Toves of the forties, as indeed they were, although there were also major differences between them and their predecessors.

You can't all have been at Cambridge? . . .

In the forties his question had been rhetorical – and defensive, since Maclaren-Ross himself had been to no university at all. Now it was redundant and had been supplanted by one that was altogether more fundamental. 'Julian, in the Wheatsheaf, was asking querulously where everyone had gone,' Dan Davin remembers.

The straight answer to that is easy. By the mid-fifties the cannier survivors of the Fitzrovian literary fraternity had long since found work and contacts in a new set of pubs, all of which were conveniently close to Broadcasting House and the various outposts of the BBC. There was the Stag's Head, a pub known as 'the Whore's Lament' in Great Titchfield street and above all the George on the corner of Mortimer and Great Titchfield streets. It was not for nothing that the George retained its nickname of 'the Gluepot' which Sir Thomas Beecham had coined in the 1930s.

But that was not really what Maclaren-Ross wanted to hear, nor even what he was trying to say. His very querulousness hints at his bewilderment at the change which had come over Soho and Fitzrovia in particular and Bohemia in general. Seemingly over-night, a corner had been turned. London had at last recovered from the war. The worst excesses of Austerity and even rationing were over, and people – and in particular, young people – were beginning to live a new life in the present. A revival of interest in music, fashion and entertainment, and a boom in consumer spending reflected this change; and it was not entirely coincidental that, in the London area at least, a second, commercial television channel began transmissions in 1955. To Julian, however, it all boiled down to the fact that the Fitzrovians' coveted spots at the end of the bar in the pubs of Rathbone Place – *their* pubs – had been usurped by younger men.

Indeed the pubs themselves had changed. Back in the forties, Maclaren-Ross had always tried to avoid the Duke of York in Rathbone Street because of its popularity with the Bums. Now it was overrun by their descendants: since the early 1950s it had been one of London's principal meeting-places for the art-school students and duffle-coated 'Outsiders' who called themselves 'beatniks' or just 'beats'. Over in Rathbone Place, the Black Horse too had succumbed. As early as 1953 it had pre-empted even Paul Lincoln and the 2i's and begun presenting live music. Its 'Ballads and Blues Club' (which, confusingly, actually presented English folk music and was initially run by Ewan McColl) had been one of the very first of the innumerable music clubs, pubs, bars, cellars and even attics which were to flourish in the pre-discotéque London of the fifties and early sixties.

Dylan Thomas was long dead, and by the mid-fifties Julian and his dwindling band of survivors were fast following in Nina Hamnett's footsteps and becoming museum-pieces in their own lifetimes. So much was this the case that when, in December 1956, the BBC broadcast a radio play about life in and around the Charlotte Street of the thirties the whole subject was treated as historically as any of Louis MacNeice's evocations of the times of Byron or Christopher Marlowe. Everyone was included; their names were disguised, but the message was clear enough. The play was even entitled *It's Long Past the Time*.

It really was; and as if proving the point Nina Hamnett (the play's 'Cynthia') was to die less than a fortnight later, on 16 December. Finally forced out of Fitzrovia by a fire in the Howland Street premises in which she had lived during the forties, she had ended up in a couple of rooms in Westbourne Terrace, Paddington. She had tried to continue working, but drink and ill-health had overtaken her. She had broken her thigh in a fall in 1953 but, even after several months in hospital, it had healed incorrectly, leaving the leg some four inches shorter than the other.

Chronically alcoholic, convinced that she was suffering a recurrence of the venereal disease she had contracted many years previously and almost incapable of walking, she fell from the window of her second-floor flat one lunch-time and impaled herself on the area railings below. There were rumours that she had been 'misusing' the window just as she had the Howland Street sink; but despite an inquest verdict of Accidental Death it was the opinion of the majority of her friends that she had simply given up, and killed herself.

If the writings of Julian Maclaren-Ross uniquely preserve the texture of life in the London of the 1940s, as to a lesser extent those of Michael Arlen and the early novels of Patrick Hamilton do for the twenties and thirties respectively, it is the 'London Novels' of Colin MacInnes – a trilogy comprising *City of Spades* (1957), *Absolute Beginners* (1959) and *Mr Love and Justice* (1960) – which best depict life in the new city of the fifties.

The son of the novelist Angela Thirkell (and a cousin of both Stanley Baldwin and Rudyard Kipling), MacInnes was in many ways a Golden Age Bohemian who had been born out of his time. He would have been a natural ally of Augustus John, Nina Hamnett and Tommy Earp in their rampaging around the wilder fringes of London in the late twenties. As it was, after a childhood spent in Australia, he only found his feet when he arrived in Britain in 1931 at the age of sixteen. And, although he was a minor, tangential member of the pre-war Fitzrovian community, he did not come of age as a Bohemian until the late forties – the period in which Bohemianism itself was beginning to wither and die.

Abrupt, unpredictable and inevitably homosexual (he had a particular penchant for young Negroes) he revelled in the opportunities presented by the fast-changing times. He worked for the BBC as a scriptwriter and in the early fifties as a contributor to the radio arts programme, *The Critics*, and penetrated as far as he could the burgeoning ethnic and artistic sub-cultures of the day.

He was, of course, a regular afternoon visitor at the Colony for, he was later to write, 'with the curtains drawn at 4 p.m. on a sunny afternoon, sipping expensive poison and gossiping one's life away, has the futile fascination of forbidden fruit: the heady intoxication of a bogus Baudelairian romantic evil.'[7] But the hours of polite Bohemianism he spent there in the company of Muriel, Francis Bacon, Daniel Farson and the other regulars were only the tip of the iceberg. In an era of clubs, MacInnes (who shunned pubs – like banks, he said, they were never open when you needed them) was the most clubbable of men. He quartered London seeking out and gaining admission to a wide range of members-only establishments.

Most, it has to be said, he visited solely in the hope of meeting and in some vague way being 'accepted' by the black community. It was, apparently, a vain hope, for the (white) jazz musician Kenny Graham recalls that 'he couldn't understand Negroes and jazz musicians, their total disrespect for everything. He would flatter, cajole, bribe all the Spade musicians. Yet they used to call him "Mr Collins" while they called me "Kenny my brother".'[8] Nevertheless, he frequented the Myrtle Bank, a 'Spade drinker' in Berwick Street and, although music and particularly jazz were 'definitely a problem for him', he was among the first writers and critics to try to keep a finger on what was happening in the jazz and 'beat' clubs which were almost as numerous as coffee-bars in the London of the middle fifties.

The 100 Club which flourished in the basement of No 100 Oxford Street in the 1960s grew out of a smaller, more casual jazz club originally called Feldman's and then Humphrey Lyttleton's (or just 'Humph's') when the old-Etonian trumpeter took it over in the mid-fifties. Like Studio 51 in Great Portland Street (whose name commemorated the year of its establishment) and later clubs such as the Flamingo (Wardour Street), the Breadbasket (Cleveland Street), Richardson's (Gerrard Street) and any number of others, they all celebrated music – anything from skiffle and the earthiest folk to the tightest jazz – and youth. For, although they have not received anything like the attention which has been paid to the sixties, the middle and late fifties were the years in which a new generation began to make itself felt.

Typically the graduates of provincial art-schools (and as time went on, of the burgeoning new 'glass-and-concrete' universities) who pitched up in London for the want of anywhere better to go, in their own eyes at least, they were the 'new Bohemians'. Imbued with elements of the Maclaren-Ross myth and their own (equally incorrect) extrapolations of The Legend of Dylan Thomas, they had arrived, like Daniel Farson, convinced that in London and above all in Soho they would magically be inspired with some purpose.

And moving amongst them, vicariously sharing their hopes and genuinely enjoying their company, was Colin MacInnes. There was something of the Ransome about his prowling – he described himself as 'a very nosey person' – but unlike Ransome he used it all to good effect. Through their fractured prose and genuine, knowing but occasionally-irritating matiness, his London novels, and *Absolute Beginners* in particular, re-create the new world with spectacular clarity:

> In Soho, all the things they say happen, do: I mean, the vice of every kink, and speak-easies and spielers and friends who carve each other up, and, on the other hand, dear old Italians and sweet old Viennesse who've run their honest, unbent little businesses there since the days of George six, and five, and backward far beyond. And what's more, although the pavement's thick with tearaways, provided you don't meddle it's really a much safer area than the respectable suburban fringe. It's not in Soho a sex maniac leaps out of a hedge on to your back and violates you. It's in the dormitory sections.
>
> The coffee-spot where I hoped I'd find my two duets was of the kind that's now the chic-est thing to date among the juniors – namely, the pig-sty variety, and adolescent bum's delight. I don't exaggerate, as you'll see. What you do is, rent premises that are just as dear as any other, rip up the linos and tear out the nice fittings if there happen to be any, put in thick wood floors and tables, and take special care not to wipe the cups properly, or sweep the butts and crusts and spittle off the floor. Candles are a help or, at a pinch, non-pearl 40-watt blue bulbs. And a juke-box just for decoration, as it's considered rather naïve to *use* one in these places.[9]

For all this, tinselly, Technicolor glamour, however, MacInnes's Soho was hardly a Bohemia – and he was hard-nosed enough to accept the fact. It was a chaotic, increasingly commercial Babylon. At the end of *Absolute Beginners* his anonymous young hero-narrator, inevitably another photographer ('street, holiday, park, studio, artistic poses and, from time to time, when I find a client, pornographic') is fittingly caught up in the Notting Hill race riots of 1956. To him and his Italian-suited peers, even the war was an historical event: something 'I can hardly remember, only a bit of the buzz-bombs at the end'.

247

Times were changing. Indeed, by the end of May 1956 the whole concept of Bohemianism was redundant. On the eighth of that month the Royal Court Theatre had premiered John Osborne's first play, *Look Back in Anger* in which the actor Kenneth Haigh first articulated the frustrated anger of Jimmy Porter. And then on the twenty-sixth the firm of Victor Gollancz, which had supported the Left Book Club in the thirties and forties, published Colin Wilson's extraordinary, uncategorisable first book, *The Outsider*.

'He's A Major Writer – And He's Only 24,' screamed the headline to one review. And as the press began to revel in the details of Wilson's own 'Bohemian' life – he'd lived rough on Hampstead Heath while writing a novel in the Reading Room of the British Museum, and then worked in a London coffee-bar – Porter's anger and Wilson's youthful energy seemed to coalesce. Out of it all came the Angry Young Man, the 'Youth Culture' which was to become such a shibboleth in the 1960s, and a duffle-coated, goatee-bearded, guitar-strumming mass 'Bohemianism' which, by its very ubiquity, was ultimately self-defeating.

Everything that they had all fought for – Mürger, Wilde, Yeats, John, Sickert, Julian, Nina and even, in his own way, Colin MacInnes – had finally come to pass. And yet, in its very hour of triumph the meaninglessness of that triumph was most apparent. For, as W. S. Gilbert had said in his libretto to *The Gondoliers*, staged only eight years after *Patience*,

> *When everyone is somebodee,*
> *Then no one's anybody.*

And typically, and ironically in view of the push-me-pull-you relationship which Bohemia had enjoyed with its parent society for the previous half-century, Colin MacInnes, who had done so much to bring the new world about, was among the first to lament the passing of the old. His friend, the playwright Bernard Kops, remembered that 'when the authentic Bohemian world broke up, Colin lost his home. When the world caught up, he lost his sense of adventure. The Soho world fitted him perfectly. He was anti-establishment. So when the establishment entered it all, he deeply resented it.'[10]

248

Gin, Whisky, Sloth, Fear, Guilt and Tobacco Revisited

HANGING from the wall in the bar of the Coach and Horses in Greek Street, Soho there is a cartoon. Actually there are many cartoons, off-prints (or originals?) of the strips which have appeared in the satirical magazine *Private Eye* for many years, commemorating that pub in particular and Soho's ever-fabled drunkenness in general. Neatly framed and fastidiously hung, they cover the woodwork around the public telephone and the entrance to the gents.

But this cartoon – on the right of the door, between the windows – is special. It shows the bar soon after opening time – a clock on the wall above the optic says five thirty-eight – and, behind it, a landlord who is just recognisable as the Coach and Horse's own Norman Balon. He is drawn in profile, his mouth open – *Beano*-style – as though a brick had just been taken from it. He is angry, as you can tell from the speech-bubble writing above his head.

'YOU'RE *!!! LATE,' he screams at his two or three customers who are cowering behind their pints and evening papers. 'YOU *@!!.' It is obviously not going to be a good evening. The telephone has already started ringing, for the handset is dangling by its wire, another speech-bubble floating above it. 'JEFF BIN IN?' someone is asking . . .

As cartoons – and even some of the other *Private Eye* strips – go the joke is rather weak; too dependent on a knowledge of the pub, the irascibility of its landlord and even the doings of 'Jeff' for it to have general appeal. It does, however, encapsulate one absolute truth: five thirty-eight in the evening is a good time to arrive at the

249

Coach and Horses. By then, the first of the regulars have indeed turned up, but there is still room to move – to examine the cartoons and bag a chair from which to observe the gathering of the new Soho clans.

They enter in ones and twos, knowingly for the most part, and make straight for the bar. One's almost beaten us to it: shoulder-length hair, duffle-coat and trainers. A student, surely. He sits at the next table, rummages for a moment in a crumpled supermarket carrier-bag and produces a battered (borrowed? second-hand?) copy of a J. M. Coetzee novel. He rifles through it, Tambi-like, as if he can assess its quality by the smell of the paper, sniffs loudly and replaces it in the bag. From his coat pocket he drags an equally-battered American-looking, saga-length book as thick as it is wide, turns to page one and begins to read . . .

'. . . shouts his arse off' – it's a golf club voice and can only be emanating from within the sheepskin jacket over there at the bar. 'Doesn't know who he's talking to, or why,' it adds, apparently referring to no one, and addressing itself to no one in particular.

Six o'clock pings from somebody's watch. Up at the bar, somebody else begins what promises to be a long explanation of the science of phrenology. 'It's really spooky . . .' Around thirty people are keeping the lone barman occupied if not busy.

Two women enter, both wearing the shapeless, nondescript black dresses which signal to those in the know that they are probably the fashion editors of mass-circulation women's magazines. Both are also heavily encumbered with any number of bangles and tapestry shoulder-bags. Giggling like schoolgirls, the bangles and their multiple earrings jangling, they carry bottles of Perrier water to one of the few vacant tables.

It is less than two feet from its neighbour, which has long been occupied by two teenage youths. Blond but crop-haired, with tight jeans specifically delineating their masculinity, black berets and studded, black leather jackets they present an image of synthetic, designer-aggression. Fifty years ago they would have been natural recruits to the *Hitlerjugend*; now they are quietly arguing over last night's *EastEnders*.

'Call me anti-social if you like,' says the sheepskin jacket. No one bothers.

'. . . it's quite infallible. Really, it is. Mmm, you've got a *very interesting* mound here,' announces the phrenologist, up to his wrists in the hair of a bright-looking Pre-Raphaelite redhead; his girlfriend surely.

But then, like wounded partridges, the wandering hands suddenly flutter ineffectually to his lap, and he falls silent as the door behind the bar opens and 'the guv'nor' appears. Ursine in a heavy camel overcoat, Norman Balon growls matter-of-factly at the barman and then turns to his customers.

'YOU *@!!,' the words hang there, unsaid . . .

It's nearly six-thirty. The pub is comfortably full. Rather more than sixty people, ranging from tired and rather faded M. Hulots to louder, ex-public school Matt Dillon look-alikes, have already arrived. There are faces you've seen on television – Richard Ingrams, a former editor of *Private Eye* – and faces you know that somehow you soon will. There are *real* editors and *real* publishers, and those who gossip knowledgeably about the business from their close reading of *Publishing News* and *The Bookseller*. There are drinkers and increasing numbers of the orange-juice brigade; smokers and those who'd 'really rather you didn't, if that's all right'.

By six forty-five Norman Balon has temporarily retired upstairs, the phrenologist has taken up where he left off and another barman has arrived. The bar is getting crowded, but Jeff's still not bin in . . .

He will be, though. At the Coach and Horses Jeff's always in; he has to be for, through his 'Low Life' column in the *Spectator*, Jeffrey Bernard has become the pub's *raison d'être*. Without him it would be like any other pub in that part of London; with him it has become the essential watering-hole for a new generation of Filofax-carrying, Tory-voting, *Guardian*-reading young 'Bohemians'; the yuppies who have rediscovered Soho in the years since Mrs Margaret Thatcher became Prime Minister. Aided by Westminster City Council which has cleaned up the sex-shops (in 1979 there were nearly two hundred, by 1988 just five) and prettified and pedestrianised a few of its streets, they have rebuilt (or more accurately redesigned and refashioned) much of the district in their own image.

Soho has become a theme park. It was not coincidence which led the *Sunday Times Magazine* to give it cover-story treatment in 1987. 'Goodbye sex, hello style', it said, trailing an account of the progress of 'Soho Nouveau . . . from topless bar to champagne bar'.[1] It was inevitable and even overdue. The signs had been there for years. Its dinky restaurants, little galleries, independent booksellers, hairdressers and designer boutiques had already made it colour-supplement chic.

But it is also 'Bohemian'; almost in spite of himself, 'Jeff' has seen to that. Though he might castigate them as 'empty-headed', the new generation of Soho-ites love him. He is a 'character', they say, and convince themselves that merely by reading his column and sipping their Perriers at the Coach and Horses they are characters too. It does not take them long, for although the old Roche and the Café Boulogne have largely been replaced by establishments such as Ed's Easy Diner and Pasta Mania ('Eat as much as you like – £2.90'), the very presence of the French-looking Soho Brasserie and a scattering of other restaurants which have taken to putting a couple of gingham-covered tables out on the pavement is enough to persuade them that, now the sex-shops have gone, Soho is just like it was in the 'olden days'.

Why, it even has its own drinking-club. The Groucho Club in Dean Street opened in 1985, and is thus now a hallowed, even venerable, part of the new Soho scene. Jeff's 'always' there too, and for the rest of its 1,400-odd members that only goes to prove how little Soho has really changed. *There were always places like this* . . .

But the visiting outsider, confronted by its lush, designer-interior, soft sofas and tasteful pastel colours, hears more than the dulcet chords of the house pianist. Two disembodied voices command attention. Wrapped around in ironies, there are the gruff tones of Groucho Marx, in whose name everything has been created, solemnly warning that he could never join any club which would have him as a member. And, more faintly, there is Augustus John remembering the 'sophisticated' Cave of the Golden Calf:

My attendance was counted upon, but I never entered the place. One look at the seething mob outside its doors, on the opening night, was enough for me. I passed on. Another miscalculation!

Notes and Sources

PROLOGUE: Cleaning the Stables

1. H. Montgomery Hyde: *The Trials of Oscar Wilde* (1948), p. 330.
2. *St. James's Gazette*, 27 May 1895.
3. Hesketh Pearson: *The Life of Oscar Wilde* (1960), p. 255.
4. Montgomery Hyde: *op. cit.*, p. 331.
5. *Ibid.*, p. 335.
   Here, however, the judge may well have been right. Although *Dickens's Dictionary of London*, compiled by the novelist's son in 1879, does not detail prices at the Savoy, it suggests that a bed, full breakfast and 'dinner with soup and joint' could be had at the Langham in Portland Place for 14/6d. At the fashionable Criterion restaurant in Piccadilly Circus a *table d'hôte* dinner in the Grand Hall was 3/6d., French dinner in the West Room 5s. and a 'joint' dinner 2/6d. It seems at least possible that a charge for further, unspecified services was added to Wilde's bill.
6. Montgomery Hyde: *op. cit.*, p. 339.

CHAPTER ONE: Scandals in Bohemia

1. *The Oxford and Cambridge Undergraduate's Journal*, 3 May 1877.
2. *A Choice of Swinburne's Verse* (1973), p. 15.
3. *The Letters of Matthew Arnold*, ed. G. W. E. Russell, 2 vols (1895), Vol. I. p. 196.
4. *Ibid.*, Vol. II. p. 43.
5. Edmund Gosse: *Portraits and Sketches* (1912), p. 11.
6. Georgina Burne-Jones: *Memorials of Edward Burne-Jones*, 2 vols (1904), Vol. I, p. 205.
7. *Punch*, 10 November 1866.
8. Daphne du Maurier: *The Rebecca Notebooks and Other Memories*. Victor Gollancz (1981), p. 59.
9. *Punch*, 14 February 1880.
10. *Ibid.*, 12 February 1881.
11. *Patience*, Act I, lines 397–404; 413–20.

Notes and Sources

CHAPTER TWO: La Vie de Bohème
1. Arthur Ransome: *Bohemia in London* (1907), pp. 20–1.
2. *Ibid.*, p. 21.
3. Daphne du Maurier: *Gerald* (1934), p. 54.
4. *Harper's New Monthly Magazine*, LXXXVIII (March 1894), p. 577. The suppressed Joe Sibley passages are also available in a modern unexpurgated edition of the novel published under the title *Svengali* by W. H. Allen, 1982.
5. George du Maurier: *Trilby* (1895), pp. 32–3.
6. See Mosco Carner: *Puccini.* Duckworth, 1974, pp. 68–9.
7. Luke Ionides: *Memories* (Paris, 1925). Quoted in Leonée Ormond: *George du Maurier* (1969), p. 445.
8. Henry Mürger: *Scènes de la Vie de Bohème* (Paris, 1882), p. 34. (My translation.)
9. Jules and Edmond de Goncourt: *Journals*, 10 May 1856.
10. Mürger: *op. cit.*, pp. 125–6. (My translation.)
11. Ransome: *op. cit.*, pp. 7–8.

CHAPTER THREE: Bohemia in London
1. Ransome: op. cit., pp. 22–3.
2. Nina Hamnett: *Laughing Torso* (1932), pp. 22–3.
3. Ransome: *op. cit.*, pp. 248; 250–1.
4. *Ibid.*, pp. 197–8.
5. *Ibid.*, p. 4.
6. George du Maurier: *op. cit.*, p. 1.
7. The details of two will suffice.
Nina Hamnett's biographer, Denise Hooker, paints a bleak picture of the 'cold and dirty' Fulham Road studio occupied by the sculptor Henri Gaudier-Brzeska in 1913: 'Bare and comfortless, it was full of stone dust and sparsely furnished with two work-benches, a table, some kitchen chairs and a canvas deckchair in which he sometimes slept.' (*Nina Hamnett* (1986), p. 54)
Fifteen years previously, in a letter home to her mother, Ida Nettleship (later the wife of Augustus John) had determinedly made the best of a Paris flat she was sharing with Gwen John. It was 'on the 5th floor – overlooking a large open space – right over the market roof. It has 3 good rooms, a kitchen and W.C. and water and gas – and a balcony. Good windows – very light and airy. Nothing opposite for miles – very high up. The woman (*concièrge*) is very clean and exceedingly healthy looking. The proprietress is rather swell – an old lady – she lives this end of Paris and we went to see her. She asked questions, and especially that *we received nobody* – 'Les dames – oui. Mais les messieurs? Non! Jamais!' . . . She wants to keep her apartments very high in

character. All this is rather amusing, but it will show you it is a respectable place. It *is* over a café – but the entrance is right round the corner – quite separate . . . We want all the paper scraped and the place whitewashed . . .' (Quoted in Michael Holroyd: *Augustus John* (1974), Vol. I. p. 87).

8. Ransome: *op. cit.*, p. 67.
9. *Ibid.*, p. 116.
10. The history of Old Compton Street is described in some detail in David Benedictus: *Streets of London*. Thames Methuen, 1985.
11. Robert Machray: *The Night Side of London* (1902), p. 96. This and the other prices quoted in Chapter Three seem risible today. To set them, and the references to prices and money in later chapters, in context, it might be useful to bear in mind some modern research on the changing value of the pound over the last one hundred years.

It has recently been computed that one pound in 1914 would have been worth £1.35 in 1895 and £1.18 in 1905. In 1925 its value had declined to 57p., but by 1935 it had rallied to 70p. Following the upsets of World War Two the purchasing power of that 1914 pound declined sharply: from 37p. in 1946 to 25p. in 1955 and 20p. in 1965. By 1982 it was worth just 4p.

12. Ransome: *op. cit.*, pp. 112–3.
13. Machray: *op. cit.*, pp. 97–8.
14. Ransome: *op. cit.*, p. 162.

CHAPTER FOUR: 'Give up Verse, My Boy'
1. W. B. Yeats: *Autobiographies* (1955), p. 300.
2. W. B. Yeats: *Memoirs*, ed. Denis Donoghue (1972), p. 36.
3. *Autobiographies*, p. 165.
4. *Memoirs*, pp. 36–7.
5. *Autobiographies*, p. 165.
6. *Memoirs*, p. 36.
7. *The Oxford Book of Modern Verse*, ed. W. B. Yeats (1936), p. ix.
8. *Pall Mall Gazette*, 12 July 1889.
9. *The Academy*, January–June 1889.
10. Letter to John O'Leary, 26 June 1894. Quoted in *The Letters of W. B. Yeats*, ed. Allan Wade (1954), p. 232.
11. *Memoirs*, p. 37.
12. *Autobiographies*, p. 167.
13. *Memoirs*, p. 89. (My italics.)
14. Bernard Bergonzi: 'Aspects of the *Fin de Siècle*', in *The Victorians*, ed. Arthur Pollard (1969), p. 373.
15. Roger Shattuck: *The Banquet Years*, 1958; Vintage Books, New York, 1968, p. 24.
16. *The Oxford Book of Modern Verse* (1936), p. xi.

17. Harold Acton: *Memoirs of an Aesthete* (1948), p. 1.
18. 'Mr Bennett and Mrs Brown', reprinted in Virginia Woolf: *Collected Essays*, Vol.I. The Hogarth Press (1966), p. 319ff.
19. John Galsworthy: *The Man of Property* (1915), p. 4.
20. *Ibid.*, p. 7.
21. *Poetry (Chicago)*, January 1912. Quoted in Noel Stock: *The Life of Ezra Pound* (1985), pp. 158–9.
22. Ezra Pound: *Collected Shorter Poems* ('Personae'). Faber and Faber, (1952); Second ed. (1968), pp. 211–12.
23. Ransome: *op. cit.*, pp. 276; 280.
24. George du Maurier: *op. cit.*, p. 221.
25. Charles Dickens: *Dickens's Dictionary of London* (1879), pp. 21–2.
26. Ransome: *op. cit.*, p. 78.
27. Machray: *op. cit.*, p. 203.

CHAPTER FIVE: Augustus and the Demi-Johns

1. William Rothenstein: *Men and Memories* (1932), p. 333.
2. Holroyd quotes the following verse which appeared in *Punch*, 27 February 1929:

    > 'Augustus Caesar,' so the poet said,
    > 'Shall be regarded as a present god
    > By Britain, made to kiss the Roman's rod.'
    > Augustus Caesar long ago is dead,
    > But still the good work's being carried on:
    > We lick the brushes of Augustus John.

    (*Augustus John*, Vol. I. p. 56)
3. Wyndham Lewis: *Blasting and Bombardiering* (1937), p. 52.
4. Holroyd: *op. cit.*, Vol. II. p. 53. The provenance of the verse is uncertain. Holroyd notes that in a letter of 1918 Ezra Pound claims to remember having heard it recited as early as 1909.
5. *Ibid.*, Vol. I. p. 91.
6. Lytton Strachey to Duncan Grant, 12 April 1907.
7. Augustus John: *Chiaroscuro* (1952), p. 41.
8. *Ibid.*
9. *Ibid.*, pp. 48–9.
10. *Pall Mall Gazette*, 13 April 1886.
11. John: *op. cit.*, p. 136.
12. *Ibid.*, p. 47.
13. Sickert's music-hall canvases are now widely scattered. Many, such as *The Brighton Pierrots* (and the earlier but somewhat similar *Lion Comique* (1887)) are now in private collections. *Noctes Ambrosianae* can be seen in the Nottingham Castle Museum. *Minnie Cunningham* is in the Tate Gallery, London.
14. Marjorie Lilly: *Sickert: The Painter and His Circle* (1971), p. 98.
15. Enid Bagnold: *Autobiography*. Heinemann, 1969, p. 75.

16. Augustus John to Lady Ottoline Morrell, 4 December 1909. Quoted in Holroyd: *op. cit.*, Vol. I. p. 324.

CHAPTER SIX: 'Welcome, Gentlemen, to Tot'nam Court'

1. Letter to Violet Dickinson. Quoted in Quentin Bell: *Virginia Woolf* (1976), Vol. I. p. 115.
2. Quoted in Quentin Bell: *Bloomsbury* (1968), p. 41.
3. *Ibid.*, p. 42.
4. Lilly: *op. cit.*, pp. 136–7.
5. Undated Omega Workshops' catalogue. Quoted in Denise Hooker: *Nina Hamnett* (1986), p. 62.
6. Wyndham Lewis: *Rude Assignment* (1950), p. 124.
7. *Daily Mirror*, 8 November 1913.
8. Unpublished letter from Winifred Gill to Duncan Grant, 4 July 1966. Quoted in Hooker: *op. cit.*, pp. 62–3.
9. Quoted in Virginia Woolf: *Roger Fry: A Biography*. The Hogarth Press (1940), p. 194.
10. Quoted in Nick Bailey: *Fitzrovia* (1981), p. 15. A brief, topographical study, this monograph is especially valuable for its account of the early history of Fitzrovia.
11. Charles Dickens: *Barnaby Rudge* (1973), p. 411.
12. Bailey: *op. cit.*, p. 46.
13. George Gissing: *The Private Papers of Henry Ryecroft* (1903), p. 32.
14. *Ibid.*
15. *Ibid.*, pp. 28–9.
16. Gissing: *New Grub Street* (1968), p. 88.
17. Jean Jacques Rousseau: *Emile.* (Paris, 1951), p. 6.
18. Charles Malato, quoted in *Café Royal: Ninety Years of Bohemia* by Guy Deghy and Keith Waterhouse (1955), pp. 56–7.
19. The theory is expounded in the late Stephen Knight's fascinating (but now generally discredited) book, *Jack the Ripper: The Final Solution* (Harrap, 1976). As the title suggests, it is only the prologue to a far more convoluted tale.

    Taking as his starting point a confession Sickert made shortly before his death to his son Joseph, Knight marshalls an impressive body of evidence in an attempt to prove that the Whitechapel Murders of 1888, usually ascribed to Jack the Ripper, were in fact part of an establishment cover-up of Eddy's marriage. Even more startlingly, from an examination of Sickert's late work, he concludes that the then Prime Minister, Lord Salisbury, had pressured the artist into becoming a part of a three-man team which was actually responsible for the murders.
20. John Heath-Stubbs, in an interview with the author, 30 May 1987.

CHAPTER SEVEN: Café Society

1. Michael J. Arlen: *Exiles* (1971), p. 64.
2. *Ibid.*, p. 74.
3. Michael Arlen: *Piracy* (1922), p. 53.
4. Michael J. Arlen: *op. cit.*, pp. 66–7.
5. Michael Arlen: *op. cit.*, p. 76.
6. Max Beerbohm: *Seven Men* (1919), p. 5.
7. W. Seymour Leslie: *The Silent Queen* (1927), p. 18.
8. D.H. Lawrence: *Women in Love* (1960), p. 429.
9. Stanza from a parody of Edward Lear's 'Jabberwocky' by Mostyn Piggott, published in *The World*, 8 May 1895, and quoted in Deghy and Waterhouse: *op. cit.*, pp. 18–19. This book is a valuable source of anecdote and legend relating to the Café Royal in the early part of this century, and the basis of many of the stories in this chapter.
10. Beerbohm: *op. cit.*, p. 39.
11. *Ibid.*, p. 20.
12. *Ibid.*, pp. 12–13.
13. Deghy and Waterhouse: *op. cit.*, p. 16.
14. Hamnett: *Laughing Torso* (1932), p. 82.
15. Lawrence: *op. cit.*, p. 7.
16. Michael Arlen: *op. cit.*, pp. 168–9.
17. Quoted in Anne Chisholm: *Nancy Cunard* (1981), p. 55.
18. Leslie: *op. cit.*, pp. 43–4.
19. Cecil Gray: *Musical Chairs* (1948), p. 102.
20. Exodus, 32:6.
21. John: *op. cit.*, p. 233.
22. Osbert Sitwell: *Great Morning* (1948), p. 208.
23. Quoted in Holroyd: *op. cit.*, Vol. II, p. 55.
24. Richard Cork: *The Cave of the Golden Calf*, an essay in the Royal Academy Catalogue *British Art in the Twentieth Century* (1987), p. 132.

CHAPTER EIGHT: At the Eiffel Tower

1. Letter to Carrington, 6 April 1914, quoted in Hooker: *op. cit.*, p. 48.
2. Quoted in Holroyd: *op. cit.*, Vol. II, p. 55.
3. *King Lear*, I.v.35–8.
4. Michael Arlen: *op. cit.*, pp. 3–5 *passim*.
5. Anthony Powell: *To Keep the Ball Rolling* (1983), p. 138.
6. Nancy Cunard: *Sublunary*. Hodder and Stoughton, 1923, pp. 94–5.
7. John: *op. cit.*, p. 137.
8. *Ibid.*, p. 136.
9. Michael Arlen: *op. cit.*, pp. 5–6.

10. The phrase is Arlen's; it occurs twice in *Piracy* (p. 7 and p. 308). But the exact repetition suggests that the novelist is here remembering a standard remark of Stulik's.
11. Tristram Hillier: *Leda and the Goose*. Longman, Green and Co., 1954, p. 72.
12. Gray: *op. cit.*, p. 216.
13. Arlen again – and again the phrase occurs twice: *Piracy*, p. 167 and p. 307.
14. See Leslie: *op. cit.*, p. 203.
15. Michael Arlen: *op. cit.*, pp. 167–8.
16. *Ibid.*, p. 6
17. Hamnett: *Is She a Lady?* (1955), p. 47.
18. *Ibid.*, p. 69.
19. The phrase is taken from Michel Georges-Michel's *Les Montparnos* and quoted in Hooker: *op. cit.*, p. 150.
20. Hamnett: *op. cit.*, p. 61.
21. *Ibid.*
22. Gray: *op. cit.*, p. 278.
23. Hamnett: *op. cit.*, pp. 61–2.
24. Elisabeth Welch, in a conversation with the author, 1 December 1987.
25. Dylan Thomas to Trevor Jones, January 1934; in *Dylan Thomas: The Collected Letters*, edited by Paul Ferris (1985), p. 94.

CHAPTER NINE: Enter Dylan Thomas

1. Louis MacNeice: *Autumn Sequel*. Faber and Faber, 1954, pp. 113–4.
2. Cyril Connolly recalled the exchange – and many similar gaffes made by Thomas during the course of a single dinner party in 1935 – in a sound recording; a transcript is now in the Lilly Library at Indiana University. It is quoted in Paul Ferris: *Dylan Thomas* (1978), p. 130.
3. Paul Ferris: *Dylan Thomas* (1978), p. 341.
4. Letter to Geoffrey Grigson, summer 1933; in Thomas: *op. cit.*, p. 19.
5. Letter to Pamela Hansford Johnson, October 1933; *ibid.*, p. 30.
6. Letter to Pamela Hansford Johnson, January 1934; *ibid.*, pp. 84–5.
7. *Ibid.*, p. 99.
8. Letter to Pamela Hansford Johnson, October 1934; *ibid.*, p. 169.
9. Letter to A. E. Trick, December 1934; *ibid.*, p. 177.
10. *Ibid.*, p. 178.
11. Thomas: *The Collected Stories*. Dent, 1983, p. 249.
12. Patrick Hamilton: *Hangover Square* (1956), p. 66.
13. Julian Maclaren-Ross: *Memoirs of the Forties* (1965), pp. 119–20.
14. Thomas to Rayner Heppenstall; quoted in Constantine Fitz-Gibbon: *The Life of Dylan Thomas* (1965), p. 145.

15. Letter to A. E. Trick, December 1934; in Thomas: *Letters.*, p. 177.
16. Ransome: *op. cit.*, p. 49ff.
17. Letter to Pamela Hansford Johnson, November 1933; in Thomas: *Letters.*, p. 56.
18. Ransome: *op. cit.*, pp. 61–2.
19. Maclaren-Ross: *op. cit.*, p. 118.
20. Unattributed story, quoted in FitzGibbon: *op. cit.*, p. 147.
21. Maclaren-Ross: *op. cit.*, p. 123.
22. Although critics habitually refer to the four poets as a group, the shorthand is misleading. Cecil Day-Lewis put things into context when he explained that Auden, Spender and he were never in the same room together until 1947. Nor are there any photographs of the quartet together. Seemingly the closest to a convenient four-shot is a snap of Auden, Day-Lewis and Spender – but even that dates from 1949 when they were delegates to a PEN club conference in Venice.
23. W. H. Auden: *Selected Poems*. Faber and Faber, 1979, p. ix.
24. *The Listener*, 27 February 1935.
25. Letter to Glyn Jones, March 1934; in Thomas: *op. cit.*, pp. 97–8.
26. Stephen Spender: *World Within World* (1977), p. 144.
27. Cyril Connolly: 'Some Memories', an essay included in *W. H. Auden: A Tribute*, edited by Stephen Spender, (1975), p. 69.
28. I have quoted only the final stanza of 'The Pilgrim' from Yeats's *Last Poems* (1936–1939).
29. Henry Reed, in an article in the June 1943 issue of *New Writing and Daylight*. Quoted in Robert Hewison: *Under Siege* (1979), p. 110.
30. See Ferris: *op. cit.*, p. 221 and note.

CHAPTER TEN: A District of the Mind

1. Hamilton: *Twenty Thousand Streets Under the Sky* (1987), pp. 16–17.
2. Caitlin Thomas in a talk broadcast on BBC Wales in 1977. Quoted in Ferris: *op. cit.*, p. 152.
3. Maclaren-Ross: *op. cit.*, p. 154.
4. Hamnett: *Is She a Lady?* (1955), p. 78.
5. *Ibid.*, p. 83.
6. Andrew Motion: *The Lamberts* (1987), p. 178.
7. See Anthony Powell: *To Keep the Ball Rolling* (1983), p. 326; and *Books Do Furnish a Room* (1983), p. 112.
8. Maclaren-Ross: *The Nine Men of Soho* (1946), p. 12.
9. Laughton can be summarily dismissed, but Lowry is an almost equally bizarre recruit to Fitzrovia. Undoubtedly an alcoholic at the end of his life (he died in 1957), he had been a heavy drinker for many years before that; but how regular a customer he was at the Wheatsheaf or elsewhere is open to question. Gordon Bowker (in *Malcolm Lowry Remembered*, Ariel Books/BBC, 1985) insists that

'in [Fitzrovian] pubs such as the Fitzroy Tavern and the Plough he became a familiar' between 1932 and 1936. But it has to be said that not only is this contradicted – in the same volume and only thirteen pages further on – by the writer John Sommerfield ('I'm not sure really if *we* did any Fitzroy work or not. Probably did, but not a lot, I think'), but also that there does not seem to be a single reference to Lowry's presence in any of the other memoirs of the time.

10. As much for what it says about him as for any other reason, it is worth reprinting Maclaren-Ross's list of the personalities of the Fitzrovian forties. Seemingly in no particular order, it is split into two columns, one on each side of his hand-lettered title page. That on the left reads: Cyril Connolly, Dylan Thomas, Graham Greene, Anthony Carson, Philip Toynbee, Norman Douglas, Gerald Kersh, John Lehmann, Woodrow Wyatt, William Sansom, George Barker, John Minton, George Orwell, Feliks Topolski, André Deutsch, Beverly Nichols, Nina Hamnett, Alan Ross, Robert Newton, Arthur Calder-Marshall.

   The right-hand column includes the names of Anthony Powell, Henry Green, Eric Ambler, Picasso, Maurice Richardson, Brian Howard, Liam O'Flaherty, James Agate, Roy Campbell, William Saroyan, Rayner Heppenstall, Jim Phelan, Peter de Polnay, Tambimuttu, Ruthven Todd, Alun Owen, Jonathan Cape, H.M. King Juan 1st of Redonda, Val Gielgud, Mulk raj Anand and Joyce Cary.

   Beneath both Maclaren-Ross has added the words 'among many others'. It is only to be regretted that he did not live even to record his encounters with all those of whom he had at first thought.

11. *London Magazine*, December 1962.
12. Maclaren-Ross: *Memoirs of the Forties* (1965), p. 159.
13. Dan Davin: *Closing Times* (1975), p. 124.
14. Maclaren-Ross: *op. cit.*, p. 159.
15. *Ibid.*, pp. 153–4.
16. John Heath-Stubbs in an interview with the author, 30 May 1987.
17. 'Oh no they don't,' said Norman Balon, landlord of the Coach and Horses pub in Greek Street, Soho in a conversation with the author, September 1987. 'I've never heard anyone call it that. Ever.' I venture to disagree with the man, well known to readers of Jeffrey Bernard's Low Life column in the *Spectator* as 'the rudest landlord in London'. In the course of researching this book, I have. Several times.
18. Maclaren-Ross: *op. cit.*, p. 113.
19. Though outwardly impenetrable, the whole letter (addressed to Earp and dated 1 July 1943) is of extreme interest to anyone

attempting the almost impossible task of following Thomas's
pub- and club-crawling in London:

'Dear Tommy:
When next shall we stumble to the stutter of our lewis-gun
    carols
From bombazine-bosomed bar to a bliss of barrels,
Two period percies friscoed with ladders and banting,
Two spooned swiss pillars, tumble falsetting and ranting?

O when, marcel-bound, shall we ruth our swine's way to
    the many-johned
Penny-fond antelope's cavern from the royal back-bar of
    beyond,
Or sinister self-mabuses ripe for the phelan of the withy,
Peggy-legged limping in bottle-dress he hooved from the
    Wardour-street smithy?'

(Thomas: *Letters* (1987), p. 506.)

As Paul Ferris points out in his explanatory note to the letter,
the fun starts when one begins trying to disentangle Thomas's
punning (Lewis guns and Lewis Carroll, and the next line's play
on the word 'barrels') from the proper names disguised among
the lower-case text. Thus the ladder refers to a drinking den
called the Ladder Club, and 'banting' is a reference to a mutual
friend, the artist John Banting. Similarly, the Antelope was a
favoured pub in Kensington, while 'mabuses' recalls the film *Dr
Mabuse*. Inflicting a spoonerism on the phrase 'swiss pillars'
converts Thomas and Earp, two undoubted pillars of the Swiss,
into 'piss swillers' . . . Nearly half a century on, it is probably
now as impossible to recover the real identities of 'marcel', 'ruth',
'john' and 'peggy' as it is to understand the significance of the
word 'phelan'. (Maclaren-Ross includes the name Jim Phelan on
the holograph title page of *Memoirs of the Forties*, but neither that
book nor any other I have consulted even mentions him.) It
seems likely, however, that they were all members of the staff or
regulars at favoured bars.

On the other hand, Ferris is surely wrong in following
Constantine FitzGibbon's theory that 'smithy' was another of
these. Taken in conjunction with the 'hooved' of the previous
line, the phrase 'Wardour-street smithy' sounds more like a
reference to the Horseshoe drinking club which had premises at
21 Wardour Street.

20. Gaston Berlemont, in a conversation with the author, November
    1987.
21. Farson's comments on the pubs and clubs of Soho, here and in
    succeeding paragraphs, come from his volume *Soho in the Fifties*
    (1987).

22. Anthony Cronin: *Dead as Doornails* (1986), p. 154.
23. See note 19 above.
24. Davin: *op. cit.*, p. 5
25. Alan Ross, in his introduction to the 1984 Penguin edition of *Memoirs of the Forties*, p. ix.
26. Maclaren-Ross: *op. cit.*, p. xv.

CHAPTER ELEVEN: Whistling in the Blackout

1. Cecil Collins, in a lecture at the Barbican Art Gallery, 1 June 1987.
2. Letter to Richard Church, 9 December 1935; in Thomas: *op. cit.*, p. 204.
3. Cyril Connolly: *The Unquiet Grave* (1951), p. 96.
4. Rattigan's *Flare Path* opened at the Apollo Theatre, London in August 1942 and ran for 679 performances.

    Coward's *In Which We Serve* (1942) – in which he served as writer, star and director – was made with official permission and the enthusiastic support of Lord Louis Mountbatten, then Chief of Combined Operations. Similarly *Henry V*, which Laurence Olivier produced and co-directed, and in which he also starred, was made in 1943 (at the then almost unprecedented cost of £500,000) as a piece of semi-official propaganda.

    Mrs Miniver (1942) was Hollywood's version of life during the Blitz. Starring Greer Garson, it did much to reinforce the sentimental view that 'Britain could take it', then held on both sides of the Atlantic.
5. Letter to John Davenport, 14 September 1939; in Thomas: *op. cit.*, p. 410.
6. Robert Hewison: *Under Siege* (1979), p. 99.

    Those magazines which went out of business on the outbreak of war are discussed on p. 11.
7. Cronin: *op. cit.*, p. 142.
8. *Horizon*, January 1940, p. 5.
9. Maclaren-Ross: *op. cit.*, p. 116.
10. *Ibid.*, p. 117.
11. Todd's career is detailed in *Ruthven Todd: A Preliminary Finding-List*, compiled by his son Christopher in October 1980 and currently unpublished.
12. Charles Wrey Gardiner. Quoted in Derek Stanford: *Inside the Forties* (1977), p. 94.
13. Charles Wrey Gardiner's career and the history of *Poetry Quarterly* and the Grey Walls Press are documented in *The Grey Walls Press – A Commentary*, an unpublished study by Alan Smith, 1981. This also includes a chronological checklist of all G.W.P. publications.
14. Stanford, *op. cit.*, p. 93.
15. *New Road*, 1944, p. 61.

16. Maclaren-Ross: *op. cit.*, p. 138.
17. *The Times*, 24 June 1983.

CHAPTER TWELVE: Te Palinure Petens
1. Cecil Beaton: *The Years Between: Diaries 1939–1944*. Wiedenfeld and Nicolson, 1965, p. 53.
2. Henry Moore, quoted in Constantine FitzGibbon: *The Blitz* (1957), illustration facing p. 224.
3. Beaton: *op. cit.*, pp. 52–3.
4. *Ibid.*, p. 213.
5. John Lehmann: *I Am My Brother* (1960), pp. 181–2.
6. Flora Isserlis, quoted in Hooker: *op. cit.*, p. 169.
7. Maclaren-Ross: *op. cit.*, p. 169.
8. Cyril Connolly: *The Unquiet Grave* (1951), p. 29.
9. Ibid., p. 31.
10. Ibid., p. 89.
11. Connolly: *Enemies of Promise* (1949), p. 4.
12. *The Unquiet Grave.*, p. 2.
13. Alan Ross: *The Forties* (1950), unpaginated.
14. *The Unquiet Grave.*, p. 45.
15. Graham Greene: *Men at Work, Penguin New Writing*, September 1940. Reprinted in Lehmann and Fuller's anthology, *The Penguin New Writing, 1940–1950* (1985), pp. 33–8.
16. *New Statesman and Nation*, 20 April 1940, pp. 526–7.

CHAPTER THIRTEEN: Sohoitis
1. Iris Murdoch: *Under the Net* (1954), p. 275.
2. *Ibid.*, p. 106.
3. George Orwell: *Nineteen Eighty-Four*, 1949; Penguin, 1954, pp. 6–7.
4. *Penguin New Writing 5*, April 1941.
5. *New Writing and Daylight II*, 1946, pp. 8–9.
6. Cronin: *op. cit.*, p. 27.
7. Maclaren-Ross: *op. cit.*, p. 138.
8. *Reynold's News*, 27 January 1957.
9. Michael Wishart: *High Diver* (1978), p. 113.
10. David Mellor: 'John Minton: The Fall of London', an essay in the Barbican Art Gallery catalogue, *The Neo-Romantic Imagination in Britain, 1935–55* (1987), p. 58.
11. George Melly, in his Introduction to Daniel Farson's *Soho in the Fifties* (1987), p. xiii.
12. *The Listener*, 13 February 1947.
13. John Craxton, in a lecture at the Barbican Art Gallery, 1 June 1987.
14. John Rothenstein: *Modern English Painters*, Vol.III (1984), p. 174.
15. *Ibid.*, p. 168.

16. Cronin: *op. cit.*, p. 160.
17. Ruthven Todd, quoted in Hooker: *op. cit.*, p. 213.
18. Undated letter written by Julius Horowitz, and quoted in Hooker: *op. cit.*, p. 232.
19. John Heath-Stubbs, in a conversation with the author, 30 May 1987.
20. Hooker: *op. cit.*, p. 223.

CHAPTER FOURTEEN: Deaths and Entrances

1. Noel Barber: *Conversations with Artists* (1964), quoted in the Barbican Art Gallery catalogue *A Paradise Lost* (1987), p. 58.
2. John Heath-Stubs, in a conversation with the author, 30 May 1987.
3. *Capital Gay*, 14 April 1987.
4. Quoted in Farson: *op. cit.*, p. 81.
5. See Tony Palmer: *All You Need is Love*, Futura, 1977, p. 212.
6. Quoted in John Platt: *London's Rock Routes*, (1985), p. 12.
7. Colin MacInnes, 'See You at Mabel's', *Encounter*, March 1957.
8. Kenny Graham, quoted in Tony Gould: *Inside Outsider* (1986), p. 140.
9. Colin MacInnes: *Absolute Beginners*, MacGibbon & Kee, 1959; Allison & Busby, 1980, pp. 61–2.
10. Bernard Kops, quoted in Gould: *op. cit.*, p. 139.

EPILOGUE: Gin, Whisky, Sloth, Fear, Guilt and Tobacco Revisited

1. *Sunday Times Magazine*, 13 December 1987.

Bibliography

Acton, Harold: *Memoirs of an Aesthete*. Methuen, 1948.
Arlen, Michael: *Piracy*. Collins, 1922.
Arlen, Michael J.: *Exiles*. André Deutsch, 1971.
Bagnold, Enid: *Autobiography*. Heinemann, 1969.
Bailey, Nick: *Fitzrovia*. Historical Publications Ltd., 1981.
Beaton, Cecil: *The Years Between* (Diaries, 1939–44). Weidenfeld and Nicolson, 1965.
Beerbohm, Max: *Seven Men*. Heinemann, 1919.
Bell, Quentin: *Bloomsbury*. Weidenfeld and Nicolson, 1968.
  Virginia Woolf, Vol. I: Virginia Stephen, 1882–1912. The Hogarth Press, 1972; Triad/Paladin, 1976.
Cecil, David: *Max Beerbohm*. Constable, 1964.
Chancellor, E. Beresford: *London's Old Latin Quarter*. Jonathan Cape, 1930.
Chisholm, Anne: *Nancy Cunard*. Sidgwick & Jackson, 1979; Penguin, 1981.
Connolly, Cyril: *Enemies of Promise*, 1938; rev. ed., Routledge & Kegan Paul, 1949.
  The Unquiet Grave, 1944; second rev. ed., Hamish Hamilton, 1951.
Coulton, Barbara: *Louis MacNeice in the BBC*. Faber and Faber, 1980.
Cronin, Anthony: *Dead as Doornails*. Calder and Boyars, 1976; Oxford University Press, 1986.
Davies, James A.: *Dylan Thomas's Places*. Christopher Davies (Publishers) Ltd, Swansea, 1987.
Davin, Dan: *Closing Times*. Oxford University Press, 1975.
Deghy, Guy, and Waterhouse, Keith: *Café Royal: Ninety Years of Bohemia*. Hutchinson, 1955.
Dickens, Charles: *Barnaby Rudge*. Penguin, 1973.
Dickens, Charles (the younger): *A Dictionary of London, 1879*. Dickens and Evans, 1879; facsimile reprint by Howard Barker Press, 1972.
Du Maurier, Daphne: *Gerald: A Portrait*. Victor Gollancz, 1934.
Du Maurier, George: *Trilby*. Osgood, McIlvane & Co, 1895.

Bibliography

Ellmann, Richard: *Oscar Wilde*. Hamish Hamilton, 1987.

Farson, Daniel: *Soho in the Fifties*. Michael Joseph, 1987.

Ferris, Paul: *Dylan Thomas*. Hodder and Stoughton, 1977; Penguin, 1978.

Fido, Martin: *Oscar Wilde*. Hamlyn, 1973.

FitzGibbon, Constantine: *The Blitz*. Allan Wingate, 1957.
The Life of Dylan Thomas. Dent, 1965.

Galsworthy, John: *The Man of Property*. Heinemann, 1906; 1915.

Gissing, George: *The Private Papers of Henry Rycroft*. Constable, 1903.
New Grub Street. Penguin, 1968.

Gould, Tony: *Inside Outsider: The Life and Times of Colin MacInnes*. Chatto & Windus, 1983; Penguin, 1986.

Gray, Cecil: *Musical Chairs*. Home & Van Thal, 1948; The Hogarth Press, 1985.

Hamilton, Patrick: *Hangover Square*. Constable, 1941; Penguin, 1956.
Twenty Thousand Streets Under the Sky. Constable, 1935; The Hogarth Press, 1987.

Hamnett, Nina: *Laughing Torso*. Constable, 1932; Virago Press, 1984.
Is She a Lady? Allan Wingate, 1955.

Hewison, Robert: *Under Siege – Literary Life in London 1939–1945*. Weidenfeld and Nicolson, 1977; Quartet, 1979.

Holroyd, Michael: *Augustus John*, Vol. I – The Years of Innocence. Heinemann, 1974.
Augustus John, Vol. II – The Years of Experience. Heinemann, 1975.

Hooker, Denise: *Nina Hamnett*. Constable, 1986.

John, Augustus: *Chiaroscuro*. Jonathan Cape, 1952.

Joll, James: *The Anarchists*. Methuen, 1964; second ed., 1979.

Knight, Stephen: *Jack the Ripper: The Final Solution*. Harrap, 1976; Grafton, 1977.

Lawrence, D. H.: *Women in Love*. Martin Secker, 1921; Penguin, 1960.

Lehmann, John: *I Am My Brother* (Autobiography II), Longman, 1960.
In the Purely Pagan Sense. Blond & Briggs, 1976.

Lehmann, John, and Fuller, Roy (eds): *The Penguin New Writing, 1940–1950*. Penguin, 1985.

Leslie W. Seymour: *The Silent Queen*. Jonathan Cape, 1927.

Lewis, P. Wyndham: *Blasting and Bombardiering*. Eyre & Spottiswoode, 1937.
Rude Assignment. Hutchinson, 1950.

Lilly, Marjorie: *Sickert: The Painter and His Circle*. Elek Books, 1971.

Linklater, Eric: *Poet's Pub*. Jonathan Cape, 1929.

Machray, Robert: *The Night Side of London*. John Macqueen, 1902; facsimile reprint by Bibliophile Books, 1984.

Maclaren-Ross, Julian: *Memoirs of the Forties*. Alan Ross Ltd, 1965; Penguin, 1984.
The Nine Men of Soho. Allan Wingate, 1946.

Motion, Andrew: *The Lamberts*. Chatto & Windus, 1986.

Murdoch, Iris: *Under the Net*. Chatto & Windus, 1954.

Mürger, Henry: *Scènes de la Vie de Bohème*. Michel Lévy Frères, Paris, 1882.

Pearson, Hesketh: *The Life of Oscar Wilde*. Methuen, 1946; Penguin, 1960.

Platt, John: *London's Rock Routes*. Fourth Estate, 1985.

Powell, Anthony: *Messengers of Day*. Heinemann, 1978.
To Keep the Ball Rolling. Penguin, 1983.
Books Do Furnish a Room. Heinemann, 1971; Flamingo, 1983.

Ransome, Arthur: *Bohemia in London*. Chapman and Hall, 1907; Oxford University Press, 1984.

Ross, Alan: *The Forties*. Weidenfeld & Nicolson, 1950.
Blindfold Games. Collins Harvill, 1986.

Rothenstein, John: *Modern English Painters* (Vol. III). Third ed., 1976; Macdonald, 1984.

Rothenstein, William: *Men and Memories: Recollections 1872–1900*. Faber and Faber, 1931.
Men and Memories: Recollections 1900–1922. Faber and Faber, 1932.

Sitwell, Osbert: *Great Morning*. Macmillan, 1948.

Spender, Stephen: *World Within World*. Faber and Faber, 1951; 1977.

Spender, Stephen (ed.): *W. H. Auden: A Tribute*. Weidenfeld and Nicolson, 1975.

Stanford, Derek: *Inside the Forties*. Sidgwick & Jackson, 1977.

Stock, Noel: *The Life of Ezra Pound*. Routledge & Kegan Paul, 1970; Penguin, 1974, 1985.

Thomas, Donald: *Swinburne: The Poet in His World*. Weidenfeld and Nicolson, 1979.

Thomas, Dylan: *The Collected Letters* (ed. Paul Ferris). Dent, 1985.

Thompson, John: *Orwell's London*. Fourth Estate, 1984.

Wharton, Michael: *The Missing Will*. Chatto & Windus, 1984.

Wishart, Michael: *High Diver*. Blond & Briggs, 1977; Quartet, 1978.

Yeats, W. B.: *Autobiographies*. Macmillan, 1955.
Memoirs (ed. Denis Donoghue). Macmillan, 1972.

Yeats, W. B. (ed): *The Oxford Book of Modern Verse*. Oxford University Press, 1936.

EXHIBITION CATALOGUES

Barbican Art Gallery: *A Paradise Lost: The Neo-Romantic Imagination in Britain, 1935–55*, (ed. by Dr David Mellor) 1987.

Christies, St James's: *The New English Art Club Centenary Exhibition*, with an introduction by Anna Robbins, 1986.
The Painters of Camden Town. 1905–1920, with an introduction by Wendy Baron, 1988.

Bibliography

Parkin Gallery: *Fitzrovia and the Road to the York Minster*, with a memoir by Ruthven Todd, 1973.

Artists of the Colony Room Club. A Tribute to Muriel Belcher, with essays by Daniel Farson, Molly Parkin and George Melly, 1982.

Royal Academy of Arts: *British Art in the Twentieth Century: The Modern Movement*, (ed. by Susan Compton) 1987.

Tate Gallery: *The Pre-Raphaelites*, with an introduction by Alan Bowness, 1984.

Francis Bacon, with essays by Dawn Ades and Andrew Forge, 1985.

Index

Acton, Sir Harold, 48
Adelphi, The, 141
Aestheticism, 2, 6, 8–9, 12, 13, 17, 21, 34, 47, 48, 105, 164, 174
Agate, James, 114
Albert Victor, Prince ('Eddy'), 97
Algerian Café, 39
Allchild, Charlie, 238, 240–1
Allinson, Adrian, 107, 108
Anand, Mulk Raj, 198
Anderson, Sir John, 204
Anglesey, The, 144, 145
Apocalyptics, The, 154, 155, 165, 182, 185, 196, 227
Archer, David, 144, 192, 196, 236
Arlen, Michael, 99–101, 104, 110, 114, 124, 125, 126, 128, 130, 144, 245
  Piracy, 100–101, 110, 124, 130
Arlen, Michael J., 99
Arnold, Matthew, 10
Artists' International Association, 183–4
Arts Council of Great Britain, 222, 223
Asquith, Herbert, 127
Asquith, Margot, 207
Auden, W. H., 150, 151, 152, 153, 154, 155, 161, 195, 207
Ayrton, Michael, 229

Bacon, Francis, 228, 230, 233, 246
Baddeley, Hermione, 122
Bagnold, Enid, 71, 103
Bailey, Nick, 89
Bakunin, Mikhail, 95
Balon, Norman, 249, 251, 261

Barker, George, 167, 181, 192, 200, 232
Baudelaire, Charles, 28, 210
BBC (British Broadcasting Corporation), 137, 155, 156, 213–14, 222, 224, 235, 243, 244, 245
Beardsley, Aubrey, 3, 43, 48, 49, 104, 106
Beaton, Cecil, 204, 206
Beecham, Sir Thomas, 112, 243
Beerbohm, Max, 43, 67, 102, 103, 104, 105, 108
Beerbohm Tree, Sir Herbert, 15, 75, 108
Beer House, The (Newman Arms), 170, 172, 238
Behan, Brendan, 174, 223, 226
Belcher, Muriel, 233, 246
Bell, Clive, 79, 80, 153
Bell, Quentin, 80, 155
Bell, Vanessa, 78, 80, 83, 152, 153
Bennett, Arnold, 50, 52, 53, 83, 101
Berlemont, Gaston, 173–4
Berlemont, Victor, 173
Bernard, Jeffrey, 251–2, 261
Bertorelli's Restaurant, 176
Betjeman, John, 191
Binyon, Laurence, 52, 53
Black Horse, 171, 244
Black, William, 227
Blast, 126, 182
Bloomsbury Group, 78–81, 153–5, 185
Boeuf sur le Toit, Le (Paris), 133, 134
Bomberg, David, 84
'Bosie', *see* Douglas, Lord Alfred
Boulogne Café, 36, 38, 252

270

Brancusi, Constantin, 133
Brandt, Bill, 204
Breton, André, 181
Brice's Restaurant, 37, 59
Bricklayer's Arms, (The Burglars), 171, 181, 202, 234
Bridges, Robert, 52
Brooke, Peter, 181, 207
Brown, Ford Madox, 67, 68
Browning, Robert, 11, 44, 66
Bryden, Ronald, 178
Buchanan, Robert, 12
Burglars, The, *see* Bricklayer's Arms
Burke, Edmund, 36
Burne-Jones, Edward, 15
Burne-Jones, Georgina, 10
Burns, John, MP, 121, 122
Burra, Edward, 182
Byron, George Gordon, Lord, 7

Cabaret Club, The, *see* Cave of the Golden Calf
Café de Paris, 144, 205, 206
Café Momus (Paris), 22, 27, 28, 57, 58, 133
Café Royal, 18, 39, 61, 75, 96, 101, 102–9, 111, 112, 113, 114, 115, 123, 125, 127, 130, 132, 133, 144, 152, 164, 173
Calder-Marshall, Arthur, 172, 181, 193, 215
Calonne, Alphonse de, 26, 28
Camden Town Group, The, 72, 77, 182, 183
Campbell, Roy, 166, 181
Carlyle, Thomas, 21, 31, 32, 55
Cary, Joyce, 62, 226
Cave of the Golden Calf, (The Cabaret Club), 114–17, 118, 122, 128, 132, 134, 175
Caves de France, 174, 175, 232
CEMA (Council for the Encouragement of Music and the Arts), 204, 222, 223; *see* Arts Council
Chamberlain, Neville, 200
Chancellor, E. Beresford, 85
Channing-Renton, E. M., 195
Charlotte Street, ix, 81, 88, 91, 92, 94, 95, 96, 106, 134, 155, 161, 169, 171, 178, 179, 202, 218, 244
Cherwell, 190, 197
Cheshire Cheese, The, 40, 41, 42–3, 46, 59, 157

Chesterton, G. K., 43, 50, 104, 180
Church, Richard, 182
Clark, Kenneth, 184
Closerie des Lilas, La (Paris), 25, 133
Club, The, 36, 41
Coach and Horses, The, 249–52, 261
Cocteau, Jean, 133, 234
Coleridge, Samuel Taylor, 7, 91, 92
Collins, Cecil, 181, 182, 227
Collins, Wilkie, 43, 91
Colony Room Club, 230, 233, 245
Colquhoun, Robert, 166, 231–3, 237, 239
Comfort, Alex, 154, 196, 197
Compton's, *see* Swiss Tavern, The
Connolly, Cyril, 153, 183, 191, 192, 193, 194, 197, 208–12, 222, 223
  The Unquiet Grave, 209–11
Constable, John, 91
Cooper, Lady Diana, 112
Coward, Nöel, 183, 219–20
Crabtree Club, 118–19
Craxton, John, 228, 232
Crisp, Quentin, 241
Cronin, Anthony, 191, 223, 226, 232–33
Crosland, T. W. H., 107, 109
Crowley, Aleister, 62
Cunard, Lady Maud ('Emerald'), 83, 111, 112, 206–7
Cunard, Nancy, 104, 108, 110, 111–13, 125–6, 127, 130, 131, 135, 162

Dali, Salvador, 181
Davenport, John, 212, 224
Davidson, John, 43, 48
Davin, Dan, 160, 167, 178, 179, 243
Day-Lewis, Cecil, 150, 155
Deakin, John, 229, 230, 233
Dean Paul, Lady Brenda (Poldowski), 126, 134, 239
Dempsey, Jack, 173
Derain, André, 133
Diaghilev, Sergei, 76
Dickens, Charles, 43, 85, 90, 91
Dickens, Charles (the Younger), 56, 102
Dieppe Restaurant, 37, 39
Dieren, Bernard van, 114
Disraeli, Benjamin, 91
Dôme, Le (Paris), 133, 234, 235
Donnegan, Lonnie, 242

Dorchester Hotel, 205–7
Douglas, Lord Alfred ('Bosie'), 4, 14, 18, 106, 109, 195
Douglas, Keith, 169
Dowson, Ernest, 43, 44, 106
Doyle, Sir Arthur Conan, 7, 43
Drummond, Malcolm 71
Dryden, John, 36
Dufy, Raoul, 134
Duke of York, The, 170, 244
Du Maurier, Daphne, 14, 23
Du Maurier, George, 14, 15, 21, 22–3, 25, 26, 39, 55, 67
  Trilby, 21, 24–6, 35, 54, 55
Durrell, Lawrence, 166, 197
Dylan, Bob (Robert Zimmerman), 139

Earp, T. W. ('Tommy'), 77, 134–5, 161, 168, 173, 245, 261–2
Egan, Pierce, 33
Eiffel Tower Restaurant, 36, 100, 114, 123–9, 130, 131, 132, 133, 134, 144, 152, 162, 169, 232
Eliot, T. S., 44, 150, 153, 155, 198, 213
Engels, Friedrich, 95
ENSA (Entertainments National Service Association), 204
Epstein, Jacob, 111, 114, 116, 117, 133
Étoile Restaurant, 176
Ewart, Gavin, 150, 169

Faith, Adam 242
Farson, Daniel, 174, 175, 176, 227, 232, 235, 241, 246
Fava's Restaurant, 176
Ferris, Paul, 139, 140, 155, 262
Firbank, Ronald, 114, 127
Fitzgerald, Edward, 45
FitzGibbon, Constantine, 146, 148, 262
Fitzroy, Charles (Baron Southampton), 86, 87, 88
Fitzroy Square, 79, 81, 82, 85, 88, 89, 114, 168
Fitzroy Street Group, 70–2, 76, 77, 78, 81, 110
Fitzroy Tavern, ix, 77, 134, 135, 144, 145, 150, 155, 160, 161, 168, 169, 170, 171, 176, 232, 234, 235, 238, 240–1
Ford, Ford Madox (Hueffer), 53, 116
Forster, E. M., 50, 80, 154, 155

French House, The (York Minster, The), 173, 174, 232, 237, 238
Freud, Lucian, 228, 229
Fry, Christopher, 197
Fry, Roger, 72, 73, 74, 78, 80, 81, 82, 83, 84, 152, 153, 183
Fuller, Roy, 155, 169

Gallienne, Richard le, 43, 45, 46
Galsworthy, John, 50
  Man of Property, The, 50–2
Gargoyle Club, 122–3, 126, 131, 144, 175, 237
Gascoyne, David, 200
Gaudier-Brzeska, Henri, 84, 234, 254
Gautier, Théophile, 9, 26, 28
Gawsworth, John, *see* 'Redonda, King Juan I of'
Gertler, Mark, 84, 114, 119, 126
Gilbert, W. S. (and Sullivan, Sir Arthur), 15, 49, 63, 248
  Patience, 15, 16, 49, 63
Gill, Eric, 115, 117
Gilman, Harold, 70, 71, 72, 107, 126
Ginner, Charles, 71, 72, 107, 116, 117
Gissing, George, 91–3, 180
Godwin, William, 91, 94
Golden Lion, The, 238, 239
Goldsmith, Oliver, 31, 32, 36, 43
Gore, Spencer, 70, 71, 72, 115, 117, 126
Gosse, Edmund, 10
Gosse, Sylvia, 71
Gough, Sylvia, 63
Gourmet's Restaurant, The, 36, 38, 39
Gower, Lord Ronald, 18, 59
Graecen, Robert, 196
Graham, W. S., 166
Grant, Duncan, 79, 152
Gray, Cecil, 113, 114, 129, 134
Greene, Graham, 215–16
Gregory, Lady, 67, 121
Grey Walls Press, The, 194, 195, 196
Grigson, Geoffrey, x, 140, 152, 153, 214
Grosvenor Gallery, 13, 16
Groucho Club, 252
Grub Street, 91

Hamblett, Charles, 181
Hamilton, Patrick, 144, 158, 245

Index

Hamnett, Nina, ix, 32, 35, 48, 71, 76, 77, 81, 83, 107, 110, 114, 119, 123–4, 125, 126, 129, 131, 132–4, 135, 149, 160, 161, 166, 167, 168, 175, 181, 185, 187, 188, 207, 234–6, 244–5, 248
Hansford Johnson, Pamela, 140, 141, 148
Hardie, Keir, 95, 121, 122
Harding, Gilbert, 214
Hardy, Thomas, 52, 91
Harris, Frank, 103, 106, 116
Hazlitt, William, 32, 41, 90
Heath-Stubbs, John, 97, 155, 166, 234, 238, 241
Hemingway, Ernest, 160
Hepworth, Barbara, 182, 185
Herbert, A. P., 211
Heseltine, Philip (Warlock, Peter), 114
Hewison, Robert, 181, 190, 191
Highlander, The (Nellie Dean, The), 172, 179, 193, 238
Hillier, Tristram, 128
Hitchens, Ivon, 185
Holroyd, Michael, 61, 63
Horizon, 165, 177, 187, 188, 190, 191, 193, 195, 202, 208, 211
Horne, Lena, 173
Horseshoe Club, 175
Hudson, Nan, 70, 71
Hughes, Trevor, 145
Hunt, William Holman, 9, 67, 68
Huxley, Aldous, 62

Image, Selwyn, 43
Ingrams, Richard, 251
Isherwood, Christopher, 153

James, Henry, 49, 53
Janes, Alfred, 143
John, Augustus, ix, 7, 35, 60–7, 68, 69, 73–7, 83, 104, 107, 108, 109, 111, 113, 114, 115, 116, 117, 118–19, 121, 122, 123, 126, 127, 128–9, 131, 132, 134, 135, 148, 149, 150, 160, 161, 167, 168, 175, 185, 234, 245, 248, 252, 254
John, Gwen, 35, 66, 110, 254
John, Ida, 66, 254
Johnson, Lionel, 43, 44, 46, 47
Johnson, Dr Samuel, 36, 40, 41, 42, 43, 55, 90, 91, 121, 178, 180

Jones, Glyn, 142, 152
Joyce, James, 50, 140, 160

Karlowska, Stanislawa de, 71
Kavanagh, Patrick, 186, 226
Kennedy, Margaret, 62
Kettner's Restaurant, 5, 101
Keynes, Maynard, 64, 80
Kingdom Come, 190, 197
King's Arms, 239
Kipling, Rudyard, 50
Kirkup, James, 197
Kleinfeld, 'Papa', 134, 136, 238
Knight, Laura, 107
Kropotkin, Prince Peter, 95

Lambert, Constant, 135, 162, 164
Lancaster, Osbert, 186, 187, 188, 189, 202
Lane, Sir Hugh, 69, 71, 73, 75, 121
Langham Sketch Club, 57
Laughton, Charles, ix, 164
Lawrence, D. H., 50, 62, 91, 100, 104, 110
Leavis, F. R., 150
Lehmann, John, 153, 167, 215, 221–3, 240
Leland, John, 36
Leslie, W. Seymour, 112, 124
Lessore, Thérèse, 71
Levy, Mervyn, 143
Lewis, Alun, 169
Lewis, Percy Wyndham, 61, 82, 84, 104, 114, 115, 116, 126, 231
Lilly, Marjorie, 81
Lincoln, Paul, 242, 243, 244
Linklater, Eric, 157
L'Isle-Adam, Villiers de, 45
Listener, The, 151, 190, 195
London Group, The, 72, 182, 183
London Sketch Club, 57, 58
Lowry, Malcolm, 164, 260
Lutyens, Sir Edwin, 123
Lyttleton, Humphrey, 246

Macaulay, Thomas Babington, 121
MacBryde, Robert, 166, 231–3, 237, 239
MacCaig, Norman, 154, 197
MacCarthy, Desmond, 80
MacColl, D. S., 74, 75
MacDonald, J. Ramsay, 122, 123
Machray, Robert, 38, 57, 58

MacInnes, Colin, 232, 233, 245–8
Absolute Beginners, 246, 247
Maclaren-Ross, Julian, ix, 146, 148,
149, 159, 160, 161, 163, 165, 166,
167–8, 169, 170, 171, 172, 173,
174, 176–80, 181, 185, 187, 188,
189, 193, 194, 194, 197, 198, 199,
200, 202, 207, 208, 215, 218, 224,
226, 229, 230, 240, 243–4, 245,
248
Memoirs of the Forties, 149, 159, 166,
167, 178, 188–9
MacNeice, Louis, 137–8, 150, 214,
224
Malatesta, Errico, 95–6
Malato, Charles, 96
Mandrake Club, 175
Mare, Walter de la, 200
Markham Arms, The, 144, 145, 169
Marnau, Fred, 181, 196
Marquis of Granby, The, 167,
169–70, 172, 186, 187, 188, 240
Masefield, John, 209
Matisse, Henri, 123
Maugham, W. Somerset, 104
May, Betty, 111, 116, 118
McColl, Ewan, 244
Melly, George, 230
Mendelson, Edward, 150
Meredith, George, 10, 18, 91
Milhaud, Darius, 133
Millais, John Everett, 9
Ministry of Information, 213,
214–16, 221
Minton, John, 166, 181, 228–31, 232,
237, 239, 240
Modigliani, Amedeo, 133, 234
Moka Coffee Bar, 241
Monckton, Lionel, 49
Arcadians, The, 49
Moore, George, 65, 75, 106, 108, 112,
113
Moore, Henry, 181, 182, 183, 184,
200, 204–5, 227
Moore, Nicholas, 154, 196, 197
Moorish Café, The, 39
Morrell, Lady Ottoline, 73, 76, 83
Morris, William, 82, 83, 95
Morrison, Herbert, 204
Most, Johann, 95
Motion, Andrew, 162
Mrs Miniver, 183, 202, 204
Murdoch, Iris, 218–19

Mürger, Henry, 25, 26, 27, 28, 30, 32,
47, 54, 55, 57, 58, 122, 248
Scènes de la Vie de Bohème, 25

Nadar, Felix, 27, 28
Nash, Paul, 84, 119, 182, 183, 184,
185, 228
Neo-Romanticism, 227–8, 235
Nerval, Gérard de, 28, 47
Nettleship, Jack, 66, 121
Nevinson, C. R. W., 107, 109
Newbolt, Henry, 52
New English Art Club, 66, 67, 68, 69,
74, 76
New English Weekly, 141, 190
New Grub Street, 92–3
New Road, 183, 196–7
New Statesman, 153, 190, 208, 215,
216–17, 222
New Verse, 150, 151–2, 153
New Writing (and *Penguin New
Writing*), 153, 167, 191, 195,
215–16
New Writing and Daylight, 190, 221
Nichols, Beverly, 165
Nichols, Daniel, 102, 103, 104, 164
Nicholson, William, 108
Nye, Robert, 10

O'Brien, Flann (Myles Na Gopaleen),
226
Odle, Allan, 106, 108, 132
O'Fáolain, Séan, 186
Old Compton Street, 36, 37, 172, 173,
176, 241
Olivier, Laurence, 183
Omega Workshops, The, 81, 82, 83,
84, 110, 126, 181
100 Club, The, 246
Orpen, Sir William, 64–5, 68, 75–6,
107, 108, 118
Orton, Joe, 179
Orwell, George, 203, 212, 214, 216,
220–1, 223, 227
Nineteen Eighty-Four, 216, 220–1,
223
Osborne, John, 248
Owen, Robert, 94–5

Palmer, Samuel, 227
Pater, Walter, 7, 9
Peake, Mervyn, 200
Pearson, Hesketh, 18

Picasso, Pablo, ix, 165
Piper, John, 181, 184, 227, 228
Piratin, Philip, MP, 203
Pissarro, Camille, 72
Pissarro, Lucian, 72
Plough, The, 145
Poetry (Chicago), 52, 191, 199
Poetry (London), 191, 198–200
Poetry Quarterly, 191, 195, 197
Post-Impressionist Exhibitions (1910, 1912), 72, 76, 78, 82, 153, 181
Poulenc, Francis, 133
Pound, Ezra, 49, 52, 53–4, 61, 126
Powell, Anthony, 123–4, 125, 129, 162–3, 179
Powell, Lady Violet, 162
Pre-Raphaelite Brotherhood, 3, 9, 11, 13, 67
Priestley, J. B., 211, 215, 222
Private Eye, 249, 251
Proudhon, Pierre Joseph, 94
Puccini, Giacomo, 21, 22, 23, 25, 58
  Bohème, La, 21–2, 25, 35, 54
Punch, 11, 14

Queensbury, Marquess of, 3
Quiller-Couch, Sir Arthur, 43
Quincey, Thomas de, 7, 90

Raine, Kathleen, 200
Ransome, Arthur, 20–1, 23, 29–30, 31–41, 42, 47, 54, 55, 57, 58, 59, 90, 146–8, 167, 178, 180, 188, 227, 247
  Bohemia in London, 31–5, 54, 55, 146, 188
Rathbone Place, 88, 90, 132, 158, 161, 163, 169, 171, 186, 187, 202, 218, 244
Rattigan, Terence, 183
Read, Herbert, 181, 182
Reade, Charles, 91
Recording Britain Project, 184, 227
'Redonda, King Juan I of' (Gawsworth, John), 165, 166
Reed, Henry, 154
Rees, Sir Richard, 141
Reynolds, Sir Joshua, 36, 43
Rhondda, Lady, 191
Rhymer's Club, The, 40, 43–7, 49, 54, 58, 109, 134
Rhys, Ernest, 43
Richard, Cliff, 242

Richards, Ceri, 200, 227
Rimbaud, Arthur, 36, 44, 210
Roberts, William, 84
Roche's Restaurant, 36, 39, 42, 59, 252
Rolleston, T. W., 43, 45
Ross, Alan, 166, 169, 237
Rossetti, Dante Gabriel, 9, 11, 12, 15, 18, 31
Rossetti, William Michael, 12, 69
Rothenstein, John, 233
Rothenstein, William, 60, 67, 70, 74, 102, 103, 104, 105
Rotonde, La (Paris), 133, 134, 234
Ruskin, John, 13, 24, 73, 183
Russell, Walter, 70
Rutherston, Albert, 70, 119

Saintsbury, George, 18
Sands, Ethel, 70, 71
Sargent, John Singer, 60, 65
Savage Club, The, 35, 41, 224
Savage, Richard, 31, 32, 178, 180
Savoy Hotel, 4, 5, 71, 127, 203, 205, 207
Scala Café, 176, 179, 202
Schmidt's Restaurant, 176
Shaw, George Bernard, 53, 79, 83, 95, 106, 110, 180
Shelley, Lillian, 111, 118
Shelley, Percy Bysshe, 8, 91, 92
Sheridan, R. B., 121
Sickert, Walter, 35, 60, 68–72, 73, 75, 76, 81, 83, 84, 97, 127, 181, 184, 185, 234, 248, 256, 257
Sisley, Alfred, 72
Sitwell, Edith, 127, 137, 153, 213, 227
Sitwell, Osbert, 114, 117, 127, 132, 227
Slade School of Art, 60, 61, 65, 66, 67, 71
'Slithy Toves', 163, 164, 165, 168, 172, 187, 197, 224, 243
Spectator, The, 74, 183
Spencer, Stanley, 62, 184
Spender, Stephen, 150, 152, 197, 203
Stag's Head, The, 243
Stanford, Derek, 181, 196, 197
Steele, Richard, 31, 32, 33
Steele, Tommy, 242
Stephen, Sir Leslie, 78–9
Stewart, Mrs, 159–60, 164, 165, 187
Strachey, Lytton, 64, 65, 79, 80, 153
Stravinsky, Igor, 76, 113

Index

Strindberg, Frida, 115, 116, 117, 118, 122, 123, 128
Stulik, Rudolf, 125, 127, 128–9, 130, 169
Subramaniam, Alagu, 167, 198
Surrealism, 154, 181–3, 227
Sutherland, Graham, 184, 200, 227, 228
Swift, Jonathan, 41
Swinburne, Algernon Charles, 9–12, 13, 15, 17, 18, 19, 44
Swiss Tavern, The, 173, 174, 198, 199, 232, 238, 239, 262
Sydney-Turner, Saxon, 79, 80
Symons, Arthur, 29, 43, 44, 45, 46, 47, 48, 58, 106, 134

Tambimuttu, J. Meary, 163, 167, 172, 173, 181, 197–200, 226
Tennant, The Hon. David, 122, 123
Tennyson, Alfred, Lord, 10, 11, 44
Thackeray, W. M., 43
Thomas, Caitlin, 160–1, 167
Thomas, Dylan, ix, 7, 128, 136, 137–49, 150, 151, 152, 154, 155, 156, 160–1, 165, 167, 172, 173, 175, 178, 182, 185, 187, 189–90, 192, 193, 195, 197, 199, 202, 208, 212–13, 215, 218, 224–5, 227, 232, 234, 244, 261–2
Thompson, Francis, 43
Time and Tide, 191
Todd, Christopher, 194
Todd, Ruthven, 128, 181, 193–5, 196, 197, 234, 235
Tonks, Henry, 66, 71, 74, 75
Torino, Café, 176
Tree, Iris, 63, 108, 110, 112
Treece, Henry, 154
Trick, A. E. ('Bert'), 143, 145, 147, 148
Twain, Mark, 43
2i's Coffee Bar, 241–3, 244

Unit One, 182, 183
Unwin, Stanley, 211
Urquhart, Fred, 166, 181

Valerie, Patisserie, 176
Vaughan, Keith, 166, 227, 237–8, 239
Vere Cole, Horace de, 108
Verlaine, Paul, 36, 44

Virgil, 209, 210–11
Vlaminck, Maurice, 133
Voltaire (François-Marie Arouet), 2, 60
Vorticism, 84, 116, 126

Wadsworth, Edward, 84
Walden, Lord Howard de, 118
Waller, Sir John, 166, 181, 197
Walpole, Hugh, 50
Walton, Sir William, 135
War Artists Advisory Committee, 184, 213
Watkins, Vernon, 197
Watson, Boris, 175
Watson, William, 43
Watts, George Frederic, 10
Waugh, Alec, 99
Waugh, Evelyn, 104
Webb, Sidney, 95
Welch, Denton, 100
Welch, Elisabeth, 135
Wells, H. G., 50, 83, 101
Wheatsheaf, The, 151, 154, 158, 159–61, 164, 166, 167, 168, 169, 177, 179, 181, 185, 188, 199, 203, 222, 223, 225, 228, 237, 238, 243
Whistler, James Abbott McNeill, 13, 15, 17, 23–4, 31, 60, 64, 68, 70, 73, 84, 106
White Tower Restaurant, *see* Eiffel Tower Restaurant
Whyton, Wally, 242, 243
Wilde, Oscar, ix, 1–5, 6, 9, 13, 14, 15, 16, 17, 18, 43, 45, 46, 48, 53, 59, 104, 106, 109, 119, 121, 122, 123, 148, 179, 239, 248
Wilson, Colin, 248
Wilson Steer, Philip, 74, 75
Wishart, Michael, 229
Wood, Sir Henry, 132
Woolf, Leonard, 79, 80, 153
Woolf, Virginia, 50, 52, 72, 78, 79, 112, 153, 155
Wrey Gardiner, Charles, 181, 194, 195–7, 199

Yeats, John B., 46, 66, 186
Yeats, William Butler, 43, 44, 45, 46, 47, 48, 49, 52, 58, 64, 66, 67, 76, 109, 113, 121, 122, 134, 154, 167, 248
Yellow Book, The, 48, 195